ERRATA

RURAL
MALAY
WOMEN
IN TRADITION
AND TRANSITION

BURMA

THAILAND

LAOS

KAMPUCHEA

VIET
NAM

PHILIPPINE
ISLANDS

EAST MALAYSIA

BRUNEI

KT

SABAH

PENINSULAR
MALAYSIA

KL

SARAWAK

SINGAPORE

0°

KALIMANTAN

SUMATRA

INDONESIA

N

JAVA

SOUTHEAST   ASIA

Heather Strange

RURAL
MALAY
WOMEN
IN TRADITION
AND TRANSITION

For Linda —
whose understanding,
affection and humor
never fail —
and always make me
feel very special —
love,
Heather

PRAEGER

PRAEGER SPECIAL STUDIES • PRAEGER SCIENTIFIC

Library of Congress Cataloging in Publication Data

Strange, Heather.
   Rural Malay women in tradition and transition.

   Bibliography: p.
   1. Rural women--Malaysia. I. Title.
HQ1750.6.S77   305.4'2'09595   81-5140
ISBN 0-03-052616-7   AACR2

Published in 1981 by Praeger Publishers
CBS Educational and Professional Publishing
A Division of CBS, Inc.
521 Fifth Avenue, New York, New York 10175 U.S.A.

© 1981 by Praeger Publishers

123456789   145   987654321

Printed in the United States of America

For my parents,

Ruby and Reg.

And for the women of Rusila.

ACKNOWLEDGMENTS

The research upon which this book is based has been carried out over a period of 14 years. Necessarily, during such a prolonged period, a great many people have made direct or indirect contributions to my work, among them professors, students, and colleagues at New York University, where I did my postgraduate work; at Rutgers-the State University of New Jersey, where I am now a faculty member; and the University of Malaya, where I taught as a senior Fulbright lecturer in Malay studies during 1978-79. Colleagues at other universities who have carried out research in Malaysia have been generous, sharing their expertise and offering advice. The villagers of Rusila and nearby kampung were accepting, curious, interested, and helpful, and Malaysian government officers from whom I sought assistance never failed to give it.

My parents, Ruby and Reg Strange, accepted my Malaysia monomania with good humor and have provided much encouragement, financial assistance, and long, newsy letters—always appreciated—when I was in the field. Other friends have been supportive in numerous ways. It is impossible to name everyone, and no one who is named bears any responsibility for the content of the book or the interpretations I have made.

My very special appreciation and thanks go to Abdullah Baginda, Fred Dunn, Cynthia Enloe, Mano Maniam, and the staff at the Malaysian American Commission for Educational Exchange (MACEE), Mohd. Taib Osman, Selamah binti Abdul Kadir, her husband Awang bin Haji Kadir and their family, and Suri binti Sulaiman.

And to Kenneth R. Anderson, Cik Rogayah, Fatimah Hamid-Don, Ruth Freed, Vera Green, Jean Grossholtz, Mazidah Zakaria, Mohamed Ali bin Yusoh, Nik Safiah Karim, Penghulu Haji Ibrahim, Puvanes, Ravee Raghavan, Terry Rambo, Rohani binti Abdullah, Yusof bin Ismail, Chaim I. Waxman, Christine Wilson, and Zahid bin Muda.

Financial support for the 1965-66 research period of 14 months was from a Fulbright-Hays fellowship (FH 4-89). During 1975 five months of research was possible because of a Faculty Academic Study Program leave from Rutgers. In 1978 preliminary work was carried out while I was an exchange lecturer through the Fulbright program and facilitated by many supportive services from the staff at MACEE. I am truly grateful for the financial and other assistance that I received.

Rhonda Breen typed the original manuscript. She did a superb job, and never complained when I returned perfectly prepared pages with requests for additions or deletions. Eileen Gnecco typed the extensive revisions beautifully, and kept her cheerful humor the while. Lynda Sharp, my editor at Praeger, has been patient, understanding, and helpful. My father, Reginald B. Strange, prepared the house plan in Figure 2; I took the photographs.

CONTENTS

LIST OF ACRONYMS AND ABBREVIATIONS

ABIM   Muslim Youth Movement

ASEAN   Association of Southeast Asian Nations

Echo   Straits Echo, an English-language daily newspaper

Fed. Const.   Federal Constitution

FELDA   Federal Land Development Authority

FOA   Farmer's Organization Authority

GNP   gross national product

HSC   Higher School Certificate, a post-secondary
                education certificate

JMBRAS   Journal, Malaysian Branch of the Royal Asiatic
                Society

LCE   Lower Certificate of Education, awarded to students
                passing examinations during the third year of
                secondary school

Mail   Malay Mail, an English-language daily newspaper

MARA   Majlis Amanah Rakyat, a federal agency

MCA   Malayan Chinese Association, a political party and
                member of the National Front coalition

MCE   Middle Certificate of Education, awarded to students
                who pass examinations during the fifth year of
                secondary school

MCP   Malayan Communist Party

MIC   Malayan Indian Congress, a political party and
                member of the National Front coalition

NACIWID   National Advisory Council on the Integration of
                Women in Development

NAWIM	National Association of Women's Institutes of Malaysia
NEP	New Economic Policy
NST	*New Straits Times*, a daily English-language newspaper
NSunT	*New Sunday Times*, the Sunday edition of the *New Straits Times*
PAS	Islamic political party
PQLI	Physical Quality of Life Index
PRB	Population Reference Bureau (Washington, D.C.)
RELA	Home Guard
RIDA	Rural Industrial Authority (former name of MARA)
SEAC	*Southeast Asia Chronicle*
SMP	Second Malaysia Plan
SunEcho	*Sunday Echo*, an English-language Malaysian newspaper
SunMail	*Sunday Mail*, an English-language Malaysian newspaper
SunStar	*Sunday Star*, an English-language Malaysian newspaper
TMP	Third Malaysia Plan
UMNO	United Malays National Organization, a political party and member of the National Front coalition

INTRODUCTION

As I write, it is the midpoint of the United Nations Decade for Women, which has "Equality, Development and Peace" as its three goals; the World Conference booklet (U.N. 1980a) for the international meetings held in Copenhagen during July 1980, called upon all governments to implement the "World Plan of Action" as a means of achieving the goals by ". . . a real transformation of society where the subordinate role of women is permanently changed to one of equality with men and full participation in all aspects of life" (p. 12).

Specific priorities for achieving equality and improving the situation of women through development--in employment, land ownership, health needs and services, representation in government and institutions dealing with development, in education, and in the upgrading of the position of rural women, particularly with regard to food production—are outlined in the booklet (pp. 13-17). The priorities emphasize the multistranded nature of development and the many ways that women's lives can be changed in the process. That little has been accomplished for most of the world's women is shown by the very need to set priorities and urge their implementation.

Like any change, development is a process, a moving from one phase, situation, or thing to another. But development is also multistranded, as shown in the "World Plan of Action" priorities, with impact upon the economy, politics, education, and other social institutions, as well as upon ecological arrangements in a country. The various aspects of development do not necessarily occur simultaneously or evenly.

This book is primarily a study of rural Malay women in one village, Rusila, and how they are affected by the structure of their society, by the development process, and by changes in the direction of attaining or not attaining equity. I have assumed that in order to see the village clearly, some background about the nation and its components, particularly the state of Trengganu and the administrative district, Marang, is necessary: changes in the village are not taking place in a vacuum. But my consideration of the larger entities is informed by my village experience. Thus, in the chapter about economics, I give brief consideration to one government agency because of its program in the village of Rusila. Government agencies are myriad, so the selection is based on parochial interest and my local involvement.

I first went to Malaysia in the spring of 1965 and arrived in
Trengganu a couple of weeks later with letters of introduction to
government officers. Encik Abdullah Baginda, then Welfare Officer for Trengganu, was deeply interested in my research topic:
village women's economic roles. Luck. I might have had intro-
ductions to ten other people who felt no or little interest. Encik
Abdullah discussed the project at length and sent me to a number of
villages with whichever of his assistants were going there. Rusila
seemed ideal; it was also one of the most beautiful places I had
ever seen. There were a government handicraft center for women,
public transportation facilities, empty houses that might be rented,
and an English-speaking Malay teacher at the local primary school
who was willing to serve as a language tutor.

I had studied Indonesian, structurally identical to Malay, but
found the Trengganu dialect almost incomprehensible. After about
five or six weeks, a neighbor one day complimented me on my use
of Malay, adding, "When you arrived here you did nothing but
smile." During those early days I understood little of what was
said to me by adults, nor did they seem to understand me. I could
communicate with children because they were studying Standard
Malay in school, but many of them were shy of interacting with a
stranger. Again, I was lucky. My landlady's eldest son, Ramli
bin Awang, a very intelligent 11-year-old with a great deal of cu-
riosity, became my shadow and self-appointed interpreter. Re-
membering his efforts makes me smile in appreciation. I was
engaged in the first of two house-to-house surveys of the village,
trying to establish who lived where, the occupations of residents,
and other basic facts. The two of us would arrive at a home; I
would introduce myself, and explain what I was doing. The person
addressed would look at Ramli. He would repeat in the local dialect
what I had just said. The householder would respond. Then I would
look at Ramli and he would repeat the response in Standard Malay.
Later, when I could communicate directly, Ramli continued to be
helpful in many ways. So were the other members of his family.

His parents, Selamah and Awang, felt responsible for me
because I was renting their house and living alone. They were my
nearest neighbors and looked after my welfare in a hundred ways.
They became close and dear friends. When I returned to Rusila
in 1975 and again in 1979, they took me into their home and treated
me as one of their family, although my presence often must have
been awkward for them. Obviously the research could not have
been carried out without the generosity, assistance, and kindness
I received from them and many others. But their names will not
be found in the text. All names used in examples are common in
Malaysia, but they do not belong to those I have written about unless

the person is acting publicly in an esteemed role. This is a small way of protecting everyone's privacy because the village is real and easily identifiable due to the presence of the government-sponsored weaving center.

Throughout the book I have used feminine/masculine forms of English (she, he, and so on) as precisely as possible. Where a term denotes sex, such as craftswoman or headman, it means that the particular status was filled only by members of the sex indicated up to mid-1979.

A dollar sign ($) always indicates Malaysian dollars (ringgit) unless otherwise specified. The value of Malaysian dollars to U.S. dollars has fluctuated, with Malaysian dollars gaining value in recent years at M$2.00-2.50 to U.S. $1.00.

The first three chapters of the book provide general background information about nation, state, village, and women's life cycle. Chapter 1 outlines history, climate and geography, government and politics—especially the role of women in politics—Islam, the Islamic and civil/criminal legal codes, and an overview of women in education, employment, and politics by a Malaysian woman journalist, Halinah Bamadhaj.

The village of Rusila and its people are the subject of Chapter 2. Trends in housing, use of services, furniture acquisition, and amenities are one focus; another is kinship, residential groups, and women's interactions. The chapter concludes with a discussion of the ways in which the village is directly tied to the larger society.

Chapter 3 deals with the life cycle and the types of change, such as health care, affecting women's lives.

Education, from national policies and patterns to contemporary behavior and attitudes in the village and how they are affecting the lives of young women, is the subject of Chapter 4.

Traditional patterns of mate selection, marriage rituals and family forms, and the changes between 1965 and 1979 are the focus of Chapter 5; divorce and polygyny are examined in detail in Chapter 6. The economy is the subject of Chapter 7, which includes recent theories and propositions that relate women's status to their economic role or to broader aspects of national development and global economy.

The final chapter of the book integrates the main changes in education, marriage patterns, the economy, and other topics, emphasizing the effects of development on the lives of village women. Traditions and changes that relate to equality/inequality between women and men are included in the analysis.

There is no separate chapter about religion, although an overview of Islam, the official religion of Malaysia, is provided in Chapter 1. Religion is fundamental to the lives of Rusila villagers, all of whom are Muslims. Islam is mentioned in every chapter, reflecting the reality of how religion is integrated with other aspects of village life. One point requires emphasis here: the difference between "the theoretical, ideological level of Islam and its practical applied level" (U.N. 1980b:5-6), the difference between what the experts say and write and what people believe and do. The gap in Rusila is narrower than in many rural areas because both the present and the former imam are (were) far more educated and learned about Islam than the average village religious leaders are said to be. The two imams have had a deep influence in expanding local understanding of Islam at the theoretical level; the former imam was responsible for the decrease of animistic practices, against which he took an uncompromising position.

My non-Muslim status was not a problem. There were two especially pious men in the village in 1965-66 who went out of their way to avoid interacting with me, but they were always polite if for some reason they could not avoid me. I knew that any physical contact between adults of opposite sex who were not married would be frowned upon and considered defiling to a man who had performed ablutions but had not yet prayed. I avoided offering to shake hands, not a Malay practice anyway, but sometimes men who knew handshaking to be a Western custom would politely offer me their hands. Touching between women who are kin or close friends during the course of a conversation is rather common, affectionate, or playful depending on the social context. But Malays value politeness. Other women did not touch me until they knew me well; then contact took the form of patting a hand or a shoulder or holding an arm.

My status as a woman was important because the research focused on women's roles and behavior. Had I been a man, I could not have had free access to women in their homes without the presence of a chaperone. As a woman I could interact freely with women, and as a foreigner I also had access to public male activities in which women did not normally participate. But it would have been improper for me to spend time alone with an adult male, however innocent the circumstances. As in any society where many activities are sex-segregated and permitted adult interactions between male and female are carefully defined, among Malays a woman researcher has a big advantage working with women. A man would have an advantage working with men.

I have attempted to be objective in presenting the material included in this book. It is possible to be most objective and straightforward when dealing with generalities: a majority of women do this, most women say that, ten women have a particular occupation. Objectivity is less likely when individual examples of behavior and attitudes are used. What is selected as an example involves judgment even when one looks for what is "typical." And the focus of a study implies a more fundamental judgment, however much one may want and try to "know everything." The initial research was dominated by my interest in women, their socioeconomic roles, and the traditional handicrafts. The model treated the parts of the sociocultural system as functionally interrelated (functionalism). In 1975, I was concerned with these subjects but also with education, because the first local women to attend secondary school had completed their courses of study, and with the effects of other aspects of development. Returning to the United States in 1975, I did not anticipate being able to go back to Malaysia in 1978. I wrote articles contrasting women's 1965 and 1975 statuses, roles, and behavior. In 1978, I found that almost as many changes had occurred during three years as during the preceding decade. It was necessary to look at the nature and direction of the changes, to update biographical information, and to contrast the lives of younger and older women.

The basic research technique was participant observation, living as a member of the community for long periods at a time and taking part in women's activities. In 1965-66 the first weeks were spent in establishing myself as a part of the community—always a foreigner, of course, but less and less a stranger. When I returned in 1975, I was accepted as an old friend by those who had known me, but I had to become acquainted with many young women who had been little girls giggling at me shyly in 1965 or who had married into the village since that time. The day-to-day interactions that are part of participant observation are crucial to being accepted as a community member, however temporary, and to learning how people think and feel about their lives, their joys, and their problems. I also conducted household surveys, two in 1965-66—the first with Ramli's assistance shortly after my arrival and the second just prior to departure—and one each during 1975 and 1979. Interview schedules were used to get specific information about women's income, both cash and kind; work performed; and attitudes pertaining to occupations, education, and change, particularly in relation to the social roles of women and men. Photography was also an essential research technique. Requests for pictures sometimes strained my budget, but many of the "family portraits" taken in 1965 had been incorporated into albums that I was shown in 1979, providing the pleasure of reminiscence and a good starting point for discussions about change.

1
BACKGROUND SKETCHES

The sketches of this chapter are a setting for the chapters that follow and a means for alerting the reader who is unfamiliar with Malaysia to some of the features of national life—such as government, politics, and women's involvement in them—that are not found or exist in a different form at the village level. That Americans generally know rather little about Malaysia was underscored recently when U.S. Secretary of State Edmund Muskie, during an address in Malaysia's capital city, spoke "to the effect that he was surprised to find that Kuala Lumpur was a bustling modern city of a million people, instead of the 'sleepy village' he had expected" (Davies 1980).

Malaysia is a rapidly developing country and, particularly since the discovery and initial exploitation of offshore oil fields in its waters, the east coast state of Trengganu is experiencing the developmental thrust. Because changes are occurring at a fast rate—transportation and communication systems throughout the nation were enormously expanded in the 1970s, for example—Rusila and its people are increasingly affected by what happens in Malaysia and in Trengganu. And the women of Rusila feel the repercussions of events occurring far beyond their village at the edge of the South China Sea. These women may at times appear extremely vulnerable; they have never been isolated.

HISTORY

The Malay Peninsula (Malaya; formally, Peninsular Malaysia or West Malaysia) is located on an ancient international trade route. Indian and Chinese influences were felt there at least as early as the

1

fifth century; Arab traders were active in the area from about the
tenth century, and Muslim Indians arrived a few centuries later.
Merchants, missionaries, and monks went there; Indian, Chinese,
and Arab, Hindu, Buddhist, and Muslim cultural elements became
mixed with the indigenous.

In Malacca, across the peninsula from Trengganu, the ruler
was converted to Islam in 1414 and Muslim missionaries were sent
from Malacca to nearby areas within a few years. But the earliest
Muslim settlement on the peninsula may have been in Trengganu:

> Islam appears to have become a state religion in
> Trengganu on the east coast of the Malay Peninsula
> early in the fourteenth century. This is inferred from
> a recently discovered stone inscribed in Malay, in the
> Arabic script known as <u>Jawi</u>. This inscription is one
> of the oldest Malay texts, and is held to be the earliest
> contemporary record of the introduction of Islam into
> any state of the Peninsula. The inscription records
> certain legal provisions and its date is Rajab A.H. 702.
> This corresponds to March 1303, but owing to the oblit-
> eration of a word in the inscription other possibilities
> arise; one such is that the date may be the year 1386
> (Rauf 1967:30).

Aside from the inscription, no information about Trengganu at
this period is recorded. Generally, Islam came to "the Malayan
world"—Malaysia, Indonesia, and the Philippines—in two stages:
". . . a stage of incubation and a stage of mass conversion." The
former took place over a long period during which Muslim trading
colonies were established in coastal areas throughout the region;
the latter occurred as the result of conscious missionary efforts
aided by political and social changes that were already under way.
The impact of Islam was uneven, often being modified by long-
established belief systems and customary practices (Ibid.:84-89).

By the fifteenth century the Malay Peninsula was already divided among several societies that had different rulers and different
histories. All of them were based primarily on agricultural production of swidden (<u>ladang</u>), sedentary (<u>sawah</u>), or both types, and production was essentially for subsistence, with little surplus. The
family was the unit of production, with village-wide labor mobiliza-
tion for tasks such as land clearance. There were no class distinc-
tions within the villages, but in the larger societies three main, indigenous classes existed: rulers, the peasantry, and debt bondsmen
and slaves. Evidence from language, rituals, and customs suggests
that this three-tier system was already an old one by the nineteenth

century. Today there are no debt bondsmen nor slaves. The peasantry and urban poor form the base of the system, with an expanding educated middle class, a political and economic elite (the "technocrats" or "administrocrats"), and the Malay royal families at the apex. There is overlap at the top because members of some royal families are members of Parliament and hold Cabinet posts (Sundaram 1977).

By the end of the fifteenth century, Malacca was established as the leading commercial power in the region primarily because of its commanding position on the Straits of Malacca, which link the Indian Ocean and the South China Sea, and are part of the route between Europe and Asia. Pepper, cloves, and nutmeg from the Spice Islands (Indonesia), silks and porcelain from China, camphor from Borneo, and fine cotton cloth from India, as well as hardwoods, gold and other metals, and an enormous variety of foodstuffs were among the goods arriving in the port. European interest in Southeast Asia grew as the region gained commercial importance. Malacca was captured by the Portuguese in 1511 and became their Southeast Asian commercial headquarters. It was taken by the Dutch in 1641 and by the British in 1795. Hostilities and competition among European nations (and later the United States) were carried into Southeast Asia—warfare, piracy and privateering, political intrigue and influence, and finally colonization.

On the Malay Peninsula the British purchased the island of Penang from the Sultan of Kedah in 1786, and in 1819 they acquired the island of Singapore from the Sultan of Johore. The three ports, including Malacca, were called the Straits Settlements by the British colonialists, and after 1867 they were administered from London.

A form of indirect rule was established by the British over the west coast sultanates of Perak, Selangor, and Negri Sembilan, and of Pahang on the east coast. The ruler of each state was under treaty to follow the advice, ". . . a word for effective British control" (McIntyre 1964:138), of a British resident in all matters except those pertaining to Islam and Malay customary practices (adat). Through an agreement signed by each of the rulers in 1895, the Federated Malay States became an "administrative union" (Ibid.:139) controlled from Kuala Lumpur.

Britain recognized Thai suzerainty over four northern sultanates—Kelantan, Trengganu, Kedah, and Perlis—until the threat of intervention in the area by other Western powers caused a policy reversal in London. Thailand ceded the four "tributary" states to Great Britain in 1909 and the present Thai-Malaysian frontier was drawn. Johore, which already had close ties with Britain, accepted a British adviser-general in 1914. These five states gradually became known as the Unfederated Malay States. The rights of the

sultans in the unfederated states ". . . were not encroached upon to
the same degree as in the federated states . . . [and] for various
reasons these states retained their Malay character" (Ibid. :140).

British control of the peninsula had been extended in piecemeal
fashion during a period of more than a century. The British maintained the Malay class structure by preserving some of the rights of
the Malay sultans in the Federated and Unfederated Malay States.
But the rulers and their subjects experienced varying degrees of
British control.

Trengganu in 1909 was ". . . very much an independent Malay
State" (Chan 1965:159), despite the former suzerainty of Thailand,
and culturally it was almost homogeneous, with a population primarily made up of Malay peasants (Allen 1968:26). There is some
disagreement in early twentieth-century British reports about life
in Trengganu at the time. W. A. Graham reported ". . . the absence of laws, courts and police, the flourishing of crime and oppression of the peasantry . . ." (quoted by Chan 1965:164), while a
report by Conlay written the same year (1909) described the government of Trengganu as "loose," then added, ". . . there does not
seem to be any oppression as a consequence" (quoted by Allen 1968:
28-29). In J. de Vere Allen's appraisal, the government was mar-
ginal to the lives of most of the people in Trengganu. Government
revenues were small; the average person contributed very little and,
in return, received very little. Local Malay leadership apparently
resided in men who had made the pilgrimage to Mecca (Hajis) or had
other Islamic statuses, such as claim of descent from the Prophet
Muhammad. Allen suggests that Islamic religious leaders were probably more important in Trengganu than in any other part of the peninsula (Ibid.:25-28). Religious education was unequaled elsewhere in
the peninsula, but only a one-teacher vernacular school for Malays
had been established in the state by 1918 (Chan 1965:185).

Although non-Malay immigrants had come to the peninsula for
centuries, Chinese and Indian immigration into Malaya was officially
encouraged during the colonial period as a means of fulfilling British
economic interests until the worldwide depression of the 1930s caused
decreased demand for rubber and tin, Malaya's major exports. Furthermore, it was during the colonial period that formerly "fluid and
accommodating" ethnic relations became rigid; and ". . . with the
subsequent development of British interests an effective division of
labour along 'ethnic' lines began to emerge, with the Malays in the
civil service and agriculture, the Chinese as miners and urban entrepreneurs, and the Indians as plantation workers" (Nagata 1979:10).

The Japanese occupation of Malaya began when troops landed
in Kelantan on December 8, 1941, and rapidly swept south. The
peninsula was never totally subjugated because local guerrillas and

British "stay-behind" units operated from jungle bases throughout the war. Nevertheless, under the Japanese, Malaya became a single administrative unit for the first time—until the Japanese returned the four northern sultanates to Thailand in 1943. On the island of Borneo, the Japanese ended the British North Borneo Company's 60 years of control in Sabah, and a century of rule by the "white rajas" of the Brooke family in Sarawak. Both of the Borneo states became British colonies following World War II. Japanese victories in Southeast Asia had important long-range consequences: they proved to other Asians that the European colonial powers were not invincible, that Asians could triumph over them. Thus Japan's military conquests, ironically, encouraged the further development of nationalism in the lands they conquered.

In Rusila the war years are remembered as a time of constant fear and food scarcity. Even in 1965 the sight of a small British military unit stopping briefly in a village coconut grove one evening led women to lock themselves and their children in darkened homes while a group of men approached the unit commander to find out what was happening. When I later inquired if Rusila people had bad experiences with the British military, I was told that was not the case. The villagers had not responded to the nationality of the soldiers, because initially they did not know their nationality; their response was to military men, a response based on both personal experiences and accounts of sexual molestation of local women by Japanese soldiers during the occupation.

The British reestablished their authority in Malaya at the end of 1945, and soon created the Malayan Union to unite the peninsula under a strong central government. The Malay rulers would have lost all but nominal power under the Union, which was finally abandoned in response to strong protests from the Malay community and, for other reasons, from non-Malays as well. An alternative plan for the Federation of Malaya was devised and effected in 1948, the same year that saw the beginning of the 12-year Emergency, when jungle-based guerrillas of the Malayan Communist Party (MCP) attempted to gain control of the country. The guerrillas were well supplied with arms, many provided by the British during the war against the Japanese. Despite the civil war, plans for independence proceeded and Malaya gained freedom from British control in 1957. Singapore and the Borneo states remained Crown colonies.

By 1957 the peninsula's population was less than 50 percent ethnic Malay. Citizenship in the Federation had previously been conferred automatically only upon Malays and indigenous peoples (orang asli), while Malayan Chinese and Indians were required to apply for citizenship unless they had been born in one of the three Straits Settlements. Citizenship might also be claimed by anyone

habitually speaking Malay, conforming to Malay customary practices (adat), and professing Islam, the constitutional definition of a
Malay (Fed. Const. XII. 160. [2]). Indonesian immigrants were the
most likely beneficiaries of this option.

Six years after independence the Federation of Malaya was
joined by three former British colonies, the Borneo states of Sabah
and Sarawak (East Malaysia), and Singapore, in the Federation of
Malaysia. Singapore seceded in 1965 and became an independent
nation.

The Malay women of Rusila live in an area that experienced
some of the earliest Islamic influence on the peninsula, an area
that, although ruled by a Malay Sultan, had passed from Thai to
British control, then to the Japanese (who returned it to Thailand),
back to the British, and finally became a state in an independent
nation.

THE COUNTRY AND THE PEOPLE

Malaysia comprises a land area of 128,553 square miles divided into 13 states: the 11 of Peninsular Malaysia and the two of
East Malaysia, separated from the mainland by the South China Sea.

The country is located just north of the equator and is part of
an area characterized by a monsoon climate, one dominated by strong
winds blowing from one direction for almost half the year and from
the other direction during the rest of the year, dividing the annual
cycle into fairly distinct wet and dry periods that occur on the east
coast and the west coast at different times. The northeast monsoon,
from November to March or April, is the stronger of the two and
makes its greater impact on the east coast. In Malay the monsoon
is called musim gelora, the season of storms, a time of powerful
winds and torrential rains.

The mountain ranges of the mainland are aligned northwest to
southeast, with a central spine almost bisecting the 460-mile-long
peninsula. Coastal plains are on both sides of the mountainous core
and form the major agricultural areas in the country. The west
coast is characterized by mangrove swamps and mud flats; along the
South China Sea of the east coast, magnificent sandy beaches with a
backdrop of casuarina trees and coconut palms are typical. Forest
and swamps cover almost four-fifths of the peninsula and a larger
percentage of Malaysian Borneo.

Rivers abound. In early times their location determined settlement patterns and some local centers of political power and trade—
both Kuala Lumpur (Malaysia's capital city, shown on the map as
K. L.) and Kuala Trengganu (the capital of Trengganu, shown on the

map as K.T.) developed at points where two rivers meet. The loca-
tions are reflected in their names, for kuala means "a confluence."

The ports—Malacca and Penang—and other cities, including
Kuala Lumpur, on the western side of the mountain ranges were
most developed during the colonial period. The northern and east
coast sections of the country experienced a much slower rate of
change.

The population of Malaysia was estimated at 13.3 million in
1979 (Kane 1979), with about 85 percent of the people living in Peninsular Malaysia. The 1970 census showed the population as 47.1 percent Malay, 33.9 percent Chinese, and 9.1 percent Indian, with indigenous peoples such as the Kadazan of Sabah, the Iban of Sarawak,
several orang asli societies on the mainland, Eurasians, and others
making up the remainder. For some official purposes Malays and
indigenous peoples are categorized together as bumiputra (son of the
soil).

Government policies are directed toward elevating the bumiputra
to a position of educational and economic equality with the members of
other major segments of the society. Thus the official identification
of an individual as a bumiputra or a Chinese or an Indian affects his
or her access to educational facilities, to civil service and other
jobs, and determines what type of business or land can be owned.

Malaysia is a polyethnic society (Nagata 1979); and the Malays,
Chinese, and Indians—be they defined as ethnic categories (Strauch
1979), ethnic groups (Wilson 1967; Enloe 1973), or races (official
records and the Malaysian press)—which account for 90 percent of
the population, are neither monocultural nor immutable entities,
despite stereotypes to the contrary. Judith Nagata has demonstrated
that the expression of ethnicity in Malaysia can be ". . . ephemeral,
volatile, and changing . . ." (1979:252), depending on a variety of
situations and circumstances. Keeping this important point in mind,
it is still possible to consider some of the differences found within
the broad census categories.

Among the Chinese ethnolinguistic types include Hakka, Hokkien,
and Cantonese, and there are also the Baba Chinese, whose residence
in the Straits Settlements dates from at least the sixteenth century,
when immigrant Chinese males intermarried with local Malay women.
There are Buddhists and Christians, categories that each have variants, and increasing numbers of Chinese converts to Islam.

The Indians include Tamils, subdivided by point of origin in
either South India or Ceylon (Sri Lanka), Pumjabis, Malayalis, and
others. They are Hindus, Sikhs, Muslims, Christians, and Bahais.

Malays share a religion, Islam, but today religious viewpoint
increasingly divides the extreme fundamentalists from moderate
Muslims. Malays also share a language, Malay, although there are

dialectical variations associated with different parts of the country. Dialectical forms are lessening as the population of the nation becomes more educated, because Standard Malay is taught in all schools. In Rusila during 1965, for example, a wedding feast was referred to as makan besar (to eat big); by 1979 even villagers with no formal education were using the Standard Malay word, jamuan (feast), for such an event. And it is Standard Malay that is shared by educated Chinese and Indians as well as Malays and others.

Malay customary practices (adat) comprise two systems, both of which modify Islamic law to some extent and determine practices associated with rites of passage. The system typical among Trengganu Malays is adat temenggong, a male-oriented system that is dominant throughout the peninsula except in large areas of Negri Sembilan and Malacca on the west coast. There, adat perpateh, a female-oriented system, is practiced by the descendants of peoples who came from Sumatra. A further division among "Malays" is that almost 5 percent of the people so classified in the 1970 census still see themselves as "Indonesians" (Nagata 1974).

TRENGGANU

The state of Trengganu covers 5,050 square miles on the eastern side of the central mountain range, and is intersected by 16 rivers. The total population in 1970 was 404,924, a density of 81 persons per square mile, almost the same as the national figure. Women are in the majority: There are 98.3 males to every 100 females in the state, a figure that reflects to some extent the out-migration of young males. Nationally there are 101.5 males to every 100 females.

The following profile of Trengganu in 1957 and 1970, and comparisons with other states in the Federation or the nation as a whole, are drawn from the 1970 population census (Table 1.1).

Trengganu has the highest percentage of Malays and the lowest percentages of Chinese and Indians of any state in the Federation, and the statistics show a communal distribution very different from that of the nation. Although it is stereotyped as a rural state, Trengganu's urban population has grown rapidly and is now 26.9 percent of the total, the same as the national percentage.

The crude birth rate is exceeded only in the states of Kelantan to the north and Sabah in East Malaysia. Trengganu has the second highest crude death rate, after Kelantan, in the Federation. Nevertheless, both rates showed a considerable decrease between 1957 and 1970, attesting to improved health care on the one hand and to more education and interest in family planning on the other.

TABLE 1.1

Comparative Statistics: Trengganu 1957
and 1970, Malaysia 1970

| | Trengganu | | Malaysia |
	1957	1970	1970
Distribution by community (percent)			
Malays	91.9	93.6	47.1
Chinese	6.6	5.5	33.9
Indians	1.1	0.7	9.1
Others	0.4	0.1	9.9*
Percent urban population	19.0	26.9	26.9
Crude birth rate (per 1,000 persons)	41.6	36.0	34.1
Crude death rate (per 1,000 persons)	14.4	9.2	7.1
Median age of females at first marriage	16.3	18.6	21.2
Literacy, any language, people 10 years and over (percent)	30.3	48.9	58.0

*Figure not provided in the source.
Source: Federation of Malaysia 1977b, pp. 21-23.

Although the median age at first marriage has risen from 16.3 years in 1957 to 18.6 years in 1970, Trengganu has the lowest median of all states in the nation, followed by Kelantan and Sabah. The others all have a median of 20 years or more.

Trengganu's literacy rate continues to be far lower than the national average, but significant gains were made between 1957 and 1970. The 1980 census is expected to show a continuation of these trends: a higher percentage of people living in urban areas; lower birth and death rates; higher median age at first marriage; and a further rise in literacy.

Trengganu is the only state in Malaysia that has a high urban population without having a metropolitan center. Five towns, including Kuala Trengganu, are classed as urban centers but not cities. The majority of people in both the nation and the state live in villages; some, close to towns and affected by urban change and an increasing demand for housing from urban workers; others, in nearly isolated villages without electricity or piped water, where transportation routes are rudimentary dirt tracks and the nearest clinic or market is a long, difficult journey away. The presence of absence of modernization features may be a function of the economy, but ultimately economic allocation within a country is political. Where Trengganu ranks in the Malaysian distribution of power—rather low to date—affects all its residents, often its women in particular.

GOVERNMENT AND POLITICS

The Federal Constitution of 1957 established Islam as the official religion of Malaysia; the right to practice other religions in "peace and harmony" (Fed. Const. I.3.[1]) is permitted, although proselytizing by members of other faiths among Muslims can be forbidden by the states. Malay is the official national language. Both federal and state governments are provided for, with federal law to prevail over state law in cases of inconsistencies between the two. But matters pertaining to Islam, religious law, and Muslim personal law are specified as within the jurisdiction of the individual states. A Supreme Head of the Federation (Yang di Pertuan Agong), a Conference of Rulers, a two-house Parliament, a Cabinet headed by a Prime Minister, and a judiciary are all defined, the structure reflecting the colonial legacy.

The Conference of Rulers has nine members, the hereditary Rulers of the former Federated and Unfederated Malay States, who continue as heads of their respective states. They select the Supreme Head of the Federation from among their number, by seniority, to serve a five-year term—a unique form of kingship.

The Rulers are men, as are the Prime Minister and the heads of those states that do not have sultans. A woman cannot be a Ruler, nor is it remotely likely that a woman would become Prime Minister in Malaysia because of the Islamic emphasis on leadership being vested in men.

The Yang di Pertuan Agong takes precedence over all persons in the Federation. His consort, the Raja Permaisuri Agong, takes precedence after the king over all persons in the Federation. Among the duties of the Yang di Pertuan Agong is the responsibility ". . . to safeguard the special position of the Malays and the legitimate interests of other communities . . ." (Fed. Const. XII.153.[1]), including the reservation of quotas for Malays in the public service, for scholarships and educational and training privileges, and for trade and business permits. The rationale for Malay quotas and other privileges was, and continues to be, their need for the opportunity to catch up economically with the "immigrant races," especially the Chinese.

Legislative authority is vested in a Parliament comprising the Dewan Negara (Senate) and the Dewan Rakyat (House of Representatives). The Senate is composed of elected members, two from each state, and 32 appointed by the Yang di Pertuan Agong. Members serve a term of six years, half being appointed or elected every three years. The House consists of 154 elected members, each representing a single-member territorial constituency, who hold office for five years. The electorate comprises all citizens, female and male, who are 21 years of age or older.

The Prime Minister is selected from the members of the House by the Yang di Pertuan Agong, who also appoints Cabinet members (from Senate or House) and the Chief Justice of the Supreme Court, usually in consultation with the Prime Minister.

Each state within the Federation has its own constitution and government, headed by either a hereditary Ruler or a Governor. There are also a popularly elected Legislative Assembly in each state and an Executive Council headed by a Chief Minister, the Council and Chief Minister appointed by the Ruler or Governor but responsible to the Assembly and selected from its ranks.

The first formal elections in Malaya were held in 1952, five years prior to independence and in the midst of the Emergency. Most parties were (and are) ethnic-based, making ethnic cooperation a necessity if a government was to be formed. The United Malays National Organization (UMNO), the Malayan Chinese Association (MCA), and the Malayan Indian Congress (MIC) joined together to form the Alliance, with UMNO as the senior partner. Parliamentary candidates stood for election under the auspices of one of the ethnic parties, but a seat in Parliament was won (or lost) for the Alliance. The Alliance gained a majority in Parliament and formed the government that saw the country gain independence with Tunku Abdul Rahman as the first Prime Minister. Opposition parties included the Pan-Malayan Islamic Party (now, PAS or PI), which has its major stronghold in the northern and east coast states with their high concentration of Malays, the Labour Party (reorganized as the Socialist Front in 1957), and several other small parties.

Riots, resulting from complex social, political, and economic discontents, followed the elections of May 1969, when opposition parties, both Malay and non-Malay, made unexpected gains in the number of votes received. The riots can be seen on one level as an expression of Malay-Chinese antagonisms; on another level it has been argued that the Chinese are a visible target for Malay frustrations growing from contradictions between expectations and realities that are basically rooted in intra-Malay class conflict (Stenson 1976:48).

A state of emergency was declared and Parliament was sus-
pended until January 1971. A broader coalition of parties forming
the government was defined as a prerequisite for reconvening Parliament. But UMNO, the largest Malay party, remained "first
among equals" in the coalition, just as it had been since 1952. Some
parties that had been among the opposition combined with those in the
Alliance to assure the two-thirds majority needed to amend the constitution: among the changes, public discussion of "sensitive issues"—
including race relations—was banned. Thus the official view that the
conflict resulted from racial (ethnic) antagonisms rather than from
economic disparities between classes became part of the Federal Constitution. The government also declared the need to restructure
Malaysian society through effecting the Second Malaysia Plan (1971-
75), with its objectives of national unity and the eradication of poverty
among all Malaysians "irrespective of race" (Federation of Malaysia
1971b:v). These goals were reiterated in the Third Malaysia Plan
(1976-80).

With the increase in the number of parties forming a coalition,
the umbrella name for them was changed from the Alliance to Barisan
Nasional (National Front). PAS, briefly a National Front member,
and the Democratic Action Party (DAP), supported mainly by Chinese,
are the most important opposition parties. The National Front retained a large majority of Parliament seats after the 1978 elections.
Because of the elections, a number of articles in the Malaysian press
focused on women in politics.

WOMEN IN MALAYSIAN POLITICS AND GOVERNMENT

"Women in politics: are we too docile?" (NST 7/4/78), by S.
Ching Ji, reported an interview with Dr. Leonore Manderson, an
Australian anthropologist, about her forthcoming book, Women, Poli-
tics and Change, based on a study of the largest women's organiza-
tion in Malaysia, Wanita UMNO, the women's section of the United
Malays National Organization.

> The political role of the majority of women is supportive
> in nature. At election time women's votes are keenly
> sought and in victory speeches their contributions are
> openly acknowledged. Women are, in the main, loyal,
> reliable voters.
> Even women leaders are loyal and make it a point
> not to rock the boat. Resolutions that are aimed at im-
> proving the lot and status of women are aired often and
> mostly behind closed doors. Matters that might prove

controversial or embarrassing are seldom taken to
the press or discussed publicly.

Although women are regarded as equal to men
by many, in general both men and women accept
women's limited participation in politics and decision
making. . . .

Changes and demands will be met slowly, with a
lot of patient bargaining. On the other hand, it is perhaps this mildness of attitude and adherence to tradition
that contributes largely to stability in a society which is
changing and evolving all the time.

Women see themselves as peacemakers within the
home. They believe that only with harmonious homes
is it possible for society to develop, and for many, this
is as much a political as a personal ethic.

Thus, despite self-determination, massive
changes in education and industrialization, women in
Malaysia seem content to continue in the part that they
see themselves playing, and in this context, the changes
in Malaysian society, economics and politics have not
really affected their traditional values and priorities. . . .

But they do want certain things, and among them,
are more seats in the Dewan Negara and possibly more
posts in the Cabinet—which are not tall orders considering that the present ratio of women [in government to
those in the population] is in the region of 1:730,000 while
the comparative figure for men is about 1:30,000. . . .

"First-timer on the campaign trail" (NST 7/2/78), by Zainah
Anuar, followed a National Front candidate, Rafidah Aziz, through
a day of campaigning. The chatty article gave a good idea of the
hectic pace demanded of a candidate as well as some of her political
views. She was later elected to Parliament and then appointed Deputy
Minister of Finance. Other articles focused on important winners
such as Datin Paduka Hajjah Aishah Ghani, who won her seat in Parliament and maintained her position in the Cabinet. She is the only
woman with the rank of Minister. Her Ministry, Welfare Services,
is said to get "the lowest priority" in allocation of funds (Star 8/30/78).
She rose to political prominence in the 1940s and "remains as the
most important woman leader in the political arena" (Khadijah
Muhamed 1978:20).

In the state of Selangor, Puan Zaleha Ismail was elected to the
State Assembly and became the first woman in the nation to be appointed an Executive Councillor. She took charge of the Works, Utili-
ties, and Water Supply Committee.

Following the national elections there were two political events of importance to UMNO: The Wanita UMNO General Assembly's elections for membership on the Wanita UMNO Central Executive Committee and the elections to the Supreme Council of UMNO.

> Puan Zaleha Ismail received the largest number of
> votes (309) in her reelection to the Wanita UMNO Cen-
> tral Executive Committee; Deputy Finance Minister
> Puan Rafidah Aziz got 307 votes. Altogether, 36 can-
> didates contested for the ten places in the committee.
> The assembly was addressed by Wanita UMNO leader,
> Datin Paduka Hajjah Aishah Ghani, who said "Wanita
> UMNO had fared well with 18 out of their 19 candi-
> dates [for positions in the House and the State Assem-
> blies] winning" (NST 9/15/78).

There were only 26 women candidates from all of the political parties; the 19 winners included 7 in the Dewan Rakyat, which has 154 members, and 12 in the State Assemblies.

Two women were among the 20 Malays elected to the Supreme Council of UMNO. Puan Rafidah Aziz placed second in the voting, with 878 votes, and Puan Zaleha Ismail was twentieth, with 425 votes. Wanita UMNO leader Datin Paduka Hajjah Aishah Ghani is also a member of the Supreme Council and one of the vice-presidents. Puan Rafidah ". . . thanked the delegates, especially the women, who although numbering only about 100, had gone round the various divisions to convince the members on the need for women to sit on the Supreme Council" (Star 9/17/78). She attributed Wanita's success to ". . . its new strategy of compromise and cooperation among members." Under the new strategy Wanita did not propose a large number of candidates (as had been done in previous years), so as to strengthen the chances of women candidates. They proposed only two; both were elected (SunMail 9/17/78).

Deputy Finance Minister Rafidah Aziz was selected to give the keynote address at the ten-day annual Commonwealth Parliamentary Association conference in Kingston, Jamaica. At the Kingston meeting a fund was established to "promote democratic parliamentary procedures." Puan Rafidah was one of four people chosen to participate in the pilot project, a scrutiny of public expenditures in parliamentary systems (NST 10/6/78).

"The need for a special women's unit in the Prime Minister's Department to handle the affairs of the 'fairer sex' . . ." was reiterated by Puan Rafidah while addressing a convention on women's role in development at the Women's Institute in Kuala Lumpur. She said the unit should have its own staff ". . . who are well versed in laws relating to women . . ." and should be able to ". . . plan and implement a strategy which will help to involve women in national development." She was particularly concerned about mobilizing rural women and with the need for upgrading training facilities related to modern agriculture for them. At the present time the participation of women in such organizations as cooperatives and district-level committees is so limited that it is ". . . a show of tokenism." Puan Rafidah denied ". . . the widely held notion that social activities and a career would lead to a broken home. 'It all boils down to how skillfully you balance your time and energy between home, career and society and how you list your priorities,' she said" (NST 10/31/78).

Puan Rafidah was the only woman among the "technocrats" featured in a Far Eastern Economic Review article by K. Das, "All the premier's bright young men" [sic] (1978:29).

Among the 58 senators there are five women (8.6 percent), all of whom are Malays. During one debate in the Dewan Negara, three of them spoke. Senator Datin Hajjah Mahimon binti Haji Harun raised the problem of unemployed young people and deteriorating discipline in the society, for which she suggested a ". . . 'Discipline Week' to arrest this unhealthy trend." Senator Zawiah binti Abdullah ". . . urged the National Front to nominate more women in future elections at parliamentary and state level" because the number of women in such positions is small. Senator Hajjah Salmah binti Sheikh Hussein (president of the women's section of PAS, an opposition party) emphasized the need for the government to be more concerned with the welfare of rural people (NST 10/26/78).

Mrs. Rosemary Chong (Madam Chow Poh Kheng), National Front (MCA) Member of Parliament for Ulu Langat and the only Chinese woman Member of Parliament, ". . . urged the Government to allow separate taxation for wives having their own business or working with their husbands as was done for couples earning salaries." She also discussed the minimum wage vis-à-vis standard of living, and welfare benefits for ". . . breadwinners who lost their livelihood through circumstances beyond their control" during debate in the Dewan Rakyat (Star 11/2/78).

Speaking at the MCA Wanita General Assembly, in her role as leader of that group, Mrs. Chong pointed out that ". . . political representation of women in the country is poor although there is no legal barrier . . ." and added that ". . . equal opportunities in every field should be given to women" (SunMail 11/26/78).

Aside from press coverage of the proceedings of the Dewan Rakyat and Dewan Negara and features in the women's pages, only three women's names appear regularly in the English language newspapers: Puan Rafidah Aziz (Deputy Finance Minister), Datin Paduka

Hajjah Aishah Ghani (Minister of Welfare Services and leader of Wanita UMNO), and Mrs. Rosemary Chong (Member of Parliament for Ulu Langat and leader of Wanita MCA). The amount of coverage that the three receive—only a small sample is included here—suggests a greater involvement of women in politics than is actually the case.

The MIC president, Tan Sri V. Manickavasagam, ". . . called on his party branches to give more opportunities to women members to serve the party and the nation." He was opening a political seminar for women organized by the Perak branch of Wanita MIC. He noted that "many complaints have been received by the party of the lack of women members on various committees." The MIC deputy president, Mr. S. Samy Vellu, speaking about complaints that MIC women ". . . were not given chances to serve as MPs and in other political positions, said the party could not do anything about it at present in view of the limited opportunities for the party" (NST 2/5/79).

The limited opportunities to which Mr. Vellu referred are related to the fact that Indians constitute less than 10 percent of the Malaysian population, although they account for significant portions of railroad and plantation workers, and medical and legal professionals. The role of women in national and state politics is limited generally, but opportunities are further circumscribed for some women by their ethnicity. Women's councils, associations, and organizations have the potential for political action and influence; the one most directly concerned with trying to influence development policy is the National Advisory Council on the Integration of Women in Development (NACIWID).

NACIWID is composed of 25 members, 15 of whom represent ministries or government agencies, and the states of Sarawak and Sabah; they are selected subject to the Prime Minister's approval. Twelve of these representatives are women. None of them are at the top of their respective government organization's hierarchy, and therefore they have little power to push for support regarding acceptance and implementation of recommendations made by NACIWID. Other representatives are from women's organizations or serve as members at large.

NACIWID has no permanent supporting staff except one secretary. This means that the work done by it is apportioned to members, most of whom hold full-time jobs. As well as those employed in the ministries, there are members like Member of Parliament Rosemary Chong and Datin Fatimah Hamid-Don, Dean of the Faculty of Education at the University of Malaya. A majority of the members are also married and have children. Considering the demands on the time of its members, it is not surprising that NACIWID has moved rather slowly.

NACIWID was formed on July 16, 1976. A Plan of Action in English was circulated in January 1978. It was minimally revised and published in Malay as Wanita dalam Pembangunan: Rancangan Tindakan in December 1978, and circulated during January 1979.

The plan covers the decade from 1976 to 1985 and sets out the objectives of NACIWID:

(1) To serve as a coordinating, consultative and advisory body to the Government and between the Government and non-governmental women's organizations;

(2) To arouse national consciousness amongst women on their role and responsibilities towards nation-building;

(3) To ensure the full integration of women in national development;

(4) To enable women to develop their potential capabilities to the maximum;

(5) To arouse the awareness of women on their rights; and

(6) To contribute towards the promotion of international peace (undated: 1-2).

The problems to be overcome in order to accomplish these objectives are outlined, and specific strategies for achieving goals in nine broad areas—including equal participation with men in every field; strengthening the family and enhancing woman's role as home-maker, wife, and mother; and improving the legal status of women—are given.

One report sponsored by NACIWID, "Income-Generating Skills for Women: Interim Report," was produced by a team from the Faculty of Education, University of Malaya, headed by Professor Fatimah Hamid-Don. It was ready for distribution in December 1978. The report places great emphasis on education as the underlying income-generating skill. By February 1979, Professor Fatimah had received proposals from several Malaysian universities with faculty members interested in studying "women's needs and aspirations." These were awaiting analysis and, if accepted, faced the question of funding because no budget had yet been allocated for the work.

Recommendations in such reports are submitted to the government and the private sector for action. NACIWID, "The Women's Cabinet," can only encourage and urge implementation. It has no power to take direct action.

The Women's Institute—officially, the National Association of Women's Institutes of Malaysia (NAWIM)—was envisioned as a non-political, nonracial, nonreligious movement when it was introduced from Great Britain in 1952. It was seen as a means of enabling women and girls, particularly those in rural areas, to participate in community development. The movement has been criticized recently for a pro-Malay tendency and for teaching ". . . week after week . . . nothing except cookery" (Siraj 1975:51-67, 133). There are no Women's Institutes in the Rusila area, nor are any other national women's organizations, except the Girl Guides, represented there.

OTHER DIMENSIONS OF POLITICS

The interrelatedness of politics, economics, ethnoreligious features, and the effects of historical forces and colonial decisions is manifest in some current regional and domestic problems. The examples must be brief, and therefore only suggest the complexities.

Wars and persecution elsewhere have continued to reverberate on Malaysia's political and ethnic dynamics, with some direct effects on the villagers of Rusila. More than 150,000 "boat people" from Vietnam and approximately 120,000 Muslims from the southern Philippines, the former landing along the east coast of Peninsular Malaysia in the states of Trengganu, Kelantan, and Pahang, and the latter making their way to nearby Sabah, arrived in Malaysia during the late 1970s. The Malaysian government has not offered permanent asylum to refugees from Vietnam; it has allowed free entry to Muslims escaping from the revolt in Mindanao against the central government of the Philippines. The reasons appear to be multifaceted.

The governments of Malaysia and Vietnam have not established diplomatic relations; pleas from the Malaysian government to leaders in Vietnam to halt the human outpouring were acknowledged, but no action was taken. It became obvious that help from the Hanoi regime could not be expected, and that the flow might continue unabated. The refugees had no hope of returning to their homeland because they were fleeing from government policies and actions that were unlikely to change in the near future. Malaysia and the Philippines have diplomatic relations and are members (along with Indonesia, Thailand, and Singapore) of the Association of Southeast Asian Nations (ASEAN), which is committed to promoting economic stability in the area. The Philippine government has been making attempts—some halfhearted—to address the grievances of Muslim revolutionaries in the South. Thus channels of communication and cooperation exist between the two nations, and the possibility for ending the internal conflict and enabling the voluntary return of a majority of the refugees to Mindanao and the Sulu Archipelago could be considered likely.

Within the context of Malaysia's internal politics, the refugee problem has been dominated by ethnoreligious considerations. The people from the southern Philippines are Muslims whose culture shares many basic similarities with Malay culture, and who speak languages related to Malay (see Kiefer 1972). Allowing them refuge is acceptable or laudable to Malays; complaints from non-Muslim Sabahans have been muted or unreported in the press.

The people arriving from Vietnam are non-Muslims, and a majority of them are ethnic Chinese. The initial Malay reaction to the "boat people" was compassion and tolerance; but as the number of refugees increased, so did the fears of local people. During the spring of 1979, when an average of 2,000 refugees per week arrived on the east coast, villagers in Rusila and nearby areas likened the situation to the Japanese invasion of 1941. They worried about being outnumbered by non-Malays and losing their land to outsiders even though refugees were being interned in camps. However unrealistic these fears, the people who expressed them believed them strongly.

The economic strain created by the massive influx of people was real enough. Although provision of food and other necessities was underwritten by international organizations, many supplies were purchased in Malaysia. Temporary shortages of some goods and higher prices for others occurred, most notably in Kelantan and Trengganu, states that have a high percentage of poor rural Malays. These states are also a stronghold of the Malay-Muslim party (PAS), UMNO's chief rival for Malay votes. That PAS played upon the fears and realities is likely because the refugee situation allowed blame to be cast on the government, particularly on UMNO. Malaysian Chinese have, for the most part, remained silent on the issue, perhaps largely out of awareness of their own vulnerability (see Strauch 1980 for a detailed discussion).

Ethnic politics combined with economic problems concerning refugees are certainly not confined to Malaysia. We need look only as far as Florida, where thousands of Cubans arrived during the summer of 1980, to find obvious parallels of international migration altering precarious ethnic/racial political and economic balance (see Burkholz 1980).

When the border between Malaysia and Thailand was fixed in 1909, it was drawn through some areas inhabited by Malays. If government was "loose," as Conlay's report suggested, an official border probably made little difference to the rural people living on one side or the other. But that has changed in recent years. Increasingly, segments of the Malay population in southern Thailand have come to see themselves as economically and educationally disadvantaged in comparison with Thais. Muslim secessionists who want their region joined with Malaysia have become more active and more violent in pressing their demands. One group, the Pattani United

Liberation Organization, claimed responsibility for a bomb explosion during June 1980 that injured 30 people in a Bangkok bus terminal. Such groups get no encouragement from the Malaysian government, which deplores their use of violence. Malaysia is concerned to maintain good relations with Thailand and to continue joint efforts against the illegal MCP, some groups of which regularly move back and forth across the border between the two countries.

Terrorist activities by MCP members within Malaysia have continued on a small scale, intermittently, although the Emergency officially ended in 1960. Malay leaders in government have always defined Islam as an essential moral force against communism in Malaysia.

ISLAM

Prime Minister Datuk Hussein Onn has expressed this view, but also acknowledged the danger of religious extremism:

We need missionaries, but not fanaticism. Islam can counter communism. If it fails, then don't talk about religion any more. Hinduism, Buddhism, Christianity, they will all be finished. But the extremists can also finish them off (Tasker 1979:23).

During January 1980, Muslim leaders of The Forces of the Righteous Path, an illegal extremist organization, were arrested. The aim of the "holy army" is to create a Muslim state based on Malay support, for the benefit of Malays. The organization was ready ". . . to resort to violent and unconstitutional methods to achieve its ends if necessary" (Das 1980:24). While such extremist groups are small, they have an effect in the society that is disproportionate to their numbers, elevating fears among non-Muslims and further jeopardizing relations between Muslims and non-Muslims, Malays and non-Malays.

A distinction must be made between groups committed to Islamic revitalization and the fanatic fringe that distorts many Muslim teachings. Revitalization is defined by Malay leaders as positive, encouraging heightened morality and strength within the Muslim community (as well as increasing opposition to communism). Fanaticism is seen as a threat to the political and legal structure, secular education, and economic progress.

The Malay Islamic revitalization or missionary movement and some of the extremist groups have been referred to as dakwah groups or part of a dakwah movement. But it is clear that there is no

unifying leadership at present and that the "movement" comprises
moderates, progressives, and extremists, those whose aims are
consciously political and those who consider themselves apolitical
although their activities may have political impact (see Kessler 1980
for an analysis of dakwah's complexities). The diversity among
dakwah proponents is not surprising, for Islam, like other widely
spread religions, takes many forms.

> Militant Islam is one form; bourgeois Islam of the
> bazaar and the middle class is another; reactionary
> Islam is yet another. Some read socialism into Islam,
> and we should not be surprised when their adversaries
> find in the same Islam high regard for private property
> and inequality (Ajami 1980:6).

There are two major denominations within Islam: the Shi'a,
divided into three sects associated with different regions of the
world, and the Sunni, comprising approximately 90 percent of all
Muslims, including those in Southeast Asia (Rasjidi 1958:418), although Clifford Geertz argues that "Sunni Islam did not, today still
does not, represent the spiritual mainstream in Indonesia" (1968:42).
Two important Sunni sects (in Saudi Arabia and Pakistan) and a number of viewpoints that range from orthodox to reformist, but have
not resulted in sectarian development, are recognized. The Sufi
orders (mystics) are not classed as sects because adherents consider themselves to be Sunni or Shi'a as well as Sufi. Further,
there are four schools of Islamic law, founded in different places at
different times, that reflect variations in theological interpretation.
The Shafi'i school, based on a moderate theology between tradition-
alism and extreme legalism, predominates in Southeast Asia (Rasjidi
1958). And in Malaysia there are two systems of customary practices (adat) that modify Islamic law.
　　The basic source for Islam is the revealed Holy Quran, supplemented by the Sunnah and reasoning about them. The Sunnah is
a codification of the advice, values, and behavior of the Prophet,
the compilation of which began about 150 years after the death of
Muhammad and was finished almost 100 years later, thus allowing
interpretation differences that persist today. The third widely, although not universally, accepted source of Islam is reasoning
". . . about the intent of the Qur'an and Sunnah by those men who
are recognized as having the training and experience which qualifies
them to reason properly" (Ibid.:403).
　　There are universals as well as alternatives within Islam.
All Muslims share the six fundamentals of belief: ". . . in God,
Angels, revealed scriptures, prophets, the Day of Judgement, and
the destiny of man for good or evil" (Ibid.:408).

Also, a Muslim has five basic duties, generally referred to in English as "The Five Pillars of Faith":

1. The profession of faith: "There is no God but God; Muhammad is the Messenger of God."

2. Prayer. Muslims observe five prescribed prayer times each day, beginning before dawn. Praying is preceded by ritual ablutions. Wherever worshippers may be, they face toward the Ka'bah, the holiest Islamic structure, which is located in the courtyard of the Sacred Mosque in Mecca, Saudi Arabia.

3. Zakat. A Muslim is required to give a percentage of income and of the value of some types of produce and property, but in Malaysia this is left to individual conscience. At the end of the fasting month, there is a special, obligatory zakat, fitrah, paid in rice or monetary equivalent. In Rusila a portion of fitrah is remitted to the state religious department and part is kept in the village to be used for assistance to the poor (although today, application to the state for welfare funds is more usual) and for maintenance of the mosque and prayer houses. Islam distinguishes between zakat, usually translated into English as "alms-giving," and charity. Zakat is obligatory; charity, while it is encouraged, is voluntary.

4. Fasting. Throughout Ramadan, the ninth month of the Muslim lunar calendar, Muslims must abstain from eating, drinking, and sexual pleasures from just before dawn until dusk. The aged, travelers, those who are ill, and women who are pregnant may delay fasting. Mentruating women must delay their fast. Fasting should promote self-discipline and reflection about one's personal behavior.

5. The haj, or pilgrimage to Mecca in Saudi Arabia. Considered as the major unifying factor in Islam, haj should be performed by every Muslim who is both physically and financially able. There is, however, a stricture against pauperizing one's family in order to perform haj. Nevertheless, many rural people sold land to pay for the pilgrimage and returned home to nothing.

An enormous change was brought about for Malaysian Muslims through a plan proposed in 1959 by Ungku Aziz, an internationally recognized economist and currently the Vice-Chancellor of the University of Malaya. A public corporation in which Muslims could invest as a means of saving for the haj without violating the Islamic proscription of usury, interpreted strictly as including fixed interest payments on investments, was formed in 1962. Profits that are not assured are acceptable. By 1978 the corporation had investments in stocks and real estate, including an oil palm estate and commercial buildings in Malaysia and some holdings in Saudi Arabia, with a total market value estimated at more than M$140 million. The corporation is far more than an instrument to facilitate a person's saving for the pilgrimage; it also organizes everything for the haj. Transportation, provision of Saudi currency for incidental expenses, a film briefing prior to departure, a medical team of 75 persons in Jeddah along with other experts to solve whatever problems may confront a pilgrim, and other needs are provided as part of a M$4,000 (U.S.$1,887) package (Nash 1978). In 1979, 9,305 pilgrims had registered to perform the haj, and made the journey to Arabia aboard DC-10 aircraft (NST 4/19/79).

Islam established equality between women and men in religious matters, in that both are held fully responsible for personal behavior and for upholding the five pillars of faith. Women, however, are "exempted"—in practice, excluded—from communal midday prayers on Friday and are forbidden (haram) to perform prayers or other religious acts—such as reading the Quran, entering a mosque, or fasting—while they are menstruating. Mutual respect and cooperation between husband and wife are emphasized, but "Men are in charge of women because Allah hath made the one of them to excel the other and because they spend of their prosperity (for the support of women)" (Pickthall 1959:83).

The greatest sin, and the only one that is unforgivable, is disbelief in God or "ascribing a partner to Him." Other sins—such as murder, adultery, gambling, lying, charging interest on loans, mistreatment of orphans or one's parents, and performing any act that is harmful to mind or body or is socially disruptive—are punished in Purgatory, from which sinners ". . . will be delivered and transferred to Paradise where they will share with their fellow Muslims eternal happiness and enjoyment" (Rauf 1964:15).

Punishments can also be meted out by rulers in this world, and are specified—for instance, severance of the hand(s) for theft, 100 lashes for fornication, 80 lashes for drinking intoxicating beverages (Ibid.), and stoning to death of adulterers. A religious court trial is required. The listed punishments are currently used in Iran, Saudi Arabia, and some other parts of the Muslim world. In Malaysia there are fundamentalist Muslims who would like to see them introduced and applied to all Malaysians, but moderates and non-Muslims strongly oppose such a change in the legal system.

THE LEGAL SYSTEM

As presently constituted, the Malaysian legal system comprises two codes. The civil/criminal code is uniform throughout the nation and applies, generally, to Muslims and non-Muslims alike. An individual of any faith who commits murder or theft is tried under the criminal code. With regard to women, the Women and Girls Protection Act 1973 pertains to all women who are both below the age of 21 and not married, allowing them to be ". . . removed to a place of refuge and there temporarily detained and brought before the Court of a Magistrate within twenty-four hours" (Ibid. III. 7. [1]). This action can be taken if the woman is being trained for immoral purposes, is living in or frequenting a brothel, or is habitually in the company of procurers or other persons connected with prostitution. She can be ". . . detained in a place of refuge for a period of three years" (Ibid. III. 8. [4][a]) and not less than one year, or committed to the care of a relative or other person selected by the court. A woman can request admission to a place of refuge if ". . . she is being threatened . . . for purposes of prostitution . . ." (Ibid. III. 9. [i][a]). The act also specifies offenses and punishments for procurers and others involved in using women for immoral purposes. Any person trafficking in women or living on their immoral earnings is subject to five years in prison, $10,000 fine, or both. A man convicted of a second or subsequent offense is also liable to whipping.

These and other crimes, as well as innumerable civil matters, fall under the jurisdiction of the system that includes magistrates, high courts, and federal courts.

For Muslims there is also a state-level system that deals with religious offenses as well as civil actions pertaining to marriage, divorce contested or initiated by women, inheritance, and other family matters. The respective state governments, such as Trengganu's, hold legislative power with regard to such matters. There is variation in investigation, prosecution, and punishments among states. Johore, which had fairly lenient laws and punishments, has made them far more strict:

> Islamic administration laws under which Muslims can be fined or jailed for committing such offences as drinking liquor in public and failing to attend Friday prayers will be enforced in Johore from February 2, 1979. The State Executive Council decided on the date . . . the laws were passed by the State Legislative Assembly last month.
>
> Among other things, the laws cover:
>
> Friday Prayers—A Muslim man who fails to attend Friday prayers at the mosque in his community for three consecutive weeks without a valid reason can be fined $100 or jailed for 15 days or both.

Drinking Liquor in public places—A fine of up
to $100 or a maximum of 15 days' jail for the first of-
fence and a fine not exceeding $250 or a maximum of
one month's jail for subsequent offences can be imposed.

Khalwat—A Muslim found guilty of this offence
can be fined an amount not exceeding $1,000 or jailed
for up to six months or made to suffer both punishments (NST 2/1/79).

Khalwat is usually rendered in English as "close proximity"
between a male and female who are neither married to one another
nor in a primary kin relationship such as father-daughter or brother-
sister. In some very conservative communities, khalwat might be
suspected of almost any other couple who spent time together, unchaperoned. However, khalwat usually implies sexual intimacy but
is a lesser crime than illicit sexual intercourse, zinah. While a
charge of zinah requires male witnesses to have seen a couple in
the sexual act, a charge of khalwat requires only that they be found
together, secluded, in questionable circumstances. Awareness of
the khalwat prohibition makes Muslims cautious in their dealings
with members of the opposite sex of any religious group: a village
woman at home alone welcomes a friend of her husband on the
verandah but does not invite him indoors—unless both of them are
quite old; a university professor leaves the office door open when
counseling a student. In both cases, activities are public, and
therefore innocent.

Khalwat is the religious offense most frequently referred to
in the press. "Girl, 14, marries after khalwat conviction—25-year-
old bridegroom pleads guilty as well" (NST 10/27/78). The young
woman went to a show in Penang with the man, who afterward took
her to a hotel, where they were arrested during a police raid. "This
is the first time the Kadi's Office here has married a couple on the
same day after they pleaded guilty to committing khalwat." Despite
the agreement to marry, the bridegroom was fined $50 and the girl
was ". . . bound over to be of good behaviour for a month."

In Seremban, Negri Sembilan, the State Religious Affairs Department was investigating rumors about factory workers having sex
during working hours.

The department's president, Encik Ahmad bin Adjamin,
said: 'Love-making during working hours should be discouraged as precious time and money are wasted.' He
called upon workers to concentrate on their jobs . . .
and noted that the only way to discourage people from

committing Khalwat and Zinah . . . would be to im-
pose stiffer penalties. Khalwat offenders face a maximum punishment of two months jail or a fine of up to
$200 or both. The penalty for Zinah offenders is six
months' jail or a fine of up to $500 (NST 2/9/79).

These examples and the article about the new laws in Johore
illustrate the penalty variations among states. In Negri Sembilan,
the maximum penalty for khalwat is $200, two months in jail, or
both; in Johore the new law imposes a fine of up to $1,000, six
months in jail, or both. Many religious officials and members of
the Muslim public do favor more stringent penalties. And there has
been a demand by some Muslim organizations to extend the khalwat
law to non-Muslims. The latter course is unlikely, but not the imposition of larger fines and longer jail terms for Muslims in some
states, because Islamic fundamentalism is gaining strength.

MALAYSIAN WOMEN: AN OVERVIEW

The ethnic categories, socioeconomic classes, and religious
denominations of which Malaysian women are a part have been mentioned in this chapter; education, family, and economic roles are
the subjects of chapters that follow. In brief, women in 1980 are
Members of Parliament, but also manual laborers. There are
women scholars and women who are illiterate. They are business-
women and bureaucrats. Many are agriculturalists. Women serve
in the armed forces, and there are a few women among the MCP
guerrilla units operating from jungle bases. There are women phy-
sicians and herbalists, artists and artisans, athletes and film stars.
The vast majority of Malaysian women are or have been married;
they are homemakers and mothers.
Changes in the society have been uneven, affecting some
women's lives drastically while leaving others untouched. An overview of some of the major changes since the 1930s appeared in a
newspaper article, "Women's role: Time for another look—Have
they really liberated themselves?" (NST 2/12/79), written by a
Malaysian woman, Halinah Bamadhaj. I quote it here at length
rather than summarizing, so as not to delete the writer's viewpoint.
It is the most outspoken piece that I found in the Malaysian press
between June 1978 and June 1979.

Malaysian women can congratulate themselves that
their educational and professional achievements put
them on par with Western women, without ever having

had to march in the streets or incinerate their under-
wear. In our subtle, feminine, Asian fashion—the
argument runs—we have liberated ourselves without
damaging the fragile egos of our men or generating
an un-Malaysian hostility between the sexes.

But amid all this smug self-contratulation, have
we ever stopped to ask who has achieved exactly what
and exactly when? . . .

The biggest quantum leap in women's education,
for instance, came immediately after the war. In
1935 there were only 5,000 girls in schools throughout
the peninsula. In 1946 there were over 60,000. The
breakthrough had been made before the war by the
graduates of the Malacca Women's Training College,
who saw it as part of their job to tramp about the
kampungs persuading parents that girls also needed
to be literate. These young women . . . proved that
education did not lead . . . to immorality; nor did
the recipients of English education automatically become Christians.

The story is the same with university education.
Shortly after independence, 25 percent of all undergraduates in the country were women—a very respectable proportion by world standards. The numbers of women in universities have increased 10-fold
since then. . . . But proportionately there has been
little change—women now make up 30 percent of the
students. . . . The change in attitude towards
women's education was made in the forties and fifties—the present generation is just benefitting [sic]
from that breakthrough.

In politics, the struggle for Merdeka [indepen-
dence] a generation ago was the high point of women's
participation. . . . Women of the calibre of Aishah
Ghani, Datin Puteh Maria and Khatijah Sidek stormed
the public platforms and put the men to shame with
their fiery oratory. But those hectic days are over.
Independence has been won and many of those women
went quietly back to their kitchens or primary school
classrooms and got on with the job of bringing up the
next generation. . . .

The biggest leap in women's participation in
this generation has been in employment. Forty percent of all Malaysian women now work. But two
thirds of them work where their grandmothers did—

in the estates and in the padi fields: in other words,
in the most lowly paid sector of the economy. Many
are simply "unpaid family workers". . . .

This generation is still following faithfully in
its mothers' footsteps. It is still role-typed. It has
taken its supportive domestic roles out of the home
and into the labour market, where it is now paid (not
very well). Women still look after the children—they
make up 40% of the teachers—and the sick; they make
up 98% of the nurses. They assist men in all sorts of
ways (as telephone operators, key punchers, librarians
and research assistants).

As new professional fields open up, role stereotypes attach themselves to these occupations too. For
instance, women now make a strong showing in public
relations (charm, verbal skills?) but they are not acceptable in personnel relations (not tough enough to
handle the unions). Our one woman Cabinet Minister
is invariably in charge of the Welfare portfolio. . . .
In 1962 women occupied two percent of all managerial
and administrative posts. Eight years later they had
made a tiny leap to three percent. . . . Women make
up almost half of the country's primary school teachers, but primary school headmasters are overwhelmingly male. . . .

In spite of advances such as equal pay and separate tax assessment, pay differentials between men
and women are extremely wide. This is partly because professions in which women predominate are
the most lowly paid (nursing and teaching), while
they are not well represented in the richest professions—they make up only 16 percent of the accoun-
tants and economists, 0.4 percent of the engineers,
and 7.4 percent of the lawyers. The only body of
women making a lot of money are those who make up
25 percent of the medical profession. . . .

Equal pay means nothing to the 13,000 women
who work in electronics factories at Bayan Lepas.
They are not unionised, and they are employed partly because, being women, they can be paid low wages—
an average of $100 a month. As if that were not bad
enough, they have become the target of such male
chauvinist abuse as "Minah Letrik," as if being
workers in a low status occupation must make them
immoral as well as exploited.

If the statistics on the role-typing, the power-
lessness and the low pay scales of women are to be
believed, then there is room for more militancy and
less self-congratulation amongst Malaysian women.
This generation of women has advanced in quantity,
but it has not yet matched the pioneering efforts of
the post-war generation in breaking into new fields or
overturning entrenched attitudes.

Entrenched attitudes are, stereotypically, associated most
strongly with people living in rural areas. Villagers are often characterized by urbanites, even some who grew up in villages, as
"backward," clinging to outmoded views about their society and the
world. Change, especially rapid, multifaceted change, is threatening to those who fear that a stable way of life, full of value and meaning for them, may be destroyed or distorted by it. But this does not
imply that village people, any more than urban people, reject the
idea of development; that all rural people react alike; or that the effects of a particular change are universal even in a small community. Women and men, parents and children, the young and the aged,
people with different occupations, may anticipate—rightly or wrong-
ly—benefits or disadvantages from change, and react accordingly.
Concrete examples of these generalizations are drawn from the
Trengganu village of Rusila, where the pace of change accelerated
rapidly during the 1960s and 1970s.

2

KAMPUNG RUSILA

Kampung Rusila is a coastal village south of Kuala Trengganu. To the casual observer it is not readily distinguishable as an entity because houses in contiguous villages are located nearby. The milestones along the highway once marked the end of one village and the beginning of another, but they were shifted after sections of road near the town were rerouted, and no longer coincide with official village boundaries.

The other boundaries of Rusila are natural ones: the South China Sea to the east and forested hills and mountains to the west. Between the beach and the highway there is a single, irregular band of houses and a sprinkling of coconut palms, casuarina trees, and pandanus patches. In 1965 the houses near the beach in this section of the village all had wind screens erected between them and the sea to give protection from seasonally strong winds, but by 1979 only a few remained. The foundations of many homes had been strengthened during the interim. Between some of the roadside houses there are groves of coconut palms and neatly arranged cash-crop gardens. To the west of these houses is a wide belt of rice fields.

The highway passing through the village was widened to two lanes and macadamized in 1962, when it became part of a coastal network extending from Kota Bahru, more than 100 miles north of Rusila, to Johore Bahru and Singapore almost 350 miles to the south. The network also includes bridges over the many rivers that flow into the sea, making it possible to drive the entire route without waiting for ferries. All of the modifications changed the travel patterns of villagers, who began to move from one area to another by land transport rather than via boats.

The highway is both a boon and a danger to the villagers. Local buses pass through the village hourly from early in the

morning until 7 P. M. , en route between Kuala Trengganu, the state
capital (with a population of over 53,000), eight to ten miles north
of the village, and the District Office at Marang, three miles south.
Interstate buses move between Kuala Trengganu and other urban
areas, including the nation's capital, Kuala Lumpur, at least twice
per week. The paving of the road bettered travel conditions for local people; gave them easier access to medical facilities, markets,
shops, and government offices in the towns; enabled them to visit
kin and friends in the villages along the way with greater frequency;
and brought tradespeople into the village more regularly. In 1965
villagers could also reach the nearest public phone at Chendering,
three miles north, without difficulty. By 1975 a telephone in a
booth had been centrally situated in the village.

But the dangers of the highway are ever present. In June
1965 a young child was killed by a speeding automobile, and several
accidents involving local bicyclists and other vehicles occurred
during the year. The loss of small livestock was considerable. By
1975 the amount of traffic had increased significantly and so had the
number of accidents and fatalities. The highway was being widened
during 1979, bringing the dangers even closer to roadside homes.

Paths wind inland from the highway, passing around gardens
and over the rice field bunds, with small bridges spanning the
irrigation and drainage canal that passes through the rice fields.
Between the fields and the elevated forest, which in this area rises
to a maximum elevation of just over 200 feet, are two of the three
hamlets that are part of Rusila although each has its own name:
Balek Bukit and Gong. The third, Belubor, is at the northern edge
of the village and on the eastern side of the highway. The hamlets
are separated from each other by some of the fields and few low-
lying rubber groves at the base of the hills. Beyond is the forest,
where areas of natural growth are interspersed with cleared areas
in which groves of rubber trees and some upland gardens of tobacco, vegetables, and hill rice are cultivated.

In 1965 public buildings in the village included the primary
school, located half a mile inland from the highway, the community center, and the weaving center (Medan Anyaman), which had
an outhouse pit toilet nearby, one of two public toilets in the village.
The three buildings were constructed by professional carpenters at
government expense. The community center is available to any
village group, though its small size limits the number of people
who can meet there. It was here that adult education classes were
held, that the local youth club met occasionally, and that other
associations or committees could gather. There were also an old
mosque and a prayer house that was built by the village men in
1965 and financed through donations from each family.

The District Officer had $100,000 in his 1979 budget to build a new mosque in Rusila, but the villagers rejected it; they had enlarged and painted the old one around 1972. Many people expressed the view that the old mosque is a symbol of the community spirit of the village, of the gotong royong (mutual assistance and cooperation) feelings among the villagers who built and maintain it, and that it represents their devotion to Islam. It is also said that government funds come from many sources, including taxes on alcoholic beverages and the sale of licenses for dogs, that are considered inappropriate for funding a mosque or prayer house—both alcohol and dogs fall under Islamic proscriptions.

Two shelters in the village are wakaf, property donated by individuals to the public in the name of Islam. One is near the highway; the other is in the larger of two village cemeteries. A rice mill, a shed where a local woman produced cement tiles and blocks, and another shed where men practiced the artistic Malay form of self-defense, bersilat, were also in the village.

As of July 1966 there were 146 houses in the village, 12 of them unoccupied, and an additional 7 houses were in various stages of construction. Four houses had been moved to new sites since my 1965 survey. Seven houses had small "general" shops attached to them, and there was one separate coffee shop near the highway. Forty-four of the homes had private wells nearby, used by owners and their neighbors, and there were public wells provided by the government, at the Medan and several other sites throughout the village.

Many changes had been effected by 1979, and others were under way. The old weaving center had been converted into a midwife's clinic and a new, extremely modern structure housed the Medan. A small post office located in a general shop, the public phone referred to above—both reflecting increased communication between villagers and the world beyond the village—an unroofed badminton court built by local youths, and a new prayer house had become part of the village. A couple of the old shops had closed, but new ones had opened.

In 1979 there were six general stores, two coffee shops, four shops selling handicrafts, and one shop specializing in household furnishings such as tables and chairs. The last two categories indicate, respectively, attempts to benefit from an increase of tourism on the east coast and a far greater demand by villagers for a wider variety of furniture.

The sheds used for cement-block production and bersilat practice during the 1960s had been demolished after their owners ended the activities that had been carried out in them. In Balek Bukit hamlet four large kilns for drying tobacco had been constructed to serve the burgeoning local tobacco industry. New homes and additional wells were dotted throughout the village, and outhouses with gravity-flow pit toilets had become commonplace.

HOUSING, SERVICES, AND APPLIANCES

Houses in the village are elevated three or more feet from the ground on posts and cement blocks. The space under many houses is utilized for storage of large tools, odd bits of lumber, and other gear during fine weather. With the arrival of the monsoon, these things are brought inside because of the possibility of flooding.

The practice of elevating houses offers positive advantages in fine and foul weather. Cooling breezes circulate around the entire structure during hot weather, floors are above normal flooding level during the wet season, and snakes and some other animals are less likely to enter. Only shops and a few kitchens are built directly on the ground.

The basic material used for all buildings in 1965 was wood, but the quality varied from commercially prepared lumber to rough wood cut in the forest. Even the rudest structure had a wooden framework and flooring, although its walls might be thatched or made from woven bamboo panels rather than boards. Roofs were made from tiles, corrugated metal, thatch, or asbestos sheets; more than one type of roofing could be seen on some houses. For example, the main section of a house might be tiled, while the kitchen had a thatched roof, or a new section added to a house might have a roofing material different from that of the old section.

The external appearance of a home usually reflects the relative affluence of a family. The simplest dwellings in the community are those of very young married couples and families with low incomes. These houses are characterized by rough construction and use of inexpensive materials. At the opposite extreme are the few very well constructed homes, built by professional carpenters and other craftsmen. They are spacious, have walls and floors made from prepared lumber, bricks, or cement, and tile roofs. Such homes are painted both outside and inside, and have glass panes or louvers in the windows instead of wooden shutters. The Rusila houses of this type would look natural in a middle-class Florida community, and have all the amenities that a middle-class American would expect in a home. They are owned by salaried government employees such as teachers.

Two of these houses cost approximately $30,000 each to build during the mid-1970s and were valued by their owners at about $40,000 each by 1979. In 1965 the nicest house in the village was valued by its owner at $5,000; it would sell for at least $10,000 today. None of the prices include the land on which the houses are situated. One villager might own both a house and its land, but in many cases a house is owned by one person while the land on which it stands belongs to one or more other people, usually relatives of the house owner, a pattern detailed in Chapter 7.

Between the two extremes is a range of house types. Figure 1 shows an example—as the house was in 1965, a year after the present occupants purchased it, already wired for overhead lighting, through a series of modifications and extensions, to the house as it was in June 1979. It is now among the largest homes in the village but is still in the middle range, valued at $25,000, because interior sections are incomplete and there are temporary expedients such as boards nailed across holes where glass windows will be installed when materials and labor can be afforded. Other middle-range homes resemble the 1965 and 1975 versions of the Figure 2 house.

The original house was roofed with thatch, which was replaced with tiles during 1966. The new roofing sections are corrugated asbestos, which can easily be replaced with tiles at some future time. There are glass-paned shutters at the western (front) and southern sides of the house, and broken wooden shutters at the eastern (back), which overlooks the sea. The house is elevated, except for the 1979 kitchen, bathing room, and toilet, which are at ground level. The well, once several yards from the house, is now inside the kitchen, a reliable source of clean, cool water to supplement water piped in from the main early in 1979. Neighbors are still free to use the well or to take water from a standpipe outside the kitchen.

The flooring is made from commercially prepared hardwood planks except in the kitchen, toilet, and bathing room, where the floors are of a smooth, brick-colored cement. Sleeping rooms (sections A-D) have been created by erecting partitions of masonite or plywood. The outside of the 1975 house was painted a few years ago, and some of the interior areas have also been painted.

Many village houses have been modified since 1965, but this one is the most extreme and an example of what is likely to become a trend during the next few years if prosperity in the area continues. In this case the wife is the one who "made it happen," from the original purchase of the house (although not the land, which her mother owns) to its later transformation, little bit by little bit, financed with savings from her own remunerative work and as much as she could put aside from what her husband gave her for household expenses.

Differences existed in 1965, but the range was greater in 1979. There were few changes in the homes of people at the low-income

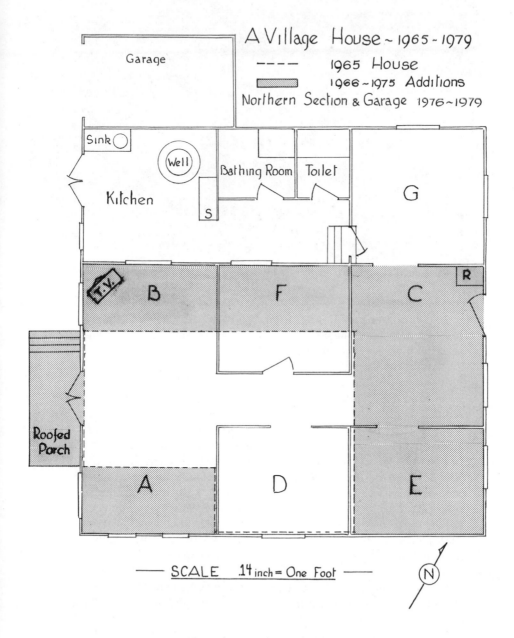

Figure 1. Floor Plans. A Village House. 1966–1979.

Figure 2. A New House (Rusila, 1979). Rozdi on the porch of his grandmother's new but traditional style house, one among the great variety of "middle range" types.

end of the spectrum, but among the affluent, elaboration was obvious: more costly materials were being used and the building was done entirely by professional carpenters and other specialists. These expensive homes have flower gardens around them and fences to keep out the cattle and goats that roam freely through the village. The only fences observed in 1965 surrounded rice seedling nurseries and some fields. Then, no one grew flowers around a home.

A seminar on Malaysian architecture sponsored by the Consumers' Association of Penang (CAP) concluded that the traditional Malay village house, with its basically wooden construction, is more suitable to a tropical climate and cheaper to build than the currently favored house built of concrete. There was some consternation among CAP members when recommendations based on the seminar were eventually directed to the Ministry of Culture rather than the Ministry of Housing (Peyman and Das 1980:44). Perhaps this was simply a channeling error. Or the "misdirection" may indicate that lower-level bureaucrats who did the channeling see traditional forms as incompatible with development.

Most houses have two or more entrances, one of which usually has a porch. Well-built houses have roofed verandahs reached by solidly constructed, railed stairways. A water container was kept near each door in 1965 so that all could wash their feet prior to entering the house. Outdoor water containers were less common in 1979 because few people went barefoot. Shoes are always removed before entering a home or other village building.

Electricity was introduced into Rusila in 1963. By 1966, 32 houses (23.7 percent of those occupied) had been wired, and by 1979 there were 120 (62.8 percent) with this service. No houses in Gong and Balek Bukit hamlets have electricity; they are so far from power lines near the highway that the cost of obtaining service is prohibitive. They continue to be lit by kerosene lamps. In 1966 electricity in Rusila was used only for lighting and radios. There were no other electric appliances. By 1975 a few homes had television sets (N = 15) and refrigerators (N = 8). When the 1979 village survey was made, there were 48 television sets and 19 refrigerators. Small appliances such as electric kettles and blenders were being used in a few homes.

In 1970 the first Rusila family had water piped into its home and a bathing room with shower built onto it. Seven homes, all close to the highway and the water pipes near it, had this luxury in 1975; by mid-1979 there were 26 homes with piped water, and 14 of them had indoor toilets.

TABLE 2.1

Services and Appliances Used in Rusila: 1965, 1975, 1979

	1965–66		1975		1979	
	Number	Percent	Number	Percent	Number	Percent
Occupied houses	134	100.0	165	100.0	192	100.0
Electricity	32	23.8	68	41.0	120	62.5
Radio	11	8.2	—	—	105	54.7
Television set			15	9.0	48	25.0
Refrigerator			8	4.8	19	9.8
Kerosene stove			78	47.2	84	43.8
Gas stove			1	.06	18	9.3
Piped water			7	4.2	26	13.5
Indoor toilet					14	7.3

The numbers and percentages, by year, for services, amenities, and major appliances are shown in Table 2.1. There has been an increase in every category between 1965 and 1979, with more households and a larger percentage of households having services and appliances in 1979. This reflects the relative affluence not only of some families in the village, but also of the village itself compared with many others in the district. Comparing 1975 and 1979, it can be seen that the increases in most categories reflect at least a doubling in both numbers and percentages except for electricity, with a 21.5 percent increase, and kerosene stoves, use of which is discussed below.

Comparative annotated data about house types, electricity, and water use for all of the villages in Marang District, of which Rusila is a part, are given in the Appendix.

FURNISHINGS

A furnishing found in almost every house that has a married couple in residence is a double bed; in 1965 this was commonly of the four-poster variety with a canopy and curtains. The curtains are more for privacy than for protection against insects, since they are usually hung only along the sides of the bed that are not next to a wall. More homes had separate sleeping rooms in 1979, so curtains for privacy were less common. Children and other household members may have wooden bedsteads, or use mattresses or sleeping mats rolled out on the floor. Infants have their own tiny mattresses and pillows with a protective covering made of netting over a wire framework, or they may sleep in rattan and bamboo cradles. Older babies and children up to several years of age sleep in a buah spring, a practical invention that is easily fashioned: a rope is hung over a roof rafter and tied to form a loop to which a heavy-duty steel spring is attached. A sarong (a skirtlike garment worn by both women and men) is hung from the spring. The child sleeps inside the sarong, which sways and jiggles in response to body movements or can be rocked by someone else. Children love sleeping in the buah spring, and relinquish it only as a concession to growing up.

Some furnishings found in 1965, such as verandah chairs and a table, reflected a family's affluence; they were, and are, by no means universal within the village. Suites of "Danish modern" sitting room furniture had become a major status furnishing in 1975, ranking just below television sets of the large, console variety (the only type to be found locally), gas stoves, and refrigerators. By 1979 more people had a wider variety of furnishings, including pieces bought at a village shop.

One item common in all kitchens in 1965 was the dapu (dapur kayu), on which indoor cooking was done. A dapu is a shallow lid-less box on four legs. The box section is filled almost to the top of the frame with packed earth or cement. Cooking fires are built directly on the top and fuel, such as wood and dried coconut shells, is stored underneath. It is usually made by a male in the household. By 1979, 84 homes (43.9 percent) had one- or two-burner kerosene stoves and 18 had gas stoves with ovens (9.4 percent). Eighty-nine kitchens (46.6 percent) were still equipped with only the dapu, and others had both kerosene stoves and the dapu, women retaining the latter for baking cakes or ember-broiling fish, and for emergencies.

It can be seen in Table 2.1 that the increase in the use of gas stoves from 1975 to 1979 is considerable. At the same time only a few more women were enjoying the convenience of kerosene stoves, and there was a decrease in the percentage of kitchens equipped with them. When these stoves were introduced, they were seen as a boon because they were relatively cheap and did not fill a house with smoke (as sometimes happens with wood fires). From a woman's point of view, they were far easier to use and she no longer had the chore of collecting fuel. A new problem has confronted her during the past few years: periodic scarcity of kerosene. This is a government-controlled commodity, and dealers are licensed so as to deter black-market activities. When a local dealer has sold the given allotment, consumers must go to Marang Town or Kuala Trengganu to look for kerosene, and are not always successful. Kerosene stoves are still considered preferable to wood, but many women have both; a gas stove is the best, but it is a very expensive appliance and, like a refrigerator and piped water, beyond the means of the average family unless the wife is committed to careful saving of small amounts of money with a long-range goal in mind. Among the poorest, even the best financial juggler cannot accumulate enough.

A kitchen also contains open shelves where cooking equipment and dishes are kept and, in the homes of the more affluent, standing cupboards for food and utensils. Even the poorest family needs cooking pots, a coconut grater, a tripod on which to elevate pots over a fire, and serving bowls, plates, and beverage containers for family members. An inventory of kitchen equipment taken in 1965 in a household where the couple had been married for over 14 years, had five children living at home, and a fluctuating but never more than moderate income, was updated in 1975 and again in 1979, a period during which the husband was regularly employed. The additions indicate this family's changed economic status in two general ways.

A number of objects in the 1965 inventory—such as a water carrier fashioned from a kerosene can, a dipper created from a fishing-net float found on the beach, a coconut grater made from a scrap of lumber and nails, a wooden "horse" to which a purchased metal coconut shredder "head" was attached, and a bamboo egg beater—had been made by the husband. A few were in use in 1979, but everything added to the kitchen since the early 1970s was mass-produced and had been purchased. The replacement of handcrafted articles by manufactured goods was obvious not only in Rusila but also in villages throughout the area. A greater variety of manu-factured goods is available today, and more people can afford them. Women and men argue that many manufactured goods are superior to handcrafted ones—certainly not all men excelled at producing things needed for kitchen use—and more beautiful.

The families who can most readily afford to replace things are those with a wage earner working outside the village five and one-half days per week. Such a man has less free time, at least seasonally, for making and repairing things in the home than if he engaged in agriculture or fishing. And households with wage earners are the ones most likely to have television sets; the occupants (and their neighbors) are using leisure time differently than during the 1960s. Among poorer villagers—prosperity is far from universal—household members still use their ingenuity to make things from materials in the natural environment or objects washed up by the sea.

A second shift is reflected in the number and types of objects used for serving refreshments. In the home where the inventories were taken, a matched set of six teacups, saucers, and a teapot, two larger teapots (all used for serving coffee more often than tea), and two big pitchers, one with matching tumblers (used for serving iced drinks), were purchased after 1975. Ice can be bought at several local shops or from some of the women who have re-frigerators in their homes. All of these things are evidence of a new style of entertaining among people who, like this family, are financially able.

Coffee, tea, or cold ades; commercial, sweet biscuits or delicacies sold by women hawkers; and fruits, both local and im-ported, are now commonly offered to anyone who comes to the home for more than a few minutes. In 1965 only visitors consid-ered important, such as the veterinarian or other government officers, were served coffee or tea with biscuits. Typically, fried yams, green coconut water, or local fruits in season would be offered to guests. Malays are very hospitable, and enjoy spending leisure time with friends; they also value politeness, and it is polite to serve refreshments to visitors. The values have not changed, but the expression of them, for the more affluent, has shifted to offering more prestigious beverages and snacks, and serving them to a greater number of people.

Certain utensils are considered necessities by a majority of women, but some households, particularly newly established ones, do not have all of them. Instead, they are borrowed from a relative or neighbor, or the tasks for which they are used are accomplished in another home.

The family living in the Figure 2 house enjoys many amenities, essentially because the woman running the household is a hard worker who saves carefully and juggles household monies adroitly. Furnishings, appliances, and services have been acquired over a period of many years.

There are three beds with mattresses in the house. They were acquired in 1950, 1966, and 1969. A suite of "Danish modern" furniture in the sitting room was purchased in 1973 so that a son attending a post-secondary school in Kuala Lumpur would not be ashamed to bring friends home. A two-burner kerosene stove (S) was bought during the same year. The television set (TV) was acquired in 1976 to satisfy the yearnings of children and husband. That purchase led a salaried daughter living elsewhere to buy her mother a refrigerator (R) in 1977, because she thought it shameful that the television set had been chosen instead of the more practical kitchen appliance.

The framework of the northern extension to the house and the makeshift garage built to protect a car belonging to a kinsman were completed between 1976 and 1978. Cement workers laid the floor of the ground-level area, set the toilet into the floor, put up cement block partitions between the toilet, bathing room, and kitchen, and constructed a water storage receptacle in the bathing room during February and March 1979. Their work completed, they were paid in full. Water was piped into the toilet and bathing rooms in April; the pipes were extended to the kitchen and a sink with a cabinet below it were installed in June. Neither the plumber nor the carpenter had finished his work at that time because there was no money to pay them. The kitchen had overhead lighting, but the refrigerator was in another part of the house because kitchen wiring was inadequate. A son who lives in Kuala Lumpur was expected to rewire the kitchen during a vacation.

Only salaried government employees can afford to have a home built and finished as a single project. They not only have regular income, but they can also borrow money from banks and other lending institutions. The average villager must take a piecemeal approach to building, finishing, and furnishing.

Piped water, refrigerators, and gas stoves are great savers of women's time and energy. In Rusila they are still seen as luxuries. Furniture creates new chores, however desirable pieces may be for comfort or prestige. I am not suggesting that women complain about the extra chores; they do not. They are proud to have the furnishings in their homes and find that pleasure in them outweighs any inconvenience. Nevertheless, mattresses, pillows, and cushions must be sunned and aired frequently; cockroaches and other insects must be dislodged from crannies between furniture frames and cushions or mattresses. In a tropical climate mildew and insects are constant problems.

LOCAL CLIMATE

All activities in the village and in each household are affected by seasonal climatic changes. In this part of Malaysia, annual rainfall is from 120 inches to 140 inches (Robinson 1967:322). During much of the year light showers or thunderstorms occur on many days, but may last for half an hour or less. These brief rains do not disturb the rounds of activity in the village very much, nor do they have a marked effect on work patterns. But the north-east monsoon, the stormy season or musim gelora, when up to 40 percent of the annual rainfall occurs (Ho 1964:29), brings many activities to a halt for varying periods of time. The strong winds and torrential rains that characterize the monsoon are interspersed with light drizzles and some clear days.

Between mid-November 1965 and mid-March 1966, the period of the stormy season, some Rusila homes suffered damage so extensive that their occupants were forced to seek refuge with relatives or neighbors. Transportation came to a halt for days at a time due to flooding of the highway. All schools in the area, as well as government offices in Kuala Trengganu and Marang, were closed. Upland vegetable gardens were swept down slopes and much of the rice crop disappeared, beaten into the ground by the force of winds and rain. Ponds and small lakes appeared overnight but stayed for many days because the stratum of clay below the sandy topsoil could not quickly absorb so much water. Many wells were rendered useless because their water was churned to mud. Gong and Balek Bukit were cut off from the main part of the village.

According to radio broadcasts, Trengganu was experiencing the worst floods in 35 years. Even so, the people of Rusila and similar coastal villages were far luckier than people living in riverside kampung where houses close to the banks were washed away and people drowned.

In contrast with the floods and destructive storms of 1965-66, the 1975 and 1979 monsoons brought only a few days of very heavy rain. Major roads were never rendered impassable, but the South China Sea was frequently too rough for local fishermen to challenge.

Work is sporadic for villagers engaged in most occupations throughout the monsoon season. Rubber tappers cannot tap because rain dilutes the latex. Fishermen cannot go out to sea. Agriculturalists, carpenters, and hawkers are immobilized for varying periods of time. Only work that is done in the home, such as mat weaving or sewing, continues completely uninterrupted by the weather.

From the end of March to November, the humidity is high, but temperatures over 90 degrees Fahrenheit are uncommon (Robinson 1967:322) and cooling breezes blow in from the sea during many days. Despite sporadic rainfall, this is the dry season. With the change in the weather there is a change in activities.

Although the weather varies seasonally, the period of daylight in this region is about the same throughout the year. The sun emerges from the South China Sea at about 6 A.M. and disappears into the forest-clad mountains about 13 hours later.

THE VILLAGERS

A villager's self-identity has three essential dimensions aside from sex and age: ethnicity (Malay, orang Melayu); natal place, Rusila or another village, usually stated as anak Rusila (child of Rusila); and membership in an extended kinship network.

The Malay identity stands in contrast with those of other large categories, such as Chinese (orang Cina) or white (orang putih), and includes the identity "Muslim" within it, because to be Malay is to be Muslim, although not all Malaysian Muslims are Malays. Local people deal with a few Chinese and Indians in the town, and over the years several village women have married Chinese or Indian Muslims—men who, if they lived in Rusila, apparently were completely accepted into the community.

In 1965 any negative comments about people in other ethnic categories were phrased in cultural/religious terms—Chinese people drink liquor, gamble, or have other behavior traits that are unacceptable to Muslims. But people were offhand in their comments; they did not socialize with non-Muslims, and so were not personally concerned with their behavior. By 1975 comments were increasingly couched in economic terms as the younger, better-educated segment of the population repeated stereotypes learned outside the village. It was suggested that Malays were poor because they were not getting the same advantages that the Chinese were getting—despite federal and state legislation favoring Malays. Chinese, Indian, and other Muslims are lauded and are excluded from the criticisms. Thus, while negative attitudes have taken on an economic dimension, religious affiliation remains an overriding concern.

The Rusila identity is most frequently used during interactions with other Malays, particularly those from Trengganu for whom village locales have meaning. Other identifying labels, such as marital status or Trengganu-person, emerge in various contexts, but being a Malay from a specific village is fundamental.

Rusila is more than a place to the people who were born there. They continue to identify with it even if they move to another area, and many feel a deep emotional attachment to it that is quite apart from the affective ties to family and friends who live there. If they live elsewhere, most return to Rusila for major ceremonial events and holidays.

Much of what Judith Djamour (1965:23-51) detailed regarding the kinship system of Singapore Malays holds equally for those of Rusila and nearby areas despite a spatial separation of several hundred miles between the two populations. Kinship is reckoned bilaterally, equal importance being accorded to mother's and father's kin. Although personal names reflect a patri-bias adopted from Arabic—a child's given name is followed by binti (daughter of) or bin (son of) and the father's given name, as in Rahimah binti Awang—there is no difference in the kinship terminology applied to maternal and paternal kin.

Both grandmothers are addressed and referred to as tok, and both grandfathers as tokki, terms that are not universal among Malays. In some parts of the country, grandfather is tok and grandmother is nek (Nagata 1979:156). Emak (mak) is mother, and ayah or bapak (pak) is father. Mother's and father's sisters are, collectively, emak saudara, while brothers of both parents are bapak saudara. However, birth order of male and female siblings of parents is recognized by their nieces and nephews: a parent's eldest sister is, familiarly, Mak Long, and eldest brother is Pak Long. There are five variants from eldest to youngest. Alternatively, an aunt or uncle may be known to a sibling's children as 'Mak or 'Pak, followed by the given name or a short form of the given name. 'Mak and 'Pak are also honorifics used for more distant kin of an older generation and for nonkin as a sign of respect.

An individual's own younger siblings are, for reference purposes, all adik, regardless of sex, while older siblings are differentiated, sisters being kakak and brothers abang. Short forms of names are appended for clarification and are normally used when addressing siblings. Rahimah routinely becomes Mah, Shamsuddin is Din, and so on. Thus, if Rahimah is one's older sister, she might be referred to and addressed as 'Kak Mah, and if younger, referred to as adik Mah and addressed simply as Mah.

Regardless of relative age, husbands are defined as senior to wives, but each should show respect for the other. Wives normally refer to a husband as suami saya (or laki-laki saya)—my husband (my man); husbands refer to a wife as my wife (isteri saya, bini saya). Within the family, short forms of names or full given names may be used.

Every person should guide his or her life by Islamic precepts, but beyond them Malays hold two interrelated values as fundamental to maintaining harmonious human relations. The closer the ties between individuals, the more important that behavior should be informed by those values: politeness and a sense of embarrassment or shame (malu) for impolite or incorrect behavior. If one acts politely, one need not be ashamed; if impolitely, one should feel ashamed. If others are rude, one feels embarrassment/shame for them and also is shamed by their discourtesy. If a member of a family is rude, everyone in the family is ashamed.

Seniority merits polite forms, although the substance of relationships is increasingly determined by considerations other than relative age. It is often the case that a young person who is formally educated finds it easier to discuss problems with an aunt/uncle who is close in age and has had similar experiences and education than to seek older kin whose experiences have been dissimilar. Increasing bureaucratization in the larger society requires villagers to submit tax forms and deal with other written material, making older illiterate persons more dependent on their literate children or younger siblings. Nevertheless, it is rare for an adult child to be openly critical of a parent or to offer unsolicited advice to an older sibling or other relative.

Ideally, relationships between parents and children are close, warm, and harmonious. When a child leaves the family of orientation to establish a household with a spouse and children, everyone concerned is pleased if the child can live nearby, preferably in the same village or one close to Rusila.

When a young woman is going to be involved in an undertaking that requires assistance, she first asks her mother, and perhaps her mother-in-law, for help. She then turns to other females among her kindred, particularly her sisters and sisters-in-law. Finally, friends and neighbors will be asked to help. A similar pattern is found in the realm of male activity.

The stepparent/stepchild relationship is difficult to general-
ize. Ideally it should be the same as that between parent and child;
when the stepparent is childless, such is usually the case. There
is more variation when the stepparent has children. Rusila women
discussed families in which a stepparent favored his or her own
children, and others where equal treatment was typical. Step-
mothers are thought more likely than stepfathers to show bias,
mainly because they have more opportunities in the family milieu:
giving or withholding special foods and money for treats, providing
new clothes for one child and not another, and generally being so-
licitous for their own children and neglecting the others in many,
sometimes subtle, ways. The same attitude is expressed in a
poignant Indonesian short story that depicts the trials of a boy,
Rahim, in the home of his stepfather. The child's mother, Marjam,
loves her son deeply, but she is powerless (penniless) against her
husband's miserly attitudes and unable to influence his behavior
toward her son. But when Rahim wishes to seek his father, Marjam
argues that living with a stepmother would be a worse misery than
her son now knows, especially if the woman has children of her
own (Amru'llah 1968).

The relationship between in-laws is characterized, minimally,
by politeness, and by deference from the younger toward the elder.
Mate selection patterns are changing, but in their traditional practice parents—especially mothers—selected a child's spouse. Choice
was based, in part, upon evaluation of the young person and her/his
parents as in-laws. Newlyweds resided with the parents of one or
the other in small homes; both child and spouse were subject to
work allocation and economic decisions made by parents/in-laws,
and many were used as unpaid or underpaid family workers. Under
such circumstances it might take years before they could establish
their own household. Many marriages did not last that long. No one
in Rusila ever suggested friction with in-laws as a primary reason
for divorce; rather, poor in-law relationships exacerbate problems
between wife and husband. And there is at least one instance of the
opposite effect: husband and wife remained married for several
years because they enjoyed excellent relations with one another's
parents. Following the divorce the intergenerational friendships
continued.

Women living in the same household share more tasks on a
daily basis than men do. Consequently there are more chances for
friction where mother-/daughter-in-law are coresidents. Women
generally preferred to reside in their parental homes, for they had
already adjusted to working with mother and sisters. But that
arrangement was not always possible. Today increasing numbers
of young people are taking a more active role in mate selection; few

of them live for more than a brief time with parents/in-laws after marrying. As the parental role in mate selection decreases, the relationship between any two in-laws becomes more formal; friction between in-laws of different generations is reduced by the establishment of separate residences.

Siblings and cousins who are the same sex and about the same age often form close ties, and it is not unusual for an individual to develop a close relationship with an aunt or uncle of the same sex and age. The closest ties between siblings of the opposite sex are usually those of older sisters and younger brothers, for the sister has served as a surrogate mother for her younger brother.

Grandparents tend to be very permissive with their grandchildren. It commonly happens that when a child's parents are displeased, the child seeks solace at the home of grandparents. Sometimes grandparents request that a grandchild be given to them if all of their children are grown and no longer living at home, but difficulties can arise if both maternal and paternal grandparents are living. Sending a child to one couple may lead to a request from the other couple and, if everyone's needs are not met, hurt feelings are the result. A widowed grandmother is given preference, so that she will not be lonely and will have help in the home. Children who cannot be cared for by their parents are taken by grandparents or other kin.

In summary, relationships between close relatives are, ideally, characterized by compatibility, mutual assistance, and affection. Often reality coincides with the ideal. When it does not, the situation is seen by others as unfortunate, bad, or even sinful, depending on the reasons for antipathy.

Advice is sought from time to time from individuals who are not part of the household or the kindred. Certain types of problems are referred directly to the midwife, the headmaster or other teacher, the imam (a Muslim religious leader), or the village headman. In the past the men who filled the latter two statuses were elders who were usually referred to and addressed with 'Pak before their names or titles ('Pak imam) as a sign of respect. The men in these statuses in 1979 were younger; the 'Pak designation was not often used for them.

The smallest residential groups in the village are households, one or more people living in the same house who share a budget and a number of common activities. There were 134 households in the village, with from one to ten members, a total of 614 persons in 1966. The number had risen to 192 households and 953 persons, with a range from one to 11 members per unit, in 1979. All of the village adults knew one another fairly well in 1965, but the rapid expansion from 134 to 192 households in 14 years—31 households

in the first decade and 27 in the following four years—has meant
that many people have little more than a polite acquaintance with
one another today. Interactions between any two persons of different households have always varied by kinship and friendship ties
as well as the proximity of their houses. The people living in each
of the hamlets continue to have more social contacts with each other
than with village residents elsewhere, and the same is true for
residents of housing clusters in the lineal section of the village.

Members of an average household are related affinally (the
married couple), consanguineally (parents and children, siblings),
and, possibly, fictively (adopted children). Kinship ties of the
three types join households to others in the village, frequently to
those of neighbors.

The most obvious reason why consanguineal ties exist between neighbors is the Islamic rule of inheritance, by which all
children of an individual have the right to inherit property, with
females each receiving half of the share inherited by males. Thus,
if a person is survived by a son and a daughter, the son receives
two-thirds of the property and the daughter gets one-third of it.
A second reason why kinship ties and propinquity are found in conjunction is the desire of children and parents to live close to one
another, a desire that is most characteristic of mothers and
daughters.

The conjunction of kinship ties and proximity is illustrated
by six neighboring households that utilized one well in 1965.
English equivalents are used for Malay kinship terms but the categories—second cousin (dua pupu) and third cousin (tiga pupu), for
example—are relationships that villagers commonly recognize.

House #1: The wife is the daughter of the married couple in #4,
           the niece of the husband (MoBro) in #2, a first cousin
           of the wife in #6, and a third cousin of the wife in #3.
           The house is located on land belonging to the wife's
           mother's brother (#2).

House #2: The married couple have a married daughter who lives
           in #6; the husband is the brother of the wife in #4, the
           uncle (MoBro) of the wife in #1, and a second cousin of
           the wife in #3.

House #3: The wife is a second cousin of both the wife in #4 and
           the husband in #2, and a third cousin to the wives in #1
           and #6. She is related to them through her mother.
           The well used by all is on this land.

House #4:   The married couple are the parents of the wife in #1;
            the wife is the sister of the husband in #2, the aunt
            (FaSi) of the wife in #6, and a second cousin of the wife
            in #3.

House #5:   The occupants are unrelated to others using the well.
            They came to Rusila from another state in 1962 and
            purchased house land from the husband in #2.

House #6:   The wife is the daughter of the married couple in #2,
            the niece of the wife (FaSi) in #4, a first cousin of the
            wife in #1, and a third cousin of the wife in #3.

When kinship ties are traced back another generation, it is
found that the father of both the husband in house #2 and the wife in
house #4 was the brother of the maternal grandmother of the wife
in house #3. Brother and sister inherited the land from their
father; the brother's share was legally divided between his heirs
at the time of his death, although their homes had been built on his
land years earlier. The elderly sister lives with her daughter in
another part of the village, but gave permission for her grand-
daughter to have a home built on the property.

The frequently expressed desire of mothers and daughters to
live near one another is reflected in the location of houses in the
cluster. The young wives in houses #1 and #6 were both living
near their mothers in 1965. However, one of the young women
had two older sisters living in other parts of the village, one of
them near her husband's parents.

As a general rule in 1965, women who shared the use of one
well had more contact with each other than they had with women
using other wells, and well-utilization groups were important
units in the women's communication network. Women gathered at
the well each morning to do their laundry and chat while working.
If a rift occurred between any of the women in the group, the
interaction at the well reflected it, as when two of the well group
outlined above had a misunderstanding about the purchase of a
chicken. The shyer of the two began using the well earlier than
her neighbors. Several women soon joined her, but two of the
original group continued to utilize the well later. Almost a month
passed before the two factions coalesced and everyone was using
the well at the same time.

Adults who live near one another, especially kin or close
friends, tend to borrow and loan household utensils and tools more
frequently than they give or take with others. They also assist one

another with greater frequency and spend more time visiting together. But daily contacts among neighbors have lessened as the wells in the village have proliferated.

An examination of the same neighbors in 1979 shows the following:

House #1:   The house was relocated next to #4 (on the wife's mother's land) in 1969, following a decision by the mother's brother (#2) to sell the part of his land where the niece's home stood. A well was dug at the new house site in 1972.

House #2:   A well was dug on the property during 1971.

House #3:   The original well is now used mainly by the occupants. During occasional periods of inadequate rainfall, when other wells have brackish or muddy water, this one continues to provide sweet, clear water (attributed to site selection by a powerful bomoh) for everyone in the neighborhood.

House #4:   A well was dug on the property in 1967.

House #5:   The land was sold back to #2 and the house to a different buyer, who relocated it elsewhere in the village during 1968. The family who lived there in 1965 moved to another village.

House #6:   The wife died after a prolonged illness in 1968. The widower remarried in 1969, and the house was moved to a site near the home of the second wife's parents. The house land was sold to another widower, who is the former brother-in-law of the husband in #3. A well was dug on the property after a house was built in 1971.

Observations made periodically during 1979 showed fewer interactions among the women living in the houses of the 1965 well-utilization group. The adult women in #1 and #4 (daughter and mother) now live next to one another, and normally have daily contact. The women living in #2 and #3 chat with each other when both are engaged in outdoor work at the same time, two to four times per week, and they visit one another at home occasionally, less than once per week. Neither of them has very much contact with the woman who lives in #4 (although #2 and #4 are sisters-in-law), and both of them see their kinswoman from #1 when she hawks breakfast foods early each morning, a time when all of the women are busy and have little time to chat. The woman now living in a house on the #6 site interacts infrequently with those in the original well group. She spends more time with peers in other nearby houses.

More families throughout the village have wells on their house land or have water piped into their homes. Fewer women must carry water for household use very far, an advantage that cannot be stressed too strongly; but the daily camaraderie previously associated with laundry chores has disappeared, and women generally have less frequent contacts with one another. The functioning of their communication networks now requires more conscious effort. Information that once flowed with the laundry water is passed now at chance meetings or when women visit in one another's homes.

Another feature of village life is reflected by the localized changes outlined above: people do move their houses. It is atypical of village patterns that three of the six houses in one small cluster were moved during a four-year period, but the reasons for the moves are typical: the land on which a house is located does not belong to the household members, and is sold to one or more persons who want to build on it; a person who owns land in one part of the village buys a house in another section and moves the house to the land; marriage bonds that made living in one section of the village preferable are broken through divorce or death, and relocation becomes a means for avoiding potentially difficult interactions with a former spouse and in-laws or, equally possible, a new marriage makes relocation desirable for social, economic, or other reasons associated with the new bond.

TIES TO THE LARGER SOCIETY

The village focuses in upon itself and outward to the larger society and beyond. The result is a range of traditional and modern views and a mixture of old and new practices. Kinship and friendship ties between the villagers and people in nearby villages and towns, and in other parts of the country, vary from one person to another and, in turn, relate to the mobility of individuals and the type of knowledge they have about the larger society. Economic patterns also affect them; the male fish peddler who obtains fish daily in a nearby village and sells it locally has a different experience than the woman who sells fresh produce in the Marang market or the male mechanic and female clerk who work in Kuala Trengganu.

Many ideas about how the larger society of which Rusila is a part functions come to the villagers through their direct contact

with government employees and, more recently, via television.
The local representative of formal government for any village is
the penghulu, a salaried civil servant who is responsible for a
section (mukim) of a district. He—there are no female penghulu
in this area—reports directly to the District Officer at Marang,
who in turn is responsible to an official at the state level.

The mukim of Rusila comprises seven villages, of which
Rusila is one. It does not coincide with the religious parish,
mukim masjid, an area served by one mosque, which today comprises two villages. The mosque is in the village of Rusila. Hence
the village of Rusila is part of the administrative mukim called
Rusila and a part of the mukim masjid Rusila. In 1966 the penghulu
and the imam both lived in the village of Rusila. After the death
of penghulu Haji Ibrahim, a series of men filled the administrative
position, but not one of them resided locally.

As a result, by 1975 local people who previously had direct
access to government services through a fellow villager were increasingly experiencing the frustrations of dealing with an impersonal bureaucratic structure. Many Rusila residents were convinced that the system of house and house land taxation to which
they had recently become subject would not have been imposed if
Haji Ibrahim were still the penghulu.

The ketua kampung (village headman) is not a salaried government employee, although he receives a small annual honorar-
ium from the government. He is appointed by the government on
the recommendation of the penghulu and District Officer, who
should select someone acceptable to the villagers. The ketua
kampung of the village of Rusila in 1965 was a respected elder and
Haji; he was replaced by a younger man in 1977. The headman is
expected to assist the penghulu as required. He is often the one to
whom villagers turn for advice and help, increasingly so since the
penghulu no longer lives in the village.

Two political parties have been active in the village over the
years. The significant changes between 1965 and 1979 were two:
a shift in the support network, from a majority favoring UMNO
(the Malay party in the governing National Front coalition) to a
majority favoring PAS (the Muslim, opposition party), and the
more divisive quality of the support.

In 1965 the majority attitude in the village was pragmatic:
support the party in power nationally and at the state level (UMNO),
with the hope of gaining economic assistance from the government
for such needs as improvement of the drainage and irrigation system upon which the padi crop depends. UMNO established a local
chapter that drew adult male membership from Rusila and two
adjacent villages. At the one 1966 meeting, there were 43 men in

attendance, less than 10 percent of the adult male population of the three villages. Women and men who are 21 or older can and do vote in elections. But no woman attended the UMNO meeting nor, to my knowledge, did any even consider doing so. Neither Wanita UNMO nor any other political affiliate had then, or by 1979, organized women in Rusila for political action.

By 1975 the government had made a number of improvements. A new system of locks had been incorporated into the drainage and irrigation system, a telephone and a midwife's clinic were located in the village, and more schools were available in the area. A greater number of people were enjoying a higher standard of living, but for many villagers the changes had little impact on their lives. Expectations had been raised but not always realized.

During the same decade an important change in local leadership occurred. Penghulu Haji Ibrahim died and UMNO lost its most influential supporter in the village, although other government employees, such as teachers, continued to be UMNO members. And when the old headman was replaced, an UMNO supporter was selected for the position.

The highly respected imam, an advocate of PAS, died in 1975. He was replaced the following year by his son, who has an M.A. degree from Al-Azhar University in Cairo and has studied Islam in several countries. The young imam, charismatic as well as learned, stood for election as a PAS candidate in 1978 and lost to a UMNO man fielded by the National Front. His candidacy and defeat polarized the strongest supporters of the two parties to the point where some individuals no longer attend feasts or ceremonies given by a member of the other faction. The imam has discouraged divisive behavior, but he also actively encourages PAS support. A majority of the villagers try to avoid extreme stands. As one woman said, "Friends are friends and politics are politics." In other words, one should not allow political views to intrude into friendship obligations. UMNO has no local voice that speaks with such authority as the imam speaks for PAS. Many people are convinced that PAS would be more responsive than UMNO to the problems of rural Malays, the problems of Muslims—their problems.

There are several committees and other official bodies in Rusila. Membership in all of them is male. The active participation of women in organized public life is nil; whatever their influence, it is exercised privately. And S. Husin Ali (1975), in his study of leadership in three Malay, agriculture-based communities—in Kedah, Pahang, and Johore—discusses male leaders, mentioning women's political participation in historical and contemporary national contexts only. The lack of women in leadership positions in Rusila and the three other communities is not surprising, in view of the Islamic emphasis on men as leaders.

The mosque committee, under the informal direction of the imam, is responsible for keeping the mosque clean and in good repair, and for mobilizing workers needed for these tasks. Members also take care of any mosque business and arrange for capable men to act as <u>muezzin</u>, making the calls to prayer over a recently installed public address system.

The Board of Governors of the primary school is expected to recommend to the District Education Officer how school funds shall be allocated and to deal with any problems concerning the school.

The Village Development and Security Committee works with the headman, who channels information about village needs to the penghulu of the mukim, who in turn should inform the District Officer. Information and directives from the government flow back to the village along the same communication lines.

Rela, the Home Guard, is responsible for local order, and should report any pro-Communist or other disruptive activities to the appropriate authorities. Members were not armed in June 1979, but rumors were circulating that the leaders would be provided with rifles.

Employees of government agencies and departments come to the village for many purposes: providing veterinary services and agricultural advice, arranging welfare payments and other assistance. One agency, Lembaga Kraftangan (Handicrafts Board), sponsors the Medan Anyaman in the village. (Because of its economic function for local women, the center is dealt with in Chapter 7.)

During the course of a year, some villagers travel many miles. They make trips to nearby villages, to the district administrative center at Marang, and to the state capital, Kuala Trengganu. They go to buy or to sell various things, to visit friends and relatives, to pawn or reclaim gold jewelry, to enjoy some form of entertainment or a feast in conjunction with a wedding ceremony, to get medical-dental-optical attention, or to attend special functions, such as the public celebrations for the birthday of His Highness the Sultan.

Friends and relatives come to the village to visit, most frequently from short distances. But for a marriage, a funeral, or other important occasion, guests arrive from other parts of the peninsula, just as Rusila residents go to other parts of the country for similar events. In 1966 no local person had been to Sabah or Sarawak, the Malaysian states on the island of Borneo. Several local men and one woman were working there in 1975 and 1979.

Villagers who made the pilgrimage to Mecca were the only local people whose direct experience of the world extended beyond

Malaysia and Singapore in 1966. Today a young couple might make a wedding trip to Indonesia or an exceptional student might be selected to continue education abroad. Many others learn of the larger society in which they live and about some aspects of the outside world from those whose experiences are more extensive than their own. Furthermore, as tourism increases more people have direct contact with foreigners, or they learn about them through television and other mass media. During 14 years the world of local villagers has expanded enormously.

3
WOMEN: THE LIFE CYCLE

I cannot begin to attempt generalizations about "the life cycle" of Malaysian women. Menarche, menstruation, and menopause provide an almost universal female experience. The vast majority of Malaysian women marry and bear children, but a few remain single and others do not reproduce. Urban women have a different experience than do rural women; the lives of rich and poor, members of different ethnic categories and religions can vary enormously.

There is not just one life cycle pattern even in a fairly homogeneous village. A generation ago formal education was not available to Rusila women; now girls routinely enter primary school at age six and a few have already gone on to earn university or college degrees. Women who continue their education beyond the secondary level (and some who do not) postpone marriage at least until their early twenties. Their mothers married between the ages of 14 and 16, a few prior to menarche. Among women of the same generation, one whose childbearing begins at 17 might well have grandchildren before she reaches 40; her life cycle has an accelerated quality compared with that of a woman who bears her first child at 25 or older. In the description that follows, I focus on major changes and differences.

THE LIFE CYCLE IN RUSILA

Children are referred to as <u>harta</u> (wealth), and are universally desired by villagers, daughters as much as sons. A daughter is more dutiful, and thus more likely to look after her parents solicitously during their later years. Anyone who has no children is

56

considered unfortunate and is pitied. Hence, it is accepted as natural for the childless, or those whose children are grown, to adopt (usually informally), borrow, or even buy a child.

Buying a child is rare: very few families in an area encompassing several villages have done it. One infant was purchased during 1966 from her parents, poor people who already had seven children, in a nearby village. The couple who took the child registered her as their own (as having been born to them). The police were suspicious. They had seen the adoptive mother daily and were sure she had not been pregnant, but the infant was registered anyway. The young woman who took her paid $30 to the biological parents to cover the midwife's fee, medicine for mother and child, and a gift to the natural mother. The adoptive mother already had a daughter of her own, and in 1969 she adopted a third girl, a child of mixed Malay-Indian ancestry. Now that the youngest is going to school, the woman is looking for another infant. She would like a Chinese baby because she, like many Malays, admires the fair Chinese skin color.

Children living with other than biological parents may be considered as adopted (anak angkat, literally "carried child") although no legal procedures have been followed. Some of the arrangements are thought to be temporary when they are made, but they may last for years. Altogether, 33 children, 10 percent of all village children, did not live with their own parents in 1966. Fifteen of them lived with their grandparents or a widowed grandmother (a situation referred to as cucu angkat, "carried grandchild"). The pattern of carrying/adoption persisted in 1979, and it was most common for a child not living with its own parents to be with a grandmother or grandparents.

INFANCY AND EARLY CHILDHOOD

Most babies are born at home with the help of a midwife. As soon as the umbilical cord is cut, the end protruding from the infant's belly is wrapped with thread. Traditionally the baby's father put a frothy paste made from leaves with magical-medicinal properties on his big toe and, with it, made an X on the child's forehead and another on its stomach to protect the infant from disease, an old, pre-Islamic custom. A grandmother of the infant then bathes it and wraps its abdomen with several turns of very soft cloth. A female infant might be circumcised at this time.

I have referred to the practice of clitoridectomy among Malays (Strange 1971). However, Fran Hosken (quoted by Daly 1978:156) distinguishes among three types of female genital mutilation, by

degree of destruction, from "Sunna circumcision" involving removal
of the tip of the clitoris and possibly the prepuce, to excision (clitoridectomy), to the even more horrifying practice of clitoridectomy and
infibulation. In Rusila a form of Sunna circumcision, either an in-
cision of the clitoris or removal of its tip, is usually performed by
the midwife. The practice reportedly was not universal even in 1965,
although informants referred to it as sunat (commendable) for Muslims.

In an article entitled "Perfectly Safe—the Way Muslim Women
Are Circumcised" (NST 5/24/79), the Mufti (a high-ranking Muslim
jurist) of the Federal Territory (Kuala Lumpur) said, in response to
a World Health Organization report condemning clitoridectomy:

> . . . the circumcision of Muslim women involves only
> a minor part of the sex organ. The practice [is] not
> mandatory in Islam. . . . [Another Muslim official]
> said that if circumcision would really endanger the
> health of an individual, especially if conducted by un-
> qualified personnel, it need not be carried out (my em-
> phasis).

The implications are obvious: if only a part of the female sex
organ is removed, the practice is defined by Muslim male officials
as acceptable, and a woman's health is not seen as endangered if
qualified "personnel" do the cutting. Although the practice is not
mandatory, it is sunat, which certainly suggests that parents will
condone, and midwives will perform, the operation, particularly in
areas where Muslim fundamentalist values are influential.

The father whispers the Islamic call to prayer, which contains the Confession of Faith, in the right ear of a son and the left
ear of a daughter. This rite is the first of a series marking the incorporation of all infants into the Muslim community. Several objects in succession are touched to the infant's lips to assure against
lying and gossipmongering during the years ahead. Anyone can perform this little ritual. The important consideration for parents when
making the selection is the person's character, in particular that she
or he has a reputation for telling the truth but is not a troublemaker.
Richard Winstedt (1961:109) notes the performance of a similar rite
in Arabia and Egypt, but suggests that it may have reached Malaya
from India.

During the first 44 days of life, the period of a new mother's
confinement, infants are breast-fed only or, if necessary, mother's
milk may be supplemented with warmed water mixed with cornstarch
(or, recently, commercial formula). Breast-feeding is done in a
relaxed, open manner by older women, but young mothers with first

babies are shy and tend to seek privacy when feeding their infants.
Since the late 1960s bottle-feeding of infants has become more common as a supplement to, or substitute for, breast-feeding, especially by young mothers who have returned to wage-paying jobs a few
weeks after childbirth. Traditionally infants might be breast-fed
for up to two years.

In rural areas nationwide, 87.5 percent of all mothers breast-
feed their babies, but only 45.1 percent were still breast-feeding
after six months and 35.9 percent after 12 months. Percentages are
much lower for urban populations in Malaysia (approximately 68 percent breast-feed and 22.7 percent continue beyond the first six months),
and considerably higher in other Southeast Asian countries that have
been studied—Indonesia (95.2 percent urban and 99.4 percent
rural women breast-feed, with 85.0 percent and 97.9 percent still
breast-feeding after six months) and Thailand (urban 76.8 percent,
rural 96.3 percent; after six months, 61.0 percent and 92.2 percent).
Tabulations based on duration of formal education show that women
with more education in all of the countries are less likely to breast-
feed, or breast-feed for a shorter period of time (Williams 1979:7-8).

Rusila mothers add small amounts of egg yolk to an infant's
diet after the 44 days. By one year of age the child is eating boiled
rice, vegetables, and fruit; at 18 months fish and meat are introduced into the diet. Some mothers say that their children aged one
and two years eat mainly commercial biscuits and milk, rejecting
most other foods. A few children are suckled until they are about
two years old, but others are transferred to a bottle before they
reach one year.

When the 44-day period ends, the placenta, which has been
stored in a clean cloth with salt, turmeric root, and bits of asam
gelugor (a type of fruit), is buried by the infant's father beneath a
coconut palm seedling. While there is believed to be a mystical con-
nection between the infant and the placenta, there is complete lack
of concern if the seedling fails to flourish. The umbilical cord,
which has dropped from the baby's navel, may be buried with the
placenta or a mother may save it, wrapped in cloth, because powerful medicine can be made from it by someone with the necessary
knowledge, such as a bomoh (Malay medical-magical practitioner).

Two rituals are performed after the 44-day period ends and,
usually, before the baby is three months old. Cukor kepala means
"to shave the head," but actually locks of hair are cut with scissors
by seven men. Women watch, but do not participate in the event beyond preparing a meal for guests. Friday is said to be the best day
for the ritual, to insure that the child will perform religious duties
seriously. One mother pointed out that of her five children, only
one is not diligent in her religious observances. The mother blames

herself for having held the cukor kepala for this child on a Wednesday. The rite is customary rather than Islamic (Wira undated:45).

Some mothers shave their infants' heads completely when the guests have departed after the ceremony, because the hair is considered unclean from having grown in the mother's womb and cannot be cleansed because of its nature. They view the practice of shaving the head as purifying. Others think that shaving a child's head will make the hair more beautiful, and that it will be more luxuriant and blacker when it grows. Traditionally a female infant had her ears pierced on the same day as the haircutting ceremony, but now it is more common for the child to be of school age. One man is adept at piercing ears without causing infections, and it is to him that little girls go, usually alone and by choice, paying 50 cents for the service.

Another ceremony may be carried out on the same day as the haircutting, though it is more likely to be done when the infant is between three and four months old. The jijak tanah (footsteps on the earth) begins when the father rubs the infant's soles with a stone brought from Mecca. Then the infant has its feet placed on "the ground" for the first time. Many people take their children to the mosque, where a tray covered with sand brought from Mecca is used; others go to the cemetery, to place an infant's feet on earth covering the grave of a highly respected person. No feast is held at this time, but those who accompany the family, usually curious children, are given snacks. Today the motive behind the ceremony is Islamic. The child first stands on sacred ground so that the path through life will be exemplary. In the ceremony use of objects from Mecca modifies pre-Islamic custom, adat (Ibid.).

A Muslim blessed with a child should give a feast to show gratitude to God (Ibid.). The feast is called akikah. Because akikah is an important event, a cow should be slaughtered for the occasion. This is a very big expense that most families cannot afford, so villagers postpone it, sometimes indefinitely; use a goat for a smaller feast; or six or seven families pool their resources to cover feast expenses.

Throughout infancy and early childhood, roughly until they begin to attend school, children are treated very indulgently. They are fondled, played with, and, while small, carried in the arms or astraddle the hips of parents and older siblings. Mothers and older sisters are particularly significant in an infant's life. Weaning and toilet training are accomplished gradually, with encouragement given for desired behavior and a shaking of the head or a "never mind" (tidak apa) for lack of it. Tots may be dressed or go nude, except for a pacifier hung around the neck, depending on the weather and the mother. Compared with 1965, it had become common in

1975 to see toddlers fully clothed in romper suits or dresses and
bonnets, and shoes and socks, especially if they were being taken
outside the village or to a special event in Rusila. Mothers' desires
to be modern (moden) created additional laundry chores, and toddlers
probably were less comfortable than their siblings had been ten years
earlier.

Walking and talking are encouraged, but not urged on a child.
The child learns to use the right hand for eating and the left for
cleaning itself (after defecating or urinating) by the mother's manipulation of its hands combined with comments about correct and incorrect behavior. The child learns to sit properly, tailor-fashion, by
having legs and feet positioned by a parent whenever an incorrect
posture is observed. Masturbation may be ignored, or discouraged
by an "ussht" sound from a parent or a light slap on the hand. Generally the early socialization process is effected in a relaxed and
gentle manner.

Indulgence extends to letting a young child eat whenever and
whatever is preferred, which may mean that more snack foods, such
as sweets and biscuits, are consumed than fish and rice. Bedtimes
also vary according to a child's mood and whether there is any special event in the village or nearby. Infants and young children are
taken almost everywhere, and can go to sleep almost anywhere. If
a toddler is sleepless during the night and want to go out, perhaps
to visit grandparents, it is likely that the desire will be granted.
Older children sometimes stay up late even though they must go to
school the next day. They hate to miss anything interesting or different. Once children are asleep, all kinds of activities, including
very noisy ones, can occur without disturbing them.

Punishments frequently are verbal or consist of a light slap
on the hands or a switching of the legs with a wand of rattan. However, if a child's behavior poses a danger, stronger punishments
are used. In particular, children must learn not to venture onto the
highway or go too near the sea. Toddlers are carefully supervised,
but sometimes a busy mother or an older sibling involved in play is
distracted long enough for a tot to stray.

One day a three-year-old, who had wandered down from his
nearby home, appeared on the beach where I was photographing some
fishing boat maneuvers. He ambled into the water before I could in-
tercept him, and was thoroughly and happily sopping by the time I
reached him, just as his mother arrived on the beach a little distance
from us. She was obviously very upset, so upset that she grabbed
him, submerged him, and then shook him, at the same time stating
the dangers of his behavior. He was so shocked by the treatment
that he screamed for almost ten minutes. This was the first punishment more extreme than a light hand slap that he had ever experienced.

If a young child picks up a sharp tool, any adult or older child who is nearby will try to provide a distraction with something less dangerous. Even an axe or a knife is unlikely to be snatched away, because if it is, the tot begins screaming. Adults occasionally warn a child against mauling a pet cat for fear the beast will retaliate, but this happens rarely. The cats usually try to escape from their young tormenters rather than attack them.

One other category of behavior elicits immediate punishment from a parent if the child is considered old enough to understand it. Behavior that Muslims consider defiling, such as touching cow dung, is punishable with slapping or shaking, combined with explanation.

Objectionable behavior is sometimes discouraged by a parent's threatening that a dog will come and carry the young child away. The threat acts as a deterrent to friendly overtures toward the stray dogs that sometimes wander into the village. It is "unlucky" to keep dogs (Skeat 1967:183), and they are unclean in the religious sense as well as potentially dangerous. An irate parent may call a misbehaving child a pig, a monkey, or use other insulting terms. However, the parent who tries to shame a child in this manner acknowledges that it is not good to do so.

Parents do their best to discourage undesirable behavior by little ones, but older siblings of eight or ten sometimes encourage tots to misbehave. If they are caught, the older children have their ears twisted or their hair pulled, or receive a slap, because they are expected to know better. The point at which a child should "know better" about behavior with younger siblings, and in the more general sense appreciate what is right and wrong, acceptable and unacceptable, is the first year or so of formal schooling. During the preschool years a child of either sex can disrupt an entire family with a temper tantrum. The same behavior from a school-age child will elicit sharp words from parents and ridicule from older siblings.

The preschool child is given the treat if there is money for only one ice cream when the vendor passes. Other children are expected to understand; they once enjoyed the same preferential treatment. Teenage or older children often show the same indulgence to their preschool siblings that parents do. The jealousy and hurt are strongest in those who have recently been replaced as the darling of the family, those who are in the throes of learning the new behavior patterns expected of them and casting off behavior patterns that they see are accepted, laughed about, and enjoyed by their parents when performed by a three-to-five-year-old. The transition appears to be very abrupt, but that conclusion may be due to the nature and length of the observations made of particular children.

Reactions to punishments or upsets from other causes also vary by age. Young children scream and cry, and will soon be

soothed by parent or sibling. Older children tend to sulk and become withdrawn, both psychically and physically, if they are punished, and seek escape through sleep if they are very upset. Sleep
serves as an escape mechanism for adults, too, when they experience shame or extreme disappointment.

Commercial toys were far more common in Rusila in 1979
than they had been even in 1975, but youngsters and adults alike
still showed ingenuity in creating playthings. Small boats, kites,
tops, slingshots, noisemakers, and other toys are constructed from
materials found in the natural environment. The only doll to be seen
in the village in 1966 was encased in its original plastic wrapper
and stood atop a closet, where it could be looked at but not played
with. A variety of molded plastic figures and several dolls were
being actively enjoyed by their young owners in 1975, but for older
children dolls had little, if any, meaning. There are infants to be
carried and cuddled, and even little girls of six or seven are expected to take some responsibility for their care. Boys also look
after younger siblings but, generally, far less is required of them
than of their sisters.

THE SCHOOL YEARS

Education and literacy have risen significantly since 1952,
when the primary school was built in Rusila. Literacy, the ability
to read and write in Malay, varies by age. By 1979 most persons
between the ages of 6 and 35 were either attending school or had at
least a primary school education. Few persons above the age of 35
are literate, nor have many had any formal secular education.

Children enter the six-year primary school program at age
six. Education at this level is open to all and is ostensibly free.
Actually each child pays a small annual school fee. Additional fees
vary at the different levels, depending on the work the children are
expected to do. Sometimes textbooks are provided for them, but
copybooks, workbooks, pens and ink, and some art supplies must
be purchased.

Each of the grade levels is taught by a different instructor.
Additional teachers are responsible for giving lessons in English
and religion to all levels receiving them. Throughout, the emphasis is on rote learning. In the first grade, children begin to read
and write Malay, using the romanized alphabet (Rumi), study arith-
metic, and participate in group games and calisthenics. They continue with these subjects through the sixth grade. As they progress,
other subjects are added: English, religion (Islam), geography,
history, Jawi (Malay written with the Arabic alphabet), arts and

crafts, and sports with more complexity. Classes begin at 7:40
A.M. and end at 12:40 P.M., a schedule that allows the children to
eat lunch at home.

Almost half of the school enrollment is accounted for by Rusila
children. The rest of the student body is made up of children from
two adjacent villages. A few local children attend a primary school
in Kuala Trengganu, where they study English as well as Malay from
the first grade.

Girls are expected to be well-behaved in class; they usually
are shy (malu) in a sexually mixed group. No one is surprised if a
boy is mischievous, because such behavior is expected of him. When
a boy is naughty, he is called up to face the class, and directed by
the teacher to bring his arms across his chest, to grasp his right
earlobe with his left hand, and his left lobe with his right hand. He
then performs kneebends, bobbing up and down for the number of
times prescribed by the teacher. After this performance he feels
embarrassed (malu) and returns to his place to sit quietly with his
head bowed. A boy who habitually misbehaves can be sent to the
headmaster for caning; by law corporal punishment "may not be
meted out to girls" (Abdul Kadir 1975:13).

Participation in extracurricular sports is encouraged. Rusila
teams compete with those of other primary schools in the district,
girls in basketball and track events, and boys in these sports and
soccer. During July 1965 the first intramural field day was held at
the school athletic field. Children of both sexes and all ages participated in appropriate events, from the 100-yard dash, broad jump,
and hurling the discus, to gunny sack races and a form of musical
chairs. Everyone in the village was present, and the District Officer and his wife, who bestowed the prizes, delighted children and
adults with their attendance. The field day has been replaced in recent years by monthly competitions that parents do not attend.

There are no girls' organizations in conjunction with the primary school. In 1965 there were two troops of Boy Scouts, but they
were disbanded during the early 1970s for lack of adult leadership.
Girl Guides and Boy Scouts are organized in some of the secondary
schools.

In addition to receiving formal religious training in school,
many Rusila children go to the home of a religious instructor for an
hour per day, six afternoons each week, to learn to recite the Quran.
Instruction sessions are held throughout the year except during the
month of Ramadan. Instructors have between 4 and 40 pupils,
women teaching girls and men giving lessons to boys. Few students
continue their studies long enough to become expert, but those who
do are lauded by village adults.

Boys have more freedom than girls. They go to another part of the village to play or to visit grandparents without informing their parents. Girls are expected to stay closer to home, especially after puberty, though they have far more freedom than their mothers had at the same age. Still, ideally, they are trained from an early age to be competent homemakers, learning to cook and perform other household chores as well as to care for infants. As a result girls have less time to play. When they do have free time, girls and boys enjoy playing at the beach. Many boys swim expertly, but few girls learn to do so. Modesty ideals constrain them. Preschoolers of either sex pull off their clothes and splash happily in the shallows under the care of older siblings. But those older siblings may not swim nude. Boys swim in the same short pants they wear to school, but a girl of nine or ten must wear a blouse and a sarong to be properly covered.

What is expected of any child depends on a parent's perceptions and on the age, sex, ability to perform a task, and the child's inclination to do so. Demands are not great in most homes, but even when one is made, a young child can ignore it without incurring more than a comment about laziness from an annoyed parent. Mothers seem far more lenient than most fathers when children fail to perform chores. Older children, boys as well as girls, are expected to do much of their own laundry and to clean their school shoes or sneakers. These chores have a built-in incentive, because no one wants to be teased by peers for wearing a dirty school uniform. A child may not respond to a request to bring water from the well for general household use, but will get water for his or her own laundry. Daughters assume more and more responsibility for meal preparations and other housework. One woman with two daughters, 18 and 20 years of age, says that she no longer does any household chores. She is enjoying her leisure, knowing that when the daughters marry, the chores will again be her responsibility.

Circumcision of males was probably performed in Malaya prior to the introduction of Islam, but today the practice is observed as a Muslim obligation (Winstedt 1961:112), although the ritual aspects of the practice are custom (adat) (Wira undated:45). This major ceremony in a male's life occurs when he is about ten years of age. Only men attend a circumcision performed in the village, which is always held outside, while women remain in their homes with all doors and windows closed.

There are two local explanations for the ban against women: women, particularly the boy's mother, would be distressed by the child's suffering; they would district the modin during his performance of the operation and that could be disastrous for the boy. Carried one step further, it can be suggested that the presence of distressed women (the mother) would counteract the symbolic separation of the boy from "the world of women" as he undergoes this rite of passage toward manhood; that the modin might be distracted also means that women are potentially distracting to him (to men), and thus dangerous to the boy (they do not want to see him pass from boyhood to manhood).

Women are excluded only from being present; there are no secret rituals being enacted that they are forbidden to know. In fact, women are active participants in the extremely detailed post-operation discussions. This underscores the likelihood, although local people do not express this interpretation, that the boy is being symbolically removed from his mother and women's domain, a separation generally expressed in male puberty rituals. In Java, for example, although the mother is present at the circumcision, when it has been completed she ". . . steps across [her son] three times, demonstrating that she . . . is free of any hidden feelings toward the boy which might hamper the necessary process of his growing emotionally away from her toward manhood" (Geertz 1960:52).

Rusila women are confined to their symbolic world, the home, while the boy takes a first step into the larger public world of men, suggested by the operation's being performed outdoors, dissociated from the women's world, with only men present. That windows and doors are closed not only emphasizes the division, but totally removes mother, the usual source of comfort and succor, from her son, who must rely on immediate support and help from other males. The boy has been separated, both physically and symbolically, from the realm of women and from his mother's psychological support. That the removal is brief—the boy returns home to mother, who looks after him—need not discredit the symbolism, for soon after the circumcision the boy takes on full adult responsibilities within the Islamic framework. He is expected to accompany his father to the mosque for the Friday prayers, for example. By 1975 circumcisions were usually performed, with anesthesia, at the Kuala Trengganu hospital, but women were still excluded.

A girl changes religious status at age nine, but strict observance of Muslim obligations and proscriptions occurs after menarche, probably during her fourteenth or fifteenth year. After that she is forbidden to perform any religious act while she is menstruating.

The menstruating woman pollutes by her presence; she is forbidden to enter a mosque or a graveyard. She pollutes by contact; she must not touch the Holy Quran. She must not pray, nor can she observe the Ramadan fast, although a special time following Ramadan is set aside for making up what was lost. Religiously a woman becomes a nonperson during mensis. Sexual relations with her husband are forbidden, and she should not allow him physical contact with her body between the navel and the knees while she is "unclean."

And the admonition to men that ". . . ye who have touched women . . . (Pickthall 1959:83) must cleanse faces and hands before praying shows that women, even when not menstruating, have the power to defile men. Ablutions are required for men and women before prayer, so the directive to men indicates that if they have performed ablutions and then touch a woman, the ablutions are negated. In other words, do not let women deter you from religious duties. Is there a similar admonition to women, or is it implicit in the one to men? I can find nothing explicit. When she is not menstruating, a woman dons a white robe (kain sembahyang) that covers her entirely, except her face, before praying. Men can wear their regular clothing, but they must cover their heads.

Figure 3. Young Weaver (Rusila, 1965). Eight-year-old Aminah weaving a small basket. She wears a sarong topped by a baju kurung.

Since the early 1960s more and more children have continued their education at the secondary level (see Chapter 4). Girls who do not so so spend their time assisting their mothers and weaving pandanus mats and basketry—a skill that some much younger girls develop—for household use or for sale. If they are not fully productive economically outside of the home, they can free a mother for such work by taking over her household responsibilities. Boys who do not go on to secondary school are more likely to be in an economic limbo. They are not big enough or strong enough to be able to work effectively as fishermen or rubber tappers, or to pursue most village occupations. They spend much of their time just hanging around, occasionally assisting their fathers. There is approximately a three-year hiatus between the time a lad finishes primary school at age 12 or 13 and the time he is big enough to perform a man's work. By age 16 a boy who is not enrolled in school is normally engaged in some kind of remunerative work, if only on a part-time basis.

MARRIAGE, PREGNANCY, AND BIRTH

Marriage, dealt with at length in a later chapter, is the major event in the life of the average young person. Change in marital status from single to married is also a social change from youth to adult. With marriage, new obligations, both social and economic, are assumed. All village Malays in this area marry unless they are drastically incapacitated. The trend noted in societies undergoing modernization, that fewer people marry (Berelson and Steiner 1964: 607), had not yet reached Rusila in 1979. However, many women and men were marrying later and had assumed full adult economic responsibilities before marriage.

When a young married woman realizes that she is pregnant, the first person she normally confides in is her mother, who tells her friends, who pass along the happy news. If a pregnant female is not married, the news is distressing, so it is kept within the family for as long as possible.

The villagers believe that a child born out of wedlock is not pure. Stigma attaches to the child even though it is the parents who have committed a sin. Yet according to Mahmoud Shaltout (1958: 131) and M. A. Rauf (1964:16), in Islam a child is believed to be born pure, bearing no responsibility for the sins of forebears. An illegitimate individual who lives in the village is subject to local beliefs rather than to orthodox theological positions, although overt discrimination is unusual. Illegitimacy is rare for three reasons aside from the aforementioned beliefs. First, there is little opportunity in the village for an unmarried couple to engage in sexual relations. Second, the mobility of the average unmarried postpubescent female is restricted. Third, every effort is made to arrange a marriage for a pregnant woman as soon as her condition is known.

If an unmarried female becomes pregnant, she and her entire family feel ashamed (malu). Her parents, especially the mother, bear the responsibility for not having supervised their daughter more carefully. Nor is the young man seen as guiltless, although the social reactions to him are less intense. There is a period of mutual avoidance between the young couple and other villagers because everyone feels awkward (malu) about the situation, but apparently local people feel no desire to punish the breakers of the moral code. Everyone shares the Islamic belief in a Day of Judgment when sinners will receive dreadful punishments in Hell and the righteous will be rewarded (Rauf 1964:9).

Pregnancy imposes a number of restrictions on a woman. Certain foods and activities must be avoided. Each taboo (pantang) is believed to assure an easy birth or a healthy baby, or to give protection from danger. There is little consensus about specific avoidances; some ideas are limited to individual family traditions, while others seem to be remembered after the fact (when a child is born with a deformity). Then there is speculation about what the mother or father did or did not do, should or should not have done.

Women give many examples of things that should not be cut during pregnancy. In particular, wood must not be split, lest the child be born with a harelip. A pregnant woman should avoid looking closely at any deformed person, and must not say anything derogatory about deformity. Otherwise, God might be angry and cause her child to be born with the same impairment. Most women agree that nothing should be closed with nails, screws, lacings, or needle and thread by the pregnant woman or her husband. If such actions are performed, the birth will be difficult because the womb will not open fully.

Village women require no special maternity garb; regular clothing serves them admirably. A sarong may be 70 inches in circumference and can be wrapped so as to accommodate expanding waistline and abdomen. Most short blouses and the longer, knee-length ones (baju kurung) fit loosely enough to be used during pregnancy.

One or two months prior to the anticipated birth, a pregnant woman who is expecting a first child returns to her parents' home, where she stays for three or four months. She receives care and emotional support from her mother. Women who already have children go home for shorter periods of time, or their mothers come to stay with them for several weeks before and after the birth. The

few women from this village who are town dwellers gave birth to
their first babies in their parents' homes. Some of their later children were born in town hospitals.

Two types of midwives are available to local women. The
bidan kampung (village midwife) learned her art from those who
practiced before her; she has also attended a government-sponsored
course to learn hygienic procedures. She can perform the necessary ceremonies as well as deliver babies. Two village midwives
live in Rusila. A government midwife (bidan kerajaan) has a secondary school education as well as a year of formal training in midwifery and infant care. During 1966 the nearest government midwife was in charge of a small clinic located three miles from the
village. By 1975 a government midwife was in charge of a clinic
located in Rusila. She could be consulted by pregnant women and
those desiring postnatal care for themselves or their infants. Her
living quarters are attached to the clinic, so she is available for
emergencies as well as during regular hours five and one-half days
each week. She is one of very few local women who rides a bicycle.
Dressed in her white uniform, she cycles through Rusila and to
other villages to visit women and infants under her care.

It is instructive to compare the government midwife available
to women in 1966 with the one who now lives in the village. The
first midwife was 20 years old. Her age and the fact that she was
not yet married were occupational liabilities because they raised
doubts about her competence in the minds of many women. The
present midwife is older, married, and the mother of several children. Women feel more confidence in her because of these personal
features. Nevertheless, for the ceremonial events associated with
pregnancy and childbirth, they still consult one of the bidan kampung.
It is now usual for two midwives—a woman of the village and the
woman who is the official government midwife—to work together and
for both to be present at a birth.

At the seventh month of a pregnancy, sirih leaves, the traditional symbol of goodwill, hospitality, and appreciation, are sent to
one of the village midwives. By her acceptance of them, she indicates that she will attend the delivery, will conduct the rites associated with pregnancy, and will participate in the postnatal care of
the mother and infant.

The seventh-month ceremony, melenggang perut (to sway the
stomach), is considered important during a first pregnancy. Everyone agrees that it wards off misfortune. Some say the ceremony
has mystical influence on the mother's body, preparing her to give
birth without difficulty; others think the influence is on the fetus,
placing the baby in the proper position for an easy birth. The ceremony is adat, but Islamic elements have been added, for ultimately

the fate of mother and baby rest with God. Pious and respected men
are invited to come to the home early on the day of the ceremony to
repeat verses from the Quran and pray, after which they are served
a festive meal. They depart, and the married female relatives of
the pregnant woman make preparations for the ceremony.

The young expectant mother lies on a bed concealed from
casual view by a screen, with the midwife squatting on the bed next
to her. A variety of objects have been assembled on trays: each is
taken in turn by the midwife and rolled gently down the pregnant
woman's abdomen. Then the ends of seven sarongs or other cloths
folded under the young woman are taken one at a time by two atten-
dants who manipulate them to sway her body. More objects are
passed over the recumbent woman, always from the direction of her
head down, the direction in which the baby must move at birth.

Then the young woman is led to the kitchen, where she is
bathed with herbal water by the midwife. Throughout she has been
wearing a sarong secured under the armpits so as to cover her torso.
Now she changes into her best clothing for the third part of the ceremony, when she sits in state behind a decorated table while the midwife touches specially prepared rice (nasi semangat) to her lips and
gives an Islamic benediction for the protection of mother and baby.
Portions of the nasi semangat are given to friends; the midwife receives payment of husked rice and a coconut used in the ceremony,
as well as a large portion of nasi semangat and some of the festive
food.

A pregnant woman who goes through this ceremony in Rusila,
even today, is normally less than 20 years old, and feels malu and
nervous about being in an unfamiliar situation and the focal point of
everyone's attention. The older women find her reactions amusing
and enjoy teasing her, occasionally in an extreme manner. The in-
tentions behind the teasing are said to be good, but the teasing itself
seems to produce more tension than it alleviates. Still, the women
reason that if the expectant mother is tense now, her feelings will
be more acute later and cause problems during the birth.

When a woman's labor pains begin, the midwives are called to
the home. The expectant mother is lying on a clean mat on the floor,
screened off from the rest of the house by a portable screen or
cloths hung from wires overhead. Some of the woman's female
relatives and friends are with her.

During the birth the woman lies with her knees drawn up and
parted. Three women hold her: one pressing her shoulders to the
floor and the others each holding one of her legs in the proper position. If she needs something to bite, a strand of her hair or a wad
of cloth is put between her teeth. A woman who screams or otherwise carries on at this time is said to be pampered or spoiled and,

because such behavior inhibits the birth process, the midwife may lightly slap the woman's face to make her stop. The others offer encouragement of the mother's efforts; the midwife grasps the emerging infant and carefully assists its entry into the world.

After the child emerges, the umbilical cord is cut and the infant is given to its grandmother, who bathes it. The midwife presses the mother's abdomen from the waist down to force out the afterbirth. Cloth is tied tightly around the mother's waist, a practice believed to keep the placenta from rising and killing her. After the expulsion of the afterbirth, the mother is bathed with warm, herbal water and covered. Men can now enter the room.

If there were difficulties with a birth in 1966, a bomoh was called, but he was limited to examining and manipulating the upper part of the expectant mother's body or her limbs. Her torso below the waist was carefully covered. By 1975 there were no longer any bomoh practicing in the village. If problems occurred, the government midwife requested medical assistance from the hospital in Kuala Trengganu. Between 1975 and 1979 several local women had given birth in the hospital, but a majority of infants were born at home with the help of midwives.

In 1965-66, 5 out of 22 Rusila infants were stillborn or died before the age of six months. There were no infant deaths during the first six months of 1979. Both statements are misleading because of the extremely small sample and the limited time periods: There is neither an infant mortality rate of 227 nor one of zero. Nationally the infant mortality rate is 44 deaths per 1,000 births (Kane 1979). But a newspaper editorial about infant deaths gave a percentage of 7.7 (a rate of 77) for some rural areas of Malaysia and attributed it to the youth of the mothers, inadequate diet associated with poverty, reluctance to give birth in hospitals, and observance of pregnancy food taboos (NST 3/9/79).

After the new mother has rested, she is massaged and bathed again. A fire is prepared in a basin filled with sand. When it becomes coals and embers, the woman stands over it, allowing the heat to rise to the vaginal area to help heal her. Bindings made from clean, soft cloth are wrapped firmly around her abdomen to aid the skin in normalizing.

Previously a special bed, made of wood with a bamboo platform in which numerous holes have been cut, has been constructed by the woman's husband or father. Pandanus matting is put atop the bamboo, and metal containers filled with hot coals are placed below it. The mother lies on this "roasting bed." She massages her abdomen with stones that have been heated in a fire, thrust momentarily into cold water, and wrapped in cloth. The woman uses the special bed on and off, day and night, for a period of 20 to 30 days. After that, as one young mother said, "How good a mattress feels!"

The village midwife is paid $15 for assisting at the birth, a fee that also covers the cost of massages and herbal baths for the mother for three days afterward. If the midwife cannot perform this part of her job, she must secure someone else, paying the other woman from her own fee. Today the government midwife is expected to oversee the health of both mother and child after the birth, so she also visits them. Because she earns a salary from the government, she is not paid any money for her services, but she is given gifts of food.

The mother must observe a number of restrictions for 44 days following the birth. She is religiously unclean during this period; hence she is forbidden to read the Quran, pray, or perform any religious duty. Physically she is said to have "cold sickness" and, therefore, she must eat no foods that are classed as "cold," but only those considered to be "hot" or neutral—plain, boiled rice, plain cake, eggs, broiled fish, cooked bananas and durian, coffee, or water prepared with herbs. She must not eat fried foods, meat, or sauces of any kind, nor should she drink plain water. (For a detailed study of this topic, see C. S. Wilson 1973). A woman may take patent medicines such as Haji Mubin's Curing Powder or ones prepared locally by a person with knowledge about the medicinal properties of plants. In 1965 such a person would have been a male bomoh, but today there are none active in Rusila. One woman herbalist began to practice outside of her nuclear family in the mid-1970s, initially treating only kinswomen, and has established a reputation as a curer of a wide variety of ailments. She now treats men (always in the presence of another adult) as well as women.

The village women go to visit the mother and to look at her baby. A new mother's activities are curtailed and she spends much of her time lying on the "roasting bed," so visitors are a welcome diversion. The women pick up the infant, examine it, point out any defects, discuss the possible taboo violations that could have caused them, give the baby to its mother to be fed, take it back, cuddle it, and replace it in its cradle.

The mother resumes a normal existence at the end of the 44-day period; she has socially returned from childbirth. Sexual relations between husband and wife can be resumed, but some women think this is undesirable because it is too easy to become pregnant again. While children are genuinely desired, there is a negative attitude about having them less than two years apart. A woman who becomes pregnant within a few months after a delivery may have her and her husband's sexual behavior likened to that of cats in heat by someone who does not like them, but most village women will pity the one who is pregnant, pointing out the physical strain and the fact that it is best to have weaned one infant before becoming pregnant again.

The government and private agencies sponsor family planning programs that appear to be having some success, especially in urban areas. In 1969 only 6 percent of the married women of reproductive age in Peninsular Malaysia were using some form of contraception; by 1975, 43 percent were using something. Almost two-thirds of the users of contraceptives have some secondary or higher education. However, more than 70 percent of all women practicing contraception are using "the pill" (Nortman 1977:11, 25).

The Chairman of the National Family Planning Board (NFPB), Tan Sri Abdul Jamil Rais, told a workshop on family planning program management that economic development in Malaysia led to the fertility decline, which was accelerated and sustained by the NFPB program. In 1966 the birth rate was 3.1 percent, and it had fallen to 2.6 percent in 1977 (NST 11/16/79). The lowered birth rate correlates with later age at marriage and better educational and occupational opportunities for women as well as men. Age at marriage remains highest for the educated in urban areas, particularly among the Chinese (Baldwin 1977:9).

There is nothing in Islam against practicing conception control (El-Zayyat 1954:11), and methods are known locally. "The pill" can be obtained from government clinics, but the side effects experienced by some women—dizziness and nausea—have discouraged them and others from using this option. Condoms are considered either expensive, impractical, or unpleasant to use. The I.U.D. and diaphragm are believed to be forbidden to Muslim women by the few people who know anything about them because complete postcoital cleansing would not be possible. Herbal beverages have been tried by some women, but no one is convinced that they are always efficacious.

The few people with whom this matter was discussed in depth are interested in family planning, and emphasized the economic difficulties when there are many children in a family, but they also viewed known conception control methods negatively. In other words, the idea is good, but the available techniques are poor. Rejection of present methods also ties in with views about adopting or loaning children on either a temporary or a more permanent basis. If a growing family presents a problem, there is more than one way of dealing with it.

Abortion is not one of the ways. No local woman admits to ever having had an abortion, although spontaneous miscarriages are not uncommon. Those who discussed abortion had varied reactions to the practice. It is considered sinful by many; others say that it is a sin only if the fetus has taken on human form (if fingers and toes can be distinguished). El-Zayyat, in his discussion of Islam, states that "abortion is considered almost as an act of murder" (1954:11).

Male infidelity is not unknown during the few months before and after a wife gives birth to a child, but it is not common either. When a man whose wife has recently borne a child is said to be involved with another woman in another place, disapproval is expressed, particularly by women, but no one seems very surprised. Gossip about the matter passes through the village, avoiding the wife and her family. Only the malicious want to cause trouble between a married couple. Perhaps, too, the wife and her family avoid hearing the gossip because then the illicit relationship can be ignored while, simultaneously, everyone hopes it will be short-lived, as it often is.

If knowledge of an infidelity reaches the wife in a blatant manner, then some sort of action is inescapable because she has been shamed. In one instance, Usman returned to his wife with a smear of lipstick on his shirt collar after spending a day in town. Halimah, his wife, was not the only one to notice it, which possibly influenced her to make an issue of it. After an argument between them, her husband left her parents' home, where both of them were staying at the time, and went to the home of his grandmother. Several individuals, including the imam, were asked by Halimah's parents to intervene, and a reconciliation was effected after a few days. Reconciliation is not always achieved, and such a rift can end in divorce.

ADULT ACTIVITIES

Adults spend a good deal of their waking hours working (discussed in a later chapter), but leisure time to spend with family and friends is very highly valued. The most common leisure activities are informal visiting and conversation with friends and neighbors— and, since the introduction of television, watching programs such as "Charlie's Angels," "The Bionic Woman," "Chips," "Hawaii Five-O," and "Wrestling from Chicago," as well as Malay cultural events and films. The long-range impact of U.S. television programs on Malay villagers has yet to be analyzed, but at least one Malaysian report about women suggests that some could provide village girls with a broader perspective of women's potential roles (NACIWID 1978).

During 1965–66 some adults participated in Quran reading and instruction at a few homes in the village. No Quran reading groups were meeting during 1975 or 1979. The adult education classes sponsored by the government where men and women could learn reading, writing, and elementary mathematics in 1965 were no longer offered in 1975. Bersilat classes conducted by a Rusila man during 1965 had also been discontinued by 1975. While a correlation can be made between the ending of bersilat and formal Quran reading/study groups and the introduction of television into the village, the latter does not appear to have caused the former. In the case of bersilat classes, for example, the instructor discontinued them after changing occupations. His new job as a manual laborer outside of the village was a financial boon, but he returned home too tired to feel enthusiastic about bersilat.

AGING

There is no local view of "middle age" as a discrete segment of the life cycle, but people in their middle years begin to joke about getting old when they can no longer see as clearly as they once did or when they feel especially tired at the end of a day of work.

It is generally accepted as normal for women to continue bearing children in their forties, despite the increased number of miscarriages, stillbirths, and deformed infants resulting from these pregnancies. It is not unusual for a woman to have some grandchildren who are older than her youngest child and, if her father has married a younger woman, she may have a sibling younger than her grandchildren.

The average woman is a grandmother when she begins menopause. Women repeat the male view of postmenopausal women: tidak ada guna (useless). The same attitude is expressed about a woman who has had a tubal ligation, hysterectomy, or other operation that is thought to render her sexless. The prevalence of the attitude explains why no local woman has had such an operation despite some instances of medical advice to do so for health reasons.

Men in their fifties and older continue to impregnate younger wives. The biological disparity between male and female supports the marriage of older men to much younger women and makes a reverse relationship seem abnormal to villagers. A woman may be "useless" after menopause, but being defined as asexual confers some of the freedom of her prepubescent years. No longer a sexual object, she can sit on her verandah in the heat of midday with her sarong wrapped under her armpits, shoulders and legs exposed, without being subject to criticism or advances. She can use her adult knowledge, giving play to her wit through double entendre with a sexual fillip; she can flirt with boys and young men. The behavior is free and lighthearted. I do not suggest that such behavior is constant or that postmenopausal Malay women become sex-obsessed. Rather, standards of modesty and related behavior patterns that were imposed prior to adolescence are once again relaxed.

The relationship between grandparents and grandchildren is usually warm and close, particularly between grandmother and

grandchild. Great-grandparents are proud of having great-grandchildren—the elders have lived long lives and seen two generations
into adulthood. But few live to see their great-grandchildren enter
primary school, so the possibility of close ties is very limited.
Elders in any kindred are consulted about important undertakings
by their children and grandchildren, though in many cases this is a
formality because their advice is not always followed. Their actual
influence in the village depends on other considerations, such as
economic and religious statuses, rather than on age alone.

Some villagers achieve the religious experience of a lifetime
when they make the pilgrimage to Mecca. A few young persons
make the haj, but the goal of doing so becomes more important with
age. The older a person is, the greater his or her chance of dying
in Mecca while in a state of grace. Married couples make the haj
together or singly. In the 1960s it was likely that if only one could
go, the husband would do so. Recently several married women went
to Mecca without their husbands, but in most cases the men had already become Hajis.

Rusila villagers consider themselves to be very religious
people. They are proud of the fact that there are more than 50
Hajis and Hajjahs in the village, and they believe that there are more
persons with those statuses in Rusila than in any other village in the
district. One man made a second pilgrimage during 1965. Four
married couples had done so by 1979, and all agreed that the experience had been far more meaningful the second time. The second
haj is thought to indicate a high degree of religiosity as well as economic well-being, although in one case children were denied secondary education while the parents saved for another haj. To some,
then, religious experience ranks far higher than secular attainments.

The villagers prefer to stay at home, surrounded by family
and friends, rather than go to the hospital when they are very ill.
But acceptance of hospitalization has become more common during
the past few years, a trend due, at least in part, to the fact that
there are no longer any powerful bomoh in the village. After death
occurs, the body is bathed ritually and then wrapped in clean cloth.
It is taken to the graveyard in a wooden coffin, and buried facing
toward Mecca. Local people say that women are buried deeper than
men because they are less pure, but I have found no Islamic prescription for the practice. Commemorative feasts, their number
and type varying from one family to another, and prayers are offered for the deceased. Women prepare cakes and other delicacies;
men pray and then partake of the food.

From birth, when the call to prayer is the first thing whis-
pered in an infant's ear, until death, Islamic beliefs and practices
punctuate an individual's life and provide ceremonial highlights to it.

But there are also various beliefs and practices in relation to the
supernatural that are not associated with Islam or are related to it
only peripherally, however well they are integrated into a person's
belief system. Major ceremonies—the marriage bersanding and the
melenggang perut during a first pregnancy—and some minor ones
are adat, although they now incorporate Islamic elements. Spells,
potions, and amulets to ward off evil are still used by villagers,
and some believe in animistic spirits, although many people say
that these are gone now because of the strength of Islam in the area.

4
EDUCATION

Education in Malaysia is a complex, multifaceted subject that, beyond a description of the system, cannot be separated from national and communal politics and long-range economic goals. Hence the rather lengthy introductory section includes a discussion of several major educational issues and a description of the system, as well as consideration of women and education.

EDUCATIONAL ISSUES

Datuk Musa Hitam, Minister of Education, has acknowledged that education in the nation "has become a sensitive and controversial subject" (NST 10/12/78). Two issues, which overlap, are continuing extension of Malay as the medium of instruction for post-primary educational levels and a concomitant decline in the standard of English, and allocation of places in universities.

Malay is the official language of Malaysia, and is now referred to as bahasa Malaysia rather than bahasa Melayu—the Malaysian language rather than the Malay language, the national language rather than the language of one segment of the population. Use of the national language throughout the educational system is conceived by the government as a major means of promoting national unity and the integration of the diverse groups that constitute Malaysia's population.

Some parts of this chapter originally appeared in "Education and Employment Patterns of Rural Malay Women," Journal of Asian and African Studies 12 (1977): 3-4, and are reprinted with the permission of the editor, Professor K. Ishwaran.

There is recognition of English as an important international language and concern about the decline in the standard of English being taught and learned. Datuk Musa Hitam discussed the matter during several interviews and acknowledged that the decline was greater than expected. He spoke of reversing the trend and placing greater emphasis on English as a second language in the schools. The Ministry of Education organized committees to review the teaching and use of English, and also obtained help from language experts in Britain and other countries to study the problem and suggest how to solve it.

Malaysia ranks high compared with most developing nations in regard to the breadth of its educational system, although the gains at the primary school end of the educational spectrum—basic literacy is enormously important—are, expectably, far greater than at the university end. Nevertheless, advances in university education are impressive. Until the late 1960s the University of Malaya was the only university in the country. Four additional universities have been built and expanded since then.

Between 1970 and 1975 college and university enrollment increased by 136.6 percent, from 13,324 students in 1970 to 31,529 in 1975 (Federation of Malaysia 1976a:387). The government has been very successful in inspiring the population to value tertiary education. One result is that demand for higher education is now far greater than the five universities, nondegree-granting colleges, and other post-secondary facilities can accommodate.

A total of 35,884 applications for admission were received by Malaysian universities and colleges for the 1978 academic year (NST 11/9/78). Those who were given places in degree-granting universities numbered 4,400: 2,881 (65.47 percent) bumiputras, 1,210 (27.5 percent) Chinese, and 309 (7.0 percent) Indians and others (NST 10/11/78).

University enrollments for 1977-78 (see Table 4.1) show that of the total 19,903 students, bumiputras accounted for 14,335 (72 percent) although they represent about 57 percent of the population. Chinese were almost 23 percent of the university population and 34 percent of the general population, while Indian students were less than 5 percent of the student population although Indians are more than 9 percent of the general population. According to Datuk Musa, "Since the launching of the New Economic Policy in 1970 . . . the Government had been giving wide opportunities for university education to bumiputra students [in order to put bumiputras on a par with non-bumiputras]. In the process, many non-bumiputra students were disappointed because they could not get places in universities despite good qualifications" (NST 12/21/78). He went on to assure non-bumiputras—essentially Chinese and Indians—that

more places would be made for them and that existing universities
would be expanded.

TABLE 4.1

University Enrollments, by Government Classification
Category: 1977-78

University	Bumiputras	Chinese	Indians	Others	Total
U. Malaya	3,487	2,775	490	100	6,852
National U.	3,926	273	85	0	4,284
U. Technology	2,882	321	58	19	3,280
U. Agriculture	2,807	205	84	3	3,144
U. Science	1,253	939	145	6	2,343
Total	14,355	4,558	862	128	19,903
Percent	72.0	22.9	4.3	0.6	100.0 (99.8)

Source: Based on information in a report to the Dewan Rakyat
by Deputy Minister of Education Haji Salleh Jafaruddin (NST
11/9/78).

What is the relation between concern about the institution of
Malay as the basic language of education and the decline of the
standard of English, on the one hand, while on the other hand there
is greater demand for tertiary education than the nation can provide?
In 1978 there were more than 36,000 Malaysians enrolled
in tertiary and other educational institutions outside Malaysia. A
large majority of them attended universities and other schools in
nations where the language of instruction is English: the United
Kingdom, Australia, New Zealand, and the United States. The
fear of Chinese and Indians, because of the admission preference
for bumiputras and an inadequate number of places for all who
qualify, is that the use of Malay as the language of education, combined with a deteriorating standard of English taught as a second
language, means that the students who must seek educational
opportunities abroad will have greater difficulty qualifying for
admission to overseas English-language universities.

THE EDUCATIONAL SYSTEM

There are three types of schools at the six-year primary
level: national and national-type, which are government-funded,
and private. In the national schools the medium of instruction is
Malay, although English is taught as a subject. National-type
schools have almost the same curriculum, but basic subjects are
taught in Chinese or Tamil. There are no longer any government-
supported English-language primary schools. Private schools set
their own language priorities.

Chinese and Indian leaders have stressed the right of children
to pursue education in their mother tongue, and have questioned
whether government-type schools are treated equitably when it
comes to funding, and whether the teachers of Malay assigned to
these schools are as capable as those assigned to teach in national
schools. Another side of the problem, according to the headmaster
of a Tamil school, is that after six years of primary education in
Tamil, "children are transferred to a Malay-medium school because there are no secondary Tamil schools for them to go to"
(Star 10/22/78), which accounts for a large number of dropouts at
the end of primary schooling because the children are not prepared
to make the shift. The same problem confronts who attend Chinese-
language primary schools. Malay will be the basic medium of instruction in all public secondary schools by 1980, and in all tertiary institutions by 1983.

Students who complete their six-year primary education suc-
cessfully can go on to secondary schools. Secondary education in
Malaysia consists of a lower level, Forms I through III, and an
upper level, Forms IV and V. Examinations for the LCE (Lower
Certificate of Education) are taken during the Form III year, and
for the MCE (Middle Certificate of Education) during Form V.
Failure at either level means that the student is denied further
public education, although private schools are a possibility for
those who can afford them. A student who fails can take the examinations again—and again—during the annual exam period. A pass
entitles a student to reapply for admission to government-supported
schools. Success in the MCE examination enables a student to continue to Form VI, a two-year program of post-secondary education
offered by the secondary schools. The Higher School Certificate
(HSC), a prerequisite for university admission, is the goal. University courses leading to bachelor's degrees are from three to
four years long, depending on the field of study. Admission to
tertiary-level vocational and professional institutions may be
granted on the basis of the MCE or other qualifications.

During the period of the Second Malaysia Plan (1970-75), total enrollment in primary schools increased from 1,682,187 to 1,897,188, almost 13 percent. Secondary enrollments increased by more than 60 percent, essentially because survival rates from the primary to the lower secondary level were improved, in part as a result of the abolition of the Secondary School Entrance Examination in 1965. Thirteen new vocational and technical schools were constructed and ten residential, secondary-level science schools were completed. More than 6,000 primary school teachers and almost 4,500 secondary school teachers were trained, but the total still fell short of the need (Federation of Malaysia 1976a:386).

The need for expansion at all levels is recognized, and plans are under way. The 14 existing teacher training colleges will be enlarged and several new ones built; all universities will be expanded; and more vocational training programs and facilities are scheduled. The development of the entire educational system is being planned to meet the requirements of an expanding economy.

WOMEN AND EDUCATION

Internationally "Women today account for 60 percent of the world's illiterate population and the number of women illiterates is increasing more rapidly than men. . ." (Orvis 1978).

An examination of the educational attainment of all women and men in Malaysia in 1970 shows that women outnumber men only in the "no schooling" category. Fifty-one percent of all women are in that category. Another 27.6 percent completed some years of primary education but did not finish their schooling at that level. Only 10.6 percent of all women completed the six years of primary school but did not go on to secondary school. The percentages decrease drastically for lower and upper secondary education for both men and women, but men are nevertheless favored (NACIWID 1978:70).

A list of some of the institutions and organizations offering education or training for women was compiled for NACIWID's "Income-Generating Skills for Women: Interim Report" by Dean Fatimah Hamid-Don's team from the Faculty of Education at the University of Malaya. The list includes the five Malaysian universities, several institutes under the auspices of MARA (a government agency), one polytechnic, the YWCA and Women's Institute, and private vocational schools offering commercial courses. The list is not exhaustive, but it does offer a good sampling of the types of courses available and the number and/or percent of women in them.

In the 33 commercial schools located in the state of Selangor, women constituted 77.8 percent of the students during 1977. They

accounted for 100 percent of the enrollees in the "private secre-
taryship" courses and were more than 90 percent of those studying
shorthand or to be telephone operators, and 86 percent of the students in typing courses. Women were 40.5 percent of the students
in accountancy and 52.4 percent of those studying bookkeeping.

The five Institute Kemahiran MARA, located in four states,
offer occupational training in various subjects in 12-, 18-, and
24-month courses. Here, enrollments in the five schools are combined and show a total of 518 students, of whom 200 (38.6 percent)
are women. The largest number of women (N = 63; 45 percent of
all students in the course) are studying "mechanical draftsman-
ship." Women are 100 percent of the students in both women's
tailoring and fashion designing, and 96.9 percent of those studying
cosmetology. They are least represented in general mechanics
(0.3 percent) and among those studying to be electricians (4.3
percent). Other areas where women are less than one-quarter of
the enrollees are electronics and refrigeration.

One young woman whose academic training is in mechanical
engineering, with a specialization in refrigeration and air condi-
tioning, took a job as a receptionist after weeks of unsuccessfully
seeking something in her field of expertise. She reported that her
applications for engineering jobs were met with incredulity, jokes,
and other negative responses during interviews (NST 12/28/78).

Hence low female enrollments may reflect a realistic appraisal of potential discrimination against women in general hiring
practices as well as cultural bias against women—by families,
peers, teachers, and others—pursuing education in some fields.

The NACIWID report includes only selected courses from the
five Malaysian universities. Three examples will suffice to emphasize that women are concentrated in some fields of study and underrepresented in others.

University of Science (Sains): the largest number and percentage of women are in education (N = 290; 47 percent), and the
fewest are in pharmaceutical science (N = 28; 25 percent).

University of Agriculture (Pertanian): Degree courses in
agriculture, veterinary science, and business agriculture have a
total enrollment of 517 persons. There are 81 (16 percent) women
in these courses. Diploma courses include home-science technology, which has 100 percent women students (N = 82), but women
make up only 17 percent of the enrollment in animal husbandry and
agriculture combined.

University of Technology (Teknologi) has 874 students in several types of engineering courses for which diplomas are granted;
162 (19 percent) are women.

Turning to the University of Malay Annual Report (Lapuran Tahunan) for 1975-76 and 1977-78, it can be seen in Table 4.2 that there were 205 fewer students enrolled in the university during the 1977 academic year than there had been in 1975, due to changes in priorities, and there were 26 more women. Women made slight gains overall during the two-year period, from 31.8 percent to 33.1 percent of the undergraduates in all fields.

Admissions officers of universities and colleges are said not to discriminate against women, and this may well be the case. There are fewer women than men seeking admission because it is only in recent years that advanced education has become a realistic goal for nonelite women, and there are still families in many parts of the country who have negative perceptions of education for women beyond the primary level.

The dimension of socioeconomic differences vis-à-vis male and female enrollment ratios is analyzed in a 1977 study by Bee-Lan Chan Wang, who hypothesizes that

> . . . "significant differences in enrollment ratios
> between males and females lead one to expect sex-
> differences in socio-economic representation."
> She finds that Indian girls tend to come from consid-
> erably higher socio-economic backgrounds than
> Indian boys; that among the Chinese, with an almost
> equal sex ratio in enrollment, there is also practi-
> cally no sex difference in socio-economic background;
> and that the Malays ". . . were between the other two
> groups in terms of the socio-economic selectivity of
> the girls who were enrolled" (quoted by Barber 1979:
> 586).

Socioeconomic differences probably also correlate with rural or urban origin. Thus, the male-to-female enrollment rations could reflect the more conservative attitudes of Malay villagers and Indian plantation workers about the education of daughters, attitudes that may not be as prevalent among the largely urban Chinese.

Admissions preference for bumiputras over Chinese, Indians, and other applicants favors bumiputra women as it does bumiputra men. It also means that fewer Chinese and Indian women (and men) have the opportunity for local tertiary education. Thus women as a category are probably not affected by the policy; Malay and other bumiputra women benefit, but Chinese and Indian women have fewer chances.

TABLE 4.2

University of Malaya Students, by Faculty and Sex: 1975–76 and 1977–78

Faculty	1975-76			1977-78		
		Total Females			Total Females	
	Total Students	Number	Percent	Total Students	Number	Percent
Economics and administration	1,344	402	29.9	1,170	391	33.4
Arts and social sciences	2,314	947	40.9	2,152	914	42.5
Law	211	103	48.8	212	86	40.6
Engineering	807	20	2.5	814	23	2.8
Dentistry	125	73	58.4	130	78	60.0
Medicine	670	149	22.2	704	169	24.0
Science	1,715	594	34.6	1,799	653	30.0
Total	7,186	2,288	31.8	6,981	2,314	33.1

Sources: Federation of Malaysia, University of Malaya 1977a, Table 5, p. 155. Federation of Malaysia, University of Malaya 1979, Table 1, p. 154.

It has been shown that some courses of study within tertiary institutions are male-dominated. The University of Malaya enrollments provide another example (see Table 4.2). Engineering has an overwhelmingly male student body, with only 23 women (2.8 percent) out of 814 students. Medicine has 24 percent female students, a gain since 1975. Women are a majority in dentistry, accounting for 60 percent of all students. This may surprise Western readers: in the United States, for example, in 1978 women were only 4.6 percent of dentists (Rule 1980), and they still have difficulties in gaining admission to courses except those leading to a specialty in dental hygiene. In Malaysia most of the small, government dental clinics are staffed by women. The importance of dental care is still not widely recognized, and dentistry is not the high-income profession in Malaysia that it has become in the United States. If that shift occurs, women may find themselves facing greater competition from men.

By ethnic categories, the greatest number of Malay women are enrolled in arts (N = 562) and economics and administration (N = 231); the greatest number of Chinese women are in the Faculty of Science (N = 439) and in arts (N = 268); the most Indian women are enrolled in arts (N = 102). Of those in dentistry, Malay and Chinese women each account for approximately half of the total; in law, Chinese women are a majority, as they are in medicine. Of the women in engineering, half are Malay and half are Chinese. Prior to the phasing out of the Faculty of Agriculture after the University of Agriculture opened, Malays were a large majority among the women enrolled.

Women are underrepresented in all tertiary institutions and in most post-secondary programs, a situation not peculiar to Malaysia. Yet Malaysian women have made educational gains during the 1960s and 1970s. Despite discrimination against them in the hiring practices common to some occupations, a few women do enroll in the relevant courses and try to break the barriers. Others choose education in fields that are culturally defined as acceptable for women: because they really want (or have been socialized to want) jobs in those fields, are more realistic about occupational opportunities for women or are less daring, or were channeled into a particular field through acceptance of government funds, such as scholarships, for their education.

The national picture can be given a diachronic perpsective by looking at female enrollments, shown as percentages of the total females in each age cohort, at all educational levels during 1957, 1967, and 1975.

Year	Primary 6-11	Lower Secondary 12-14	Upper Secondary 15-16	Upper Secondary 17-18	University 19-24
1957	80.0	15.0	11.0	—	—
1967	91.0	52.0	16.0	5.0	1.0
1975	96.0	66.8	31.6	6.9	1.5

Source: Federation of Malaysia, NACIWID 1978: Table 1.14, p. 48.

Only 80 percent of females in the 6-11 age group were in primary school in 1957. An 11 percent increase was achieved during the following decade, and by 1975, 96 percent were enrolled. Impressive increases also are recorded for those in lower secondary school—from 15 percent to 52 percent to 66.8 percent—with the big jump occurring during the first decade following independence. Although the gains by women are far smaller in the upper secondary and university categories, they nevertheless exist. The trend is a positive one. With more schools being built, transportation facilities being improved, and more families becoming aware of the need to educate their daughters as well as their sons in the rapidly modernizing society, gains by women in upper secondary and beyond should show a marked upswing during the 1980s. Two shifts at the national level would affect, perhaps reverse, the trend: stagnation of economic development and increasing influence of Islamic fundamentalism.

EDUCATION FOR WOMEN: TRENGGANU

The statistical picture that emerges for Trengganu (Table 4.3) holds few surprises if one remembers that Trengganu is among the least developed states on the peninsula. Over 58 percent of all women, 59 percent of all Malay women, and 62 percent of all women living in communities with less than 1,000 population have had no schooling, while over 22 percent in each category had some years of primary schooling. Compared with the national figures 7 percent more Trengganu women had no schooling, and 5 percent less of them had some primary schooling, than women in the nation as a whole.

It is therefore surprising to find that a higher percentage of Trengganu women than women in the nation completed primary school: 11.9 percent compared with 10.6 percent. Even more surprising is the fact that in communities with less than 1,000 population, the percentage is above 11. Although Trengganu has been among the least developed states, primary schools—the majority of which are located in villages—may have been built earlier here than in some other parts of the nation for political reasons.

TABLE 4.3

Highest Level of Primary and Secondary Schooling Completed: Trengganu, 1970

Level of Schooling	Total Population				Total Malay Population				Malays, Areas of Population 999 or Below			
	Total Persons	Females			Total Persons	Females			Total Persons	Females		
		Number	Percent of Level	Percent of Female Grand Total		Number	Percent of Level	Percent of Female Grand Total		Number	Percent of Level	Percent of Female Grand Total
No schooling	211,687	118,958	56.19	58.24	203,009	114,115	56.21	59.21	135,327	74,763	55.16	64.12
Primary												
Some years	100,257	46,583	46.46	22.80	92,914	43,640	46.96	22.64	58,059	26,877	46.29	22.33
All years	55,805	24,379	43.68	11.93	51,559	22,769	44.16	11.82	32,495	13,853	42.63	11.51
Total	156,062	70,962	45.47	34.74	144,473	66,409	45.96	34.45	90,554	40,730	44.97	33.84
Secondary												
Form I-II	14,363	6,134	42.70	3.00	12,741	5,458	42.83	2.83	5,775	2,391	41.40	1.98
Form III	6,945	2,917	42.00	1.42	5,917	2,452	41.43	1.27	2,487	1,008	40.53	0.83
Lower Certificate	3,801	1,382	36.35	0.67	3,384	1,202	35.52	0.62	1,304	395	30.29	0.32
Form IV	3,244	1,174	36.18	0.57	2,817	1,005	35.67	0.52	1,107	379	34.23	0.31
Form V	2,655	1,067	40.19	0.52	2,217	892	40.23	0.46	893	312	34.93	0.25
Middle Certificate	4,819	1,270	26.35	0.62	3,783	952	25.16	0.49	1,245	265	21.28	0.22
Form VI (lower)	529	172	32.51	0.08	436	141	32.33	0.07	245	81	33.06	0.06
Form VI (upper)	303	83	27.39	0.04	193	53	27.46	0.02	85	24	28.23	*
Higher School Certificate	516	103	19.96	0.05	241	38	15.76	*	59	9	15.25	*
Total	37,175	14,302	38.47	7.00	31,729	12,193	38.42	6.33	13,200	4,864	36.84	4.04
Grand total	404,924	204,222	50.43	100.00	379,211	192,717	50.82	100.00	239,281	120,357	50.30	100.00

*Below 0.01 percent.
Note: Percentages calculated by the author.
Source: Federation of Malaysia 1977b, Table 2.10, pp. 114-15.

At all other levels Trengganu women are less represented than are women in the nation as a whole. If Trengganu women are compared with men on the same level, it can be seen that they are a majority only in the "no schooling" category. Nevertheless, while only 11.9 percent of women in the state completed primary school and were not educated beyond that level, women account for 43.68 percent of all persons in that category and they represent at least a third of the persons in lower secondary and several upper secondary levels. These figures serve as a reminder that formal education for almost everyone was lacking or restricted to the primary level until the 1960s or 1970s. Once facilities were available, males made greater and faster gains than females, particularly in small, mostly rural communities. This situation was—and still is—due primarily to the reluctance of many families, based on cultural values and attitudes, to allow females post-primary education.

Nevertheless, even in the interior of Trengganu, an area subject to fewer modernizing influences than the coastal area, the educational position of women is improving. Dr. David McKay carried out medical-anthropoligical research in 11 inland villages. He surveyed households with children under age 15, and collected educational information for all children below the age of 20 in those households. He found that 133 boys had finished primary school and 56 (42 percent) continued on to secondary school; 145 girls had completed primary-level schooling and 43 (30 percent) went on to secondary school. More girls than boys, and a higher percentage of girls than boys, went to secondary school from four of the villages; the numbers and percentages were reversed in seven villages (personal correspondence 1979).

There were 250 students from Trengganu enrolled at the University of Malaya during the 1975-76 academic year, and only 70 (28 percent) of them were women. In 1977-78 women were 80 (30 percent) of 260 Trengganu students. If each of the 13 states of Malaysia were equally represented, there would be almost 7.7 percent Trengganu women, but during both academic years they were just over 3 percent. They had better representation at the National University and the University of Agriculture. Trengganu is both overwhelmingly Malay in population composition and still basically an agricultural—rural—state. Both of the universities mentioned and the University of Technology have a much higher percentage of Malay students than the University of Malay has.

An examination of statistics from the 1970 Trengganu census shows that a total of seven women living in the state had attained university degrees at that time. An additional 96 had finished training in nondegree-granting tertiary institutions to become teachers, midwives, and other professionals (Federation of Malaysia 1977:122-123). The statistics do not reveal whether these women are from Trengganu or how many Trengganu women with post-secondary qualifications reside in other states. For example, four women - two with teaching diplomas and two with B.A. degrees - whom I know from Marang district in Trengganu now work in Kuala Lumpur. And there are women now living in Marang district who have diplomas or other postsecondary qualifications who come from other states.

Nevertheless, few women in the state had post-secondary qualifications at the time of the census and, even more recently, Trengganu women were underrepresented in the University of Malaya and some other tertiary institutions. There are no post-secondary educational facilities in Trengganu. The situation is changing, as will be seen in the discussion of educational patterns in the village.

EDUCATION OF RUSILA CHILDREN

The value of primary education is universally acknowledged in Rusila and nearby coastal villages. Primary education encourages mastery of the "3 R's," which literate and illiterate parents alike recognize as important skills for their children in today's world.

There is far less agreement about the need or desirability for education beyond the primary level. Secondary education takes place outside of the village context, which worries some parents because the schools and the contacts made in them could be disruptive to village patterns and values without leading to any status change for the individual. Nevertheless, larger numbers of local children are continuing their education beyond the primary level.

A primary school was built in the village in 1952. Since that time almost all of the children from Rusila and two contiguous villages have attended it, raising the literacy rate sharply in the area. However, few adults above the age of 35 can read and write.

A child who has a formally educated parent enjoys a great advantage, in that the parent understands the need for study and can check homework. However well-meaning and education-oriented an illiterate parent may be, there is no real comprehension of the idea of studying. I have watched youngsters barely settle down with their homework before being called to run an errand, answer a question, get a glass of water for father, call other siblings from play - usually several interruptions per attempt to complete an assignment. The child is rarely given the time to concentrate on what must be done. In such circumstances it is impressive when the child of illiterate parents excels, as is sometimes the case.

Children who complete the primary school program, as most do, may attend one of several secondary schools located between four and ten miles from the village. Today 62 percent of them do so, a significant increase since 1965-66 and 1975 (see Table 4.4).

In 1965, of 94 local young people between the ages of 12/13 and 18, 43 (46 percent) were enrolled in secondary schools. Several types of education were available in the area. One English-language and two Malay-language schools were located six to ten miles from the village. A fourth school, referred to as madrasah Arabiah ("Arab school") in 1965 and now called sekolah agama (school of religion), was three miles away. Entrance requirements were least stringent for the Arab school, total fees paid were lower, and transportation was cheaper because the school was near. It was preferred by some pious families because the curriculum focused on religious training, but many parents gave financial reasons for sending a child to the madrasah. The greatest number of local students (25) attended the Arab school; fewest (5) were going to English-language schools.

There were 48 males in the secondary school-age group, and 56 percent of them (N = 27) attended secondary school in 1965. Eighteen males did not continue beyond the primary level. The figures are more than reversed when female enrollment is examined. Of 46 girls, 35 percent (N = 16) were attending secondary school; 65 percent (N = 30) did not go beyond the primary level.

Girls who did not attend secondary school spent their time helping their mothers and weaving pandanus mats and basketry for sale, a pattern that is unchanged today; four were already married. Twenty girls were each paid 50 cents per day for studying and working at the government-sponsored Weaving Center, enabling them to earn a small but regular income for an activity in which they would have engaged anyway. Boys who did not go to secondary school were in economic limbo; they were no longer schoolboys, nor were they productive adults.

By 1975 two additional Malay-language secondary schools had been built in the area, one only four miles from the village. The proximity of the latter school is very important for financial reasons: bus transportation costs for a pupil are half of those to any other school except the madrasah, and most boys can ride their bicycles to the school. Proximity, combined with an increasing appreciation by many local parents for education emphasizing academic subjects, explains the big shift of student attendance into Malay-language schools and away from the religion-focused madrasah Arabiah. In 1965 just over half of the males in secondary schools were attending the madrasah; almost 70 percent of the females were enrolled there. Today 88 percent of the young women and 89 percent of the

TABLE 4.4

Education of Rusila Children 13-18 Years of Age: 1966, 1975, 1979

	1966			1975			1979		
	Females	Males	Total	Females	Males	Total	Females	Males	Total
Students enrolled in secondary schools									
"Arab" school	11	14	25	6	4	10	5	3	8
Malay-language	4	9	13	25	27	52	53	49	102
English-language	1	4	5	2	3	5	program discontinued		
School of science (Malay-language)	not yet opened			1	2	3	1	1	2
Polytechnic	0	0	0	0	0	0	0	1	1
Private*									
Review	0	0	0	0	0	0	0	2	2
Commercial	0	0	0	0	0	0	2	1	3
Total	16	27	43	34	36	70	61	57	118
Percentage of persons in cohort	(35)	(56)	(46)	(46)	(52)	(49)	(62)	(62)	(62)
Hiatus**	0	0	0	3	2	5	2	4	6
Secondary school dropouts	0	3	3	5	6	11	10	11	21
Primary education only	30	18	48	32	25	57	25	19	44
Grand total	46	48	94	74	69	143	98	91	189

*Students enrolled in private schools have failed exams in the government-supported public schools. The review schools prepare students for reexamination; commercial schools offer courses in bookkeeping, typing, and other commercial subjects.

**Students who have failed examinations and intend to retake them, but are not attending any school during the interim.

men enrolled in standard secondary programs attend Malay-language schools, most students going to the one nearby. The other new Malay-language school is a school of science, a boarding school located in Kuala Trengganu. Selected students, including one girl and one boy from Rusila, have all educational expenses paid by the government and receive a monthly allowance of $30 for miscellaneous expenses. Another young man completed the course of study there and now attends the University of Science.

While secondary education has become more easily available to local teen-agers, it is still a privilege rather than a right. The difficult examinations during the third and fifth years of secondary schooling must be passed if a student is to continue. Some children respond to the pressure with physical ailments and temporary mental breakdowns. The latter are said to be insane (gila) from too studying. Students who fail the exams, for whatever reasons, can take them again during the following year. Meanwhile, they may not attend government-supported schools. A new phenomenon in 1979 was attendance by two local youths at private "review" schools in Kuala Trengganu where academic work is essentially memorization of materials needed by students to pass the exams. The form of this education may be questionable, but at least the students have a structured involvement with education. Children who must pursue their studies on their own find it enormously difficult. Three other students who failed examinations, two women and one man, were attending private commercial schools, also a new practice and one based on recognition of the importance of skills needed by women (as well as men) for occupations outside the village milieu.

Males who fail the third-year exams are more likely than females to take them again—one young man passed them on his fourth attempt. Women are more likely than men to drop out of school after a first failure. They have had less expectation of success because of the lack of female role models until very recently, and they have been conditioned by the frequently expressed opinions of older villagers that there is no use in educating them beyond the primary level. In addition, girls have more demands made on them for helping with housework and sibling care, which means that they have less time than males of the same age to devote to studying.

It also seems likely that males who enter secondary school are pushed to succeed more than most females. Males are certainly more likely to express the feeling that their families expect them to achieve academic success. "Their hopes are on me," was a typical statement in 1975. Although most village women engage in some form of remunerative work and use part of their earnings to meet household expenses, it is still the Malay ideal that a man support his family. Therefore more importance is placed on male educational success. A woman or a man who fails may suffer equally great disappointment and have the life course changed, but occupation is of greater concern to the man. A woman's primary goal is marriage and children. Whether or not she passes school examinations, she will marry.

Nevertheless, predictions of success on the fifth-year exams on the basis of passing the third-year exams are better for women than for men, judging by the performance of former students. Of six women who passed the third-year exam, five passed the fifth-year exams prior to 1975, and the sixth was successful in 1975. Fifteen males in the same age cohort passed the third-year exams, but only eight passed the fifth-year exams. Several males failed the fifth-year exams; others left school before completing the upper secondary years because they obtained jobs in the private sector outside the village area; males had, and continue to have, greater mobility and freedom to seek such work without parental opposition. Hence it seems that women have more to lose by a fifth-year failure. At the same time, having passed the third-year exams, they know that academic success is possible.

The greatest number and percentage of females, both in 1965 and in 1975, did not attend secondary school; in 1979, 62 percent of females and males between the ages of 12/13 and 18 were enrolled in secondary schools, a majority in lower secondary (pre-LCE). Some young people, including a few who did well at the primary level, have no desire to continue schooling. But salaried or wage-paying employment is increasingly seen as desirable by a large number of youngsters and their parents, and the avenue to such jobs is at least a secondary-level education.

In the 1960s a Malaysian who passed the third-year exams had a fair chance of getting a wage-paying job. This is rarely the case now, because larger numbers of students are successful at the fifth year and beyond. As a result, by 1979 there were half a dozen young men in the village who were highly discontented. They had envisioned themselves as government employees with regular salaries. They failed the examinations, and were confronted with the prospect of becoming village workers like their fathers. There may be other alternatives for them, but the young men have a limited perspective of the possibilities. They could be found together most evenings, just "hanging out" and complaining, increasing each other's frustrations. Their parents and the parents of some younger boys worried about them and their influence. There was talk among adults about their use of marijuana, unknown in the village five years earlier. Generally, the group was perceived as a local problem for which no one had a solution.

LOCAL ARGUMENTS AGAINST SECONDARY EDUCATION

Education for education's sake does not have many supporters
in any age group within the village. Hence, even if their children
want to continue their schooling, parents do not always encourage
them. Some discourage them from entertaining scholastic plans
beyond the primary level. Of the several reasons given by children
and parents for a child's not continuing, financial problems headed
the list in 1965 and continue to be first today. This reason is used
in reference to both males and females. Some families giving this
reason have better-than-average housing and furnishings; several
had the necessary funds, a few years after stating a financial reason in 1965, for both parents to make the pilgrimage to Mecca.
Religious experience continues to rank higher for many than does
academic knowledge, having eternal rather than ephemeral value,
in their view. Other parents have denied their own desires in order
to finance secondary education for a child.

The family of a child attending even a Fully Assisted Secondary
School must buy some school supplies, pay for transportation, buy
uniforms, and pay for recreation and major examination fees, or
apply for welfare assistance to cover them. When the cost of
snacks or lunch at school is added, the amount is sizable for the
average village family. Mother's as well as father's income, and
mother's secret savings, all become important.

A reason given only for females not continuing to secondary
school was that they were needed to care for younger siblings and
to look after the home while their mothers engaged in other work.
The eldest daughter in a family, regardless of her birth order, is
most likely to be denied education for this reason. Such a decision
is backed by other women. One woman whose eldest child, a
daughter, now holds a salaried position, had to contend with criticism from friends, neighbors, and some kin when she encouraged
and financially supported her daughter's desire for secondary education. When the young woman was sent by the government to
another part of the country for advanced study, the criticism increased because she was so far from home. Now that the daughter
has a salaried job, a few women who were critical have a very different attitude; several have told the mother they wish they had
followed her example. So do some of their daughters.

Another often-heard reason for a girl's not getting a secondary
education in 1965 was "it has no use" (tidak ada guna). A female
"just sits in the kitchen" (duduk di dapur saja) anyway: an old argument in more than one cultural context, but an argument heard infrequently in Rusila in 1979.

Several reasons may be combined: the family lacks the financial resources to send a child to school and, as a girl, the child is
needed at home to help, which is more useful training than school
because she will be a wife and mother one day.

The reasons given by parents in 1965 and in 1975 have not
changed very much, although there is a tendency to combine the
"no money" argument with some statement about primary school
providing enough education for a person who is going to live in the
village. There is an implication here of people acknowledging their
position in society, of not getting above themselves, not becoming
arrogant (sombong), a term sometimes used in reference to the
educated person who has taken on "town ways." The attitude covers
a multitude of possibilities, from a child not wanting to continue
education to parental fear of education outside of the village context. Villagers know all of the young men and women who have
been educationally successful and now hold good jobs. Some see
the success negated by its having taken the young people far from
the village and their families. This attitude is breaking down as
more individuals of both sexes work outside the village.

Some of the young people who were not given the opportunity
to continue their schooling, especially those who did well at the
primary level, feel resentment about having been denied. In con-
versations about education they tend to compare themselves with
their successful peers, pointing out that while in primary school
they had done as well as or better than the friend who now has a
white-collar job.

Pro-education arguments are pragmatic and take cognizance
of changes in the larger society as well as in the village. Some
parents hope that their children have fewer economic problems
than is possible when income is based on village work. Others
admit to self-interest; one man told me that he wants all of his
seven children to go to secondary school and then get good jobs.
When he and his wife are old, each child should be able to send
them $100 monthly, enough for them to live comfortably.

CHANGES FOR WOMEN, 1965 TO 1979

In 1965 the first girls from Rusila were students on the lower
secondary level. By 1975 three of them had passed the MCE or
had professional training and were salaried workers—two teachers
and one dental nurse-dentist who was in charge of a small clinic.
Two women from the village had obtained B.A. degrees by the
summer of 1979; another woman is a university student in

administration, and two are attending courses in teachers' colleges.
The numbers are small, but the accomplishments are enormous,
particularly when one realizes that the mothers of these young
women are all illiterate, as are most of their fathers.

Of the women in the 1965 cohort (those who were 12/13 to 18)
who did not go beyond the primary level or dropped out of school
in lower secondary, all but three were married by age 18 or 19.
Several are now divorced and living with their parents; others have
contracted second marriages. Most of them have children. The
same is true for almost half of the females who were 17 or older in
the 1975 cohort. Women of both groups reside in the village or in
other rural areas; their lives, responsibilities, and socioeconomic
roles are little different from those of their mothers. But basic
literacy has conferred upon them a greater awareness of the world
beyond the village. Their literacy, combined with greater exposure
to the mass media, including television during the past few years,
and increased mobility, has given them a taste for some of the
satisfactions of their better-educated peers without the means for
meeting their desires.

Three secondary school dropouts in the 1965 cohort had not
yet married in 1975; one lived with her parents, and the others had
clerking jobs. In comparison, eight females in the 1975 cohort
(about half of those who were 17 or older) who did not go beyond
primary school held jobs outside the village during 1975. They
worked as clerk, salesgirl, handicraft instructor, factory worker,
or "mother's helper." The three girls in the latter occupation
were the youngest of the eight; they were engaged in the same work
they would otherwise have been doing in their parents' homes.
They lived as family members ("younger sisters") with the people
for whom they worked, helping and providing companionship for
young married women from their own village who had moved to
towns. Each earned less than $40 per month but had room and
board provided, enjoyed the conveniences of piped water and indoor
toilet facilities, and had ready access to television and other forms
of mass media. This was a new pattern for village girls, just as
employing such helpers was new to young women from this village.

Another new pattern in 1975 was shown by two self-supporting
unmarried men (1975 cohort, primary education only) who maintained their own own residences with female co-workers, although
one of them worked only ten miles from the village. Some older
villagers considered this a shocking departure from the traditional
values that kept a woman with her family of orientation until she
married. From their viewpoint, it is bad enough that a female
teacher or other government employee can be assigned to work,
and therefore reside, away from her family, but for a woman to

make such a choice herself is beyond understanding. The influence of female government employees living away from the village prior to marriage is acknowledged by one of these young women. However strong the influence, they could not have moved without the economic stability and independence gained from wage-paying jobs.

The attempt to isolate characteristics shared by all of the women who were educationally successful by 1975 gave inconclusive results. Five of the seven are the daughters of parents who have not been divorced during the child's lifetime. But there are other intact families who have not encouraged their children to go beyond primary school. Two of the seven women have literate fathers, men with better than primary school education; only one has a literate mother, a woman born in another part of the country. Women who have enjoyed secondary school success are too young to have children of secondary school age. However, all men with secondary education or better, whose children are old enough, have encouraged or insisted that daughters and sons continue beyond the primary level.

Four of the females have older brothers with better than secondary education; none has an older sister in that category. Again, there are other families where an older brother is educated while younger siblings of either sex are not. Birth order of the seven females includes firstborn, youngest, and middle; all have siblings of both sexes.

Among the fathers' occupations are various types of village work, such as fisherman and agriculturalist. One man is a teacher. Two of the mothers claim the "housewife only" status, an indicant that financial problems do not exist in these families. The other mothers perform village work.

Discussions indicate that for each educationally successful young woman there has been one person who has been particularly important in encouraging secondary education. In three cases this significant other was the father; in two cases, an older brother; and in one case, the father's younger brother. Only one female considered another female, her mother, as most influential. The example was referred to earlier in this chapter: a mother facing opposition to and criticism of her daughter's education beyond primary level. Importantly, one person did not oppose her: her husband. He thought, however, that secondary education for his daughter was financially impossible. It was left to the girl's mother to get the necessary money. And get it she did, through utilizing secret savings, by adding various remunerative activities to those she normally pursued, and by making some household necessities, such as coconut oil, rather than purchasing them. This example is neither average nor atypical. The details differ, but other village women have, through their industry and secret savings, enabled their children to continue education.

Young people of both sexes who go to secondary school usually think in terms of getting government jobs if and when they are able to finish their programs. This is the road to security, and there are now local role models of both sexes to encourage them. The adults they know who work in the private sector are, with few exceptions, associated with village work, which is often economically unreliable and has little, if any, prestige.

While a salaried job is the goal of the educated of both sexes, for women marriage and children continue to be more fundamental goals. Because only one educated Rusila woman was married and had her own home in 1975, I sought others from nearby villages. Two women, one a teacher and the other an analyst for a bank, were contacted. My aim was to find the common elements in their lives that contrasted with those of their illiterate mothers and less-educated peers in the village. In 1979 I saw them again, and also visited two other urban-dwelling women from Rusila who had completed some form of post-secondary education and had married since 1975. The lifestyles did not differ markedly from those observed in 1975, although color television sets had replaced black-and-white receivers in two homes.

All of these women married four or five years later than the average village female of their age. Two of the women and all of the husbands have university degrees. Three of the women made their own decisions about who they would marry, one breaking an engagement to the man selected by her parents; they all met their husbands while both were students. All but one departed further from tradition by refusing to participate in the bersanding ceremony and other, minor ritual events traditionally associated with marriage. All took honeymoon trips to other parts of Malaysia or to Indonesia, a practice unknown in the village little more than a decade ago but common among the Malaysian elite.

These young women and their husbands work regularly scheduled hours; they employ housekeepers or "mother's helpers" to care for their children and homes. The combined income for any couple was over $800 per month, equivalent to the yearly income of some village families, in 1975 and over $1,200 in all cases by 1979. All of them give occasional financial assistance to one one or more grandparents, parents, and/or siblings.

The women live in towns or cities, in houses equipped with conveniences still considered unattainable by most villagers, such as running water, or considered dream appliances by rural women, such as refrigerators or gas stoves. Two of the three women in the 1975 sample drove automobiles owned jointly with their husbands, the first female drivers from their respective villages. By 1979 four women were driving; two owned cars. All of them have large wardrobes that contain clothes reflecting their lifestyles: traditional, formal attire as well as sarongs, maxis (a word now in the Malay vocabulary for any floor-length, one-piece dress), and in two cases, uniforms. They wear little gold jewelry, in contrast with village women, who use it as a form of savings.

All of the women read magazines, particularly fashion and women's magazines, regularly, read newspapers at least occasionally, and watch television most evenings. Socially they have developed a town style of entertaining. They dine out with their husbands, as couples, both in restaurants and at the homes of friends, and attend social functions related to their own or their husbands' occupations. They and a few close friends sometimes invite one another for a casual meal rather than always to celebrate an important occasion, as has been typical in the villages.

But just "dropping in" for a visit with neighbors and kin, a common village practice, is not an integral part of these young women's urban social pattern. Only one of the interviewees has more than a polite, superficial acquaintance with any of her neighbors; the others say that jobs outside the home and family demands within it leave them no time for establishing neighborhood friendships, and note that their neighbors are also employed outside the home. None of the women have kin living nearby. This social isolation within their neighborhoods is a source of worry to the young women's mothers, and is totally alien to the village lifestyle. When the women return to their villages, they enjoy the informal coming and going of friends and kin. Two women have purchased house land in their natal villages and plan to build homes one day.

Three of the couples have children of their own; another informally adopted a daughter and recently had a son. Unlike most of their village peers, these young women worry about not spending enough time with their children. As one sadly said about her six-month-old daughter: "She likes her grandmother; she doesn't like me. I rarely see her." The infant had lived with her paternal grandmother since she was a month old. She was eight months old when her mother finally secured a full-time housekeeper who could also care for the child.

These young women feel the sometimes conflicting demands of home and job commonly acknowledged by their Western peers. However, the availability of live-in help from the home village mitigates the conflict to some degree. But factory work and other job opportunities are becoming available near many towns, so it is questionable how long this solution will be possible.

The influence of the educated is greatest on their families of orientation and on nonfamily members of their own sex who are their peers or slightly younger than themselves. The most readily observable influences are perhaps superficial, though I believe they are important for the recipients; a younger sister provided with new school shoes or a pretty dress; a mother blossoming with an almost traditional but subtly different hairstyle that her town-dwelling daughter arranged and wearing the traditional type of formal attire cut with the latest flair that her daughter had made for her, feeling a bit self-conscious but pleased. Then there are the younger siblings who know that their lessons will be examined, albeit sporadically, by a literate older brother or sister who cannot be fooled as illiterate parents can. Family and friends are exposed to ideas.

These young educated women no longer live in the village, but they do visit at least several times per year. Their behavior patterns are observed, sometimes criticized, and always talked about. And there is a female secondary school teacher, from another part of Malaysia, who is married to a local man (also a teacher) and lives in the village. Their lifestyle is similar to the ones described and, while their social life is mainly with colleagues outside the village, it is similarly observed and commented upon. All of the couples are models of a lifestyle alternative to the one that has been typical in the village. Not everyone wants the alternative. Many young people continue to enjoy the village lifestyle and consciously select it. But those who do not, now have role models, female as well as male, for a different choice.

5
MATE SELECTION, MARRIAGE, AND THE FAMILY

The establishment of a new domestic family begins with mate selection—which, in Malaysia, normally involves the couple who will eventually wed far less than it involves their parents and other kin. Arrangements vary by social class, ethnic category, religious affiliation, sex, age, education, and whether the marriage is a first or subsequent one.

Two legal codes affect marriage and the family: the Islamic code pertains to all Muslims, differs slightly from one state to another, and is modified by pre-Islamic adat; the civil code applies to non-Muslims in all states. The Law Reform (Marriage and Divorce) Act, 1975, for non-Muslims was passed by Parliament during 1975, but it had not been implemented by early 1979, despite complaints from non-Muslim women. Government spokesmen claimed insufficient administrative organization to effect the changes as reason for the delay.

The main provisions of the act that pertain to marriage include establishment of monogamy for all non-Muslims; prohibition of marriages between close kin, with the exception that among Hindus a man may marry his sister's daughter; setting age 18 as the minimum for persons of either sex to contract a marriage, but

———

Sections of this chapter were originally published in "Continuity and Change: Patterns of Mate Selection and Marriage Ritual in a Malay Village," Journal of Marriage and the Family (August 1976). The article was copyrighted in 1976 by the National Council on Family Relations. Reprinted by permission.

allowing a 16-year-old woman to obtain a special license to marry (NST 8/10/78); allowing either party to petition for divorce on the ground of "irretrievable breakdown of the marriage"; and permitting divorce by mutual consent (Foo 1976:32).

PATTERNS OF MATE SELECTION IN RUSILA

Patterns of mate selection in Rusila changed significantly, for. a few, in the 1970s. They had been quite stable and predictable up to and including the time of the first study in 1965-66. Choices were made by parents, and children were expected to accept them. Elopement was not unknown in the area, but it was unusual—only two couples during a period of more than ten years. The changes observed in 1975 and 1979 constitute a trend, albeit one that thus far is affecting a small number of individuals: increasingly, young people are taking an active role in mate selection.

The changes for local women began among those who continued their education beyond the secondary level outside of Trengganu (see Chapter 4). Within a few years, others—young women with wage-paying jobs who were able to be self-supporting although still living with parents—were voicing opinions. Two women who refused fiancés chosen by their parents have no formal education beyond primary school, but they do earn regular income as handicraft instructors at government facilities outside the village. But secondary or more education is the usual route to wage-paying jobs. Being able to support oneself is fundamental to, but insufficient for, an unmarried woman's personal independence, because the idea is circumscribed by cultural values.

Women—mothers, grandmothers, and matchmakers—are pivotal to the mate selection process when it is carried out in the traditional manner. A father has influence, but generally village men credit women with being more astute at choosing a child's first mate and more clever in conducting preliminary negotiations. (The example fits Ortner's generalization [1974:81] that ". . . the feminine personality tends to be involved with concrete feelings, things, and people, rather than with abstract entities; it tends toward personalism and particularism.") And it is the women's network that passes information within and between villages about who is seeking a wife or husband for a child. It might be predicted that a mother's involvement would give daughters an active role in picking their husbands, because mothers and daughters normally have close affective ties. But such was rarely the case in the past, and is not the norm today.

Most women now in their thirties or older, and some who are considerably younger, say they were not consulted when a choice was made for them—nor did they expect to be consulted. They were young, ignorant about such matters, and had few opportunities to interact with members of the opposite sex outside of their immediate village neighborhoods. If they had opinions, they did not venture them, because even to hold one implied an unacceptable brazenness. They trusted their parents to make a careful decision on their behalf or simply hoped for the best.

The traditional pattern still affects a majority of young women and some men. Parents or guardians make decisions, trying to pick someone who matches well with their child. But they are also strongly influenced by their own feelings about prospective in-laws. It was once rare for a daughter or a son to oppose parents, but a man normally had a greater voice than a woman had in decision making. Legally both should consent to a marriage, but pressures can be exerted on an obstinate young person, most easily on a dependent daughter. The consent of a virgin given in marriage by her father or paternal grandfather is not essential under Islamic law (Foo 1976:27). The idealized rationale is the following:

> The requirement that a woman can only be given in marriage by a guardian . . . is beneficient and is laid down for the purpose of ensuring that a woman . . . is suitably matched to the right man. If a woman were left to marry solely according to her own choice and decision . . . she would run a much greater risk of falling into the wrong hands than if her marriage had been with the blessing of those whose sole considerations are her happiness and well-being (Abdul Kadir 1975:2-3).

Most Rusila parents would be in full agreement with these views. But even in 1966 some parents conceded that, although they tried to do what was best for their children, many arranged marriages ended in divorce before a year had passed. Others recognized that increased education was bringing their children into more and closer contact with members of the opposite sex, contact that might lead to the formation of affective relationships and the desire to participate in the mate selection process. The fear of this possibility influenced some parents against allowing their daughters secondary education, although other reasons were, and still are, given.

There is greater fear when the child is educated outside of Trengganu, because then he or she may develop strong feelings for someone from another part of the country. Potential problems loom in parents' minds: each spouse will want to visit her/his parents

for Hari Raya and other holidays, so it is possible that their child
and grandchildren will not visit them; when spouses are from different areas of the country, it will cost a lot of money for them to go
back and forth between two families of orientation for visits, a
wasteful situation; people from some parts of the country are too
modern and no longer respect traditional values, so one's child
might be alienated from what is locally acceptable; people from
some areas engage in magical practices through which they can control another person, possibly even force a spouse to forget obligations to parents.

Because of such fears, parents are ambivalent about an unmarried child's studying (or working) in another part of the country.
Some balance their fears against the realistic assessment that their
society is changing very rapidly, and that it is the educated person
who will have occupational opportunities with a degree of security
unknown to a village agriculturalist, fisherman, or shopkeeper.
The daughter or son who gets the education is still a "child of Rusila"
with roots in the village. Parents seek to strengthen a child's ties to
traditional values, to family, and to kampung through appropriate
mate selection. A person from Rusila or a nearby village is ideal.

Parents tend to evaluate a child's strengths and weaknesses as
well as their own socioeconomic and religious status (Muslim: very
pious or "the same as most people") in a realistic, straightforward
manner. They seek a spouse for their child who has a similar background and accomplishments, and compatible personal traits. For
example, when a child has the advantage of a secondary or better
education, a person with a similar education is sought as a marriage
partner. If equity is not possible, the man should be better educated
than the woman. Concern about level of educational attainment became increasingly important during the 1970s, and the trend shows
no sign of faltering.

Balance between the qualities and characteristics of male and
female is so highly desirable because balance is the cornerstone of
harmony, and harmony is the basic component for good interpersonal
relationships. Ideally, both female and male should be industrious
and capable within the spheres that the traditionally accepted division
of labor allots to them: she should be a competent cook and housekeeper, and show promise of being a good mother; he should manifest potential for becoming a good provider. They should have un-
blemished reputations; she must be a virgin. The appearance of
each is appraised vis-à-vis the other. If both young people are attractive, everyone is pleased by the aesthetic balance; certainly
everyone compares their relative attributes. Also, they should have
pale brown skin that is evenly pigmented. The ideal woman has well-
shaped ankles and feet, and straight posture. The young man is not

hirsute. Both are free from physical deformities; neither should be
fat or too thin. Realities are another matter, but when disparities
are very obvious, parents emphasize a child's or in-law's compensating qualities—for instance, "He is not as attractive as she is, but
he is very generous."

It is usual for first marriages to be contracted between young
people whose ages are close; the man should be two or three years
senior to the woman. In 1966 adults in their thirties or older had
married at about 14-15 for women and 17-18 for men. Their children were marrying later: the average age of a virgin female (anak
dara) at the time of marriage was 17; that of a youth (teruna), 19.
When a 20-year-old woman married for the first time in 1965, it was
said that she was comparatively old. Today she would not be atypical.

The marriageable age for females and males is still rising,
partly because more young people are continuing their education beyond their teen years. In Rusila the age at first marriage had risen
for all females, from a mean of 17 years in 1966 to a mean of 18
years by 1975 for normal women with only primary school education.
Women who continued schooling at the upper secondary level or beyond were marrying at 22 years or older. "The 21.9 [years] average for West [Peninsular] Malaysia in 1970 was higher than the
median age at first marriage of U.S. women in 1975 (21.1)" (Baldwin
1977:2). During 1979 some Rusila women married during their late
teens, but it was striking that 24 normal women between the ages of
20 and 26 had not yet married, and that five of them were over 23
years of age.

If a man of any age marries a woman more than a year or two
his senior, the union is thought to be peculiar and, unless the woman
is exceptionally attractive and financially well-off, probably due to
her use of magic. The male is defined as the head of the family
within Islam; his age seniority buttresses his position.

A divorced man may or may not be an acceptable match for an
anak dara, but a divorced woman is defined as an unacceptable mate
for a teruna. The consensus reflects the ideal that a woman should
not be more sexually experienced than her husband. Yet the final
household survey carried out in 1966 showed that of 120 married
couples, there were eight (6.6 percent) examples of divorced women
married to teruna.

In rare instances several of the ideals might be flouted simultaneously. When a 19-year-old teruna became enamored of a 23-
year-old divorcée whom he had encountered in the town bus station,
his parents were perturbed and refused permission for the marriage.
The lad eloped with his choice in spite of her divorced status, the
difference in their ages, and his parents' disapproval. The parents
were embarrassed by the marriage but accepted it gracefully when

the young couple returned to Rusila several months later, and seemed to give their daughter-in-law every consideration.

Parents evaluate a divorced man by the same criteria that are used for a teruna, plus what is known about his prior marriage and divorce, when they are looking for a daughter's prospective husband. They are wary of any man who has been divorced more than once or who has another wife.

It is unthinkable for a normal person to remain single, so if parents have difficulty finding a spouse for their child, they begin to overlook negative qualities of prospective mates.

All of a young woman's qualities per se and compared with those of the man determine the amount of bridewealth (mahr or mas kawin) she receives. Bridewealth is a gift "sincerely offered" by the groom to his bride. Some publications—the Malaysian National Museum's program for the "Traditional Malaysian Weddings" show, for example—refer to bridewealth as "dowry" (1978:20) but dowry "is in many ways the opposite of bride-wealth" (Fox 1967:238). It is provided by the bride's, rather than the groom's, family, a practice found among Indians but not Malays.

Rusila women now in their forties received bridewealth ranging from $70 to $150, the mean and the median being closer to the lower amount, when they married in the late 1940s and 1950s. The amount commonly paid during 1966 was $150. The lowest bridewealth that year was $100 to a woman from a relatively poor family whose appearance was regarded as plain; $700, a record high, was paid by the family of a teacher to a strikingly beautiful, educated woman from another state. Bridewealth inflation continued. By 1975 a woman from a nearby village who had a B.A. degree received $1,000, and since then one Rusila woman has gotten that amount, but a range from $250 to $400 was said to be common. Because bridewealth is a gift from the groom to the bride, the amount should vary according to his means as well as his and her qualities. A woman contracting a subsequent marriage receives only token bridewealth, or perhaps nothing: she is no longer a virgin.

All local marriages are between Muslims, and all but a few of them are unions between Malays. Two older women have Muslim Indian husbands, only one of whom lives in the village; three others were once married to Muslim Indians. One Rusila woman, living elsewhere, is married to a Chinese Muslim who is senior to her by more than ten years and had another Malay wife and two children before he married her. His alleged affluence was said to compensate for these negative features. Only one other woman, an elderly widow, has ever been married to a Chinese.

Villagers are ambivalent about converts to Islam, especially those who take Malay wives soon after conversion. On the one hand, they have very strong, positive views about conversion; on the other, they evince reactions from faint suspicion to subtle cynicism about the reason for conversion when marriage is at stake. In 1966, it was common for Malays to say that a convert masuk Melayu—literally, became a Malay. By 1979, the phrasing had changed (in Rusila at least) to masuk Islam, became a Muslim. Religious affiliation and ethnic identity are no longer equated.

Young women have greater freedom than their mothers had after reaching puberty. Women now in their late thirties or older were largely confined to their homes after menarche if not before, venturing beyond their immediate village neighborhoods only when accompanied by a mother or other adult female chaperone. Still, the average postpubescent female today does not have relaxed social contacts with young men, or even chat with them freely, for fear of jeopardizing her reputation. Ideally, young Malay women are shy in the presence of men who are not close kinsmen, and the ideal has a high degree of congruence with reality.

Marriages between first cousins are definitely not preferred in Rusila; the preference is against them because of a belief that difficulties between married cousins will have negative repercussions on the social relationships of their parents and other kin.

There are a few couples in the village whose parents made marriage decisions for them when they were young children, but such long-range planning is no longer practiced. Rather, as a young person approaches marriageable age, the parents begin to evaluate prospective spouses. The process is always discussed in terms of finding a wife for a young man, because women should be sought rather than seeking, but parents with an eligible daughter make the fact known. There are no professional matchmakers in Rusila, but two women with extensive social networks have reputations for making good choices and some other women play the go-between role for friends. They receive no fee for their services, but gifts are usually given to them once arrangements are finalized.

With or without the aid of a matchmaker, it is ultimately the young man's mother who approaches the woman's mother with a proposal, very subtly, in order to avoid embarrassment if there is no interest. Even when a matchmaker has established that a woman's parents are interested, one can never be certain of acceptance. A refusal is equally indirect, and involves reasons that do not reflect negatively on the youth or his family: the young woman is going to continue her education, so it is premature to make a decision, or it is hinted that a prior proposal is under consideration, which makes it inappropriate for another to be accepted. A positive response is soon followed by discussion of bridewealth and wedding date.

Prospective spouses who come from the same or nearby villages have at least seen one another, and probably attended the same primary school. But if they come from different places, they may be strangers. Men, being more mobile, can usually arrange to see a future bride, if only surreptitiously. Stories are told about men concealing themselves near a woman's home or her bathing place in order to see her prior to the marriage. Women do not have the same freedom. In 1966 one bride was so dismayed when she saw her husband for the first time—after they were married—that she initially refused to have anything to do with him.

During the early 1970s it became common for the young people at least to see photographs of one another, or for the young man's parents to take him to his intended bride's home for a visit with her and her family. While the two can look one another over, they probably will not interact beyond exchanging polite greetings and good-byes.

The following example illustrates many aspects of mate selection today, both the traditional expectations of parents and why they are not always realized. Ali, a Rusila man who had completed two years of post-secondary education and was working in Kuala Lumpur, had an informal agreement to marry—in two or three years—Faizah, a woman from Malacca who had been his classmate. Faizah's urbanite parents knew Ali and had accepted the match, although they had no part in arranging it. Ali's mother, Baidah, was very upset when she learned that her son had a special friend whom she did not know. That Faizah was from the west coast, far from Trengganu, made the matter worse. Baidah blamed herself for not arranging Ali's formal engagement to a Trengganu woman before he went away to school, but each time she had mentioned the subject of marriage, he had talked about his studies. Baidah had postponed a decision. Now she had to find someone who would make him forget his Malaccan friend. Her husband, Zakariah (Zak), refused to take Ali's commitment seriously, considering it a passing fancy that would disappear when his son realized the displeasure of his parents.

Baidah's friends in other villages and her acquaintances in the town were reminded that her son was 23, had a good job, and was not married. Soon she was getting information about young women who might be suitable for Ali. Some of the women's parents were already known to her or her husband, and between they they made inquiries about other couples. There is no sense considering women whose parents are unknown, because the relationship between the two older couples is important and their socioeconomic situation should be similar. Otherwise, interactions are complicated by status differences. Status disparity between her family and the Malaccans was another reason for Baidah's negative feelings about Ali's friend.

Faizah's father is a civil servant; the mother has never worked outside the home. Baidah was sure they would think average village
people beneath them.

When the parents of prospective brides were acceptable to
Baidah and Zak, Baidah made further inquiries about their daughters.
After approximately three months she located a young woman who
seemed ideal: Samillah was described to her as a shy, well-man-
nered, and very attractive person with above-average skills in the
home. The young woman had finished the fifth year of secondary
school but failed the MCE exams, decided not to take them again,
and instead was attending a secretarial school in Kuala Trengganu.
Baidah knew Samillah's mother slightly, and was impressed with
her reputation as an exemplary mother and homemaker. Zak and
Samillah's father had several brief, work-related encounters.
Baidah's husband found the other man pleasant and rather witty, and
knew he was respected for his scrupulous honesty. He was also
said to be a good Muslim but not overly pious, thus matching Zak's
perceptions of himself. They decided to investigate further.

Baidah visited an acquaintance who lived near Samillah's family, and found a pretext for going to the young woman's home with
the neighbor. It was midafternoon, and Samillah and her younger
siblings were at home. Baidah was impressed with the family, the
cleanliness of the house, and the hospitality. Nothing was said about
Ali or the real purpose for the visit. A couple of weeks later, on a
Friday afternoon, Baidah and Zak called upon Samillah's family.
During the course of the visit, Baidah mentioned that her eldest son
worked in Kuala Lumpur and showed his photograph to her hostess,
who passed it to the others. Everyone agreed that Baidah and Zak
were fortunate to have such a fine son. Baidah briefly mentioned
his best qualities and a few faults, and then complimented Samillah
indirectly by referring to the preparation and serving of the refreshments. The point had been made. Marriage was never mentioned.

More than a week passed before Samillah's mother returned
the visit. Too much eagerness might be interpreted as desperation.
She said that she was going to the Marang market and, as Baidah's
home was along the way, she decided to call. The women had tea
and talked about their children. It was established that Samillah
would soon be 20, a good age to marry. The mothers agreed that
it was desirable for a child to marry someone from Trengganu and,
preferably, someone who had a village rather than a town background.
The topic of bridewealth was introduced by Baidah through reference
to the recent marriage of a Rusila woman. Samillah's mother expressed surprise at the low amount and gave an example of a woman
in Marang who had only three years of secondary education but had
received more. The women eventually agreed that an amount roughly

between the two examples was probably fair for village people.
They parted amicably after Baidah confided that Ali was coming
home for a few days in the near future, and Samillah's mother expressed interest in meeting him. No direct statement about a possible match between Ali and Samillah had been made, but both
women knew they were engaged in negotiations, however tentative.
They had previously discussed bridewealth with their husbands and
then worked out an acceptable amount between themselves. It remained for Ali and Samillah to meet—and to like one another.

As soon as Ali's arrival date was known, Baidah informed
Samillah's mother. They agreed that late Friday afternoon was a
good time for the visit. Ali reached home Thursday evening. Baidah
welcomed her son and took him to the kitchen to chat while she prepared his favorite type of fried rice. They exchanged news, and
Baidah told him about the very nice family she had recently met and
about their lovely daughter. Ali was polite, but expressed no particular interest. When his mother persisted with the topic, Ali
realized her intent, and parried by telling about a visit to Faizah's
family in Malacca, how much he had enjoyed their hospitality, and
how well he thought his mother would get along with them. Baidah
was dismayed, but did not indicate it. Instead, she commented on
the importance of having good friends to visit. She also made it quite
clear that she expected Ali to accompany her and his father on a visit
to their friends, Samillah's family, the following day. When Zak returned later, his pressure was added: a dutiful son should try to
please his parents, especially when they are acting in his best interest. A son may be brought into line by parents refusing to pay bridewealth to a woman they find unacceptable, but such a threat is meaningless when the son earns more than the father.

Ali was in a dilemma. He had a serious commitment to Faizah,
although there was no formal engagement. They had spent many
hours together, talking about their hopes for the future. They were
in harmony, a state that both defined as essential for marriage. Ali
had hoped to win his parents' approval during this holiday, and had
planned to coax his mother to go to Malacca with him the following
month or, at least, to invite Faizah and her mother to Rusila. He
could simply marry Faizah because she had her father's approval,
but he did not want to act against his parents' wishes. Nor did he
intend to marry a stranger just to please them. If he went to meet
Samillah, he could probably find many shortcomings in her or her
parents to use in arguing against the match. But Ali is a sensitive
man. It would be a cruel thing to do to the young woman. Even if
she was uninformed about the purpose of the visit, Samillah would
suspect it as soon as he and his parents arrived. Then, if the engagement was not forthcoming, she would know she had been rejected

and feel ashamed. He would feel ashamed to go to her home when there was no interest in his heart. He refused.

His mother wept; his father yelled; Ali fled to his maternal grandmother's home. If his grandmother would support him, Ali might yet marry Faizah without causing a rift in the family. While the men were at the mosque the next day, Ali's grandmother went to see Baidah, her daughter. The two women talked and prepared the afternoon meal. The grandmother acknowledged that it was preferable for Ali to marry someone from Trengganu, but she also pointed out that he has a good job in Kuala Lumpur, far closer to Malacca than to Trengganu. It could be advantageous for him to have in-laws nearby. And the fact that the young couple would be able to visit Faizah's family on weekends might well mean that they would feel obliged to return to Trengganu for longer holidays. Baidah finally agreed, grudgingly, to invite the young Malaccan woman and her mother to visit Rusila. Since they had apparently accepted Ali already, there was no reason for her to seek them in Malacca. She would be a gracious hostess, but she would carefully evaluate her visitors. If Faizah turned out to be lazy or her mother snobbish (sombong), Baidah determined to fight the match in every possible way. I do not know the outcome.

Zak went to Samillah's house to cancel the visit, using the excuse that they had unexpected guests (the grandmother) at home. Ali returned late that evening. His father was still angry, but his mother acted normally and, in passing, noted that she would like to meet Faizah and her mother. Samillah was not mentioned.

It remained for Baidah to make another visit to Samillah's home. She went several days later, during the morning, when Samillah's mother would be alone except for her youngest child. Baidah was very embarrassed. She talked about modern young people and vanishing traditions; she related a story about a friend whose daughter refused to marry the young man selected by her parents; she hoped that Samillah would secure a good job when she finished her secretarial studies. No reference was made to Ali.

The example of Ali and Samillah illustrates a number of points:

1. The importance of women in the traditional mate selection process. It was Ali's mother who initiated inquiries about appropriate women, called upon Samillah's mother to get an idea of what she was like in her home surroundings and to evaluate her housekeeping, and introduced the subject of her son into conversation at the second visit; Samillah's mother also made a visit to Baidah to see her at home and to indicate interest in the match. Although the women had already discussed bridewealth with their husbands, it was they who reached a compromise—without making any direct

reference to either of their children. Later, it was Ali's grandmother who was able to influence her daughter to consider the young
Malaccan woman. And when the match for Ali and Samillah was no
longer in the offing, it was Baidah who had the unpleasant task of informing Samillah's mother. The only woman who had almost no role
in the proceedings was Samillah.

2. The importance of matching qualities and attainments. In
this example, education was important because Ali had completed
secondary school and had post-secondary training. Baidah was concerned to find a woman who had at least some upper secondary education. Both young people had village backgrounds and were close
in age, with Ali a few years senior, and both were judged to be physically attractive. Ali had the potential for being a good provider;
Samillah should be well trained in running a home because her mother
was an excellent housekeeper. Also, Samillah earned Baidah's compliments on her preparation and serving of refreshments. Neither
had been previously married. The fathers were engaged in similar
work, and Baidah concluded that their socioeconomic statuses were
similar after seeing Samillah's home. Both families were "good,"
but not extremely pious, Muslims.

3. The importance of indirection and subtlety. Marriage arrangements and bridewealth were discussed without any direct statement about Ali and Samillah being made. Had Ali accepted his parents' choice for him, a date would have been set for the marriage or
the young couple would at least have been betrothed. The match
would become public knowledge. Ali did not accept. The fact that
no open agreement had been reached between the families made it
easier for Baidah, despite her embarrassment, to break off negotiations.

4. The importance of the concept of shame/embarrassment
(malu). The main reason for emphasizing indirection and sublety is
to avoid either causing or being subject to shame or embarrasment.
Ali refused to go to Samillah's home although it would have pleased
his parents and he probably could have found reasons for not accepting Samillah after visiting her family. He knew that rejection after
a visit for the obvious, if unstated, purpose of seeing her would
shame Samillah and, he felt, himself. He refused to go. Baidah
and her husband experienced shame because their son refused to do
what they wanted and they had to indicate his disobedience to Samillah's
family as a reason for ending negotiations. Baidah was embarrassed
to have to end the negotiations.

In this example the traditional role of the parents is shown
along with some of the types of changes occurring as young people
increasingly insist on consideration of their own preferences.

Although not listed as another point, it is notable that Faizah and Ali met in school, a school far from Trengganu. The women from Rusila and nearby villages who have had post-secondary education and then married men of their own choice met their future husbands while both were students. In those three cases the women, if not the men, were far removed from the immediate influence of their families and from the behavioral norms of village life. They had more freedom than would have been possible had they been living with parents or even in a nearby town. The same holds true for unmarried women who find work far from home. I emphasize the idea of "possible" with regard to freedom of action, for not all students (or workers) from rural areas feel at ease with the idea of personal autonomy and the lack of family and community definitions of correct behavior. Many young Malay women, away from home for the first time, find campus (urban) life and the casual interactions between men and women threatening; they adopt a very conservative mode of dress as a means of creating social distance between themselves and other students. But those who want more autonomy find the possibilities are there, for it is not just seeing persons of the opposite sex in classes and on campus that builds affective relationships and leads to women as well as men wanting to select their own spouses.

My first exposure to the contrast between a person's behavior in the village and with college peers came in Kuala Lumpur in 1975, the night before I was leaving Malaysia. I invited a young Rusila man and four of his friends, all Malays, whom I had met previously to spend the evening with me. The group of five was composed of two women and three men (including the one from Rusila), with one man and woman from urban areas and the others with village backgrounds. The uneven number is more socially acceptable than even numbers of males and females, for it suggests to any observer a group of friends rather than one made up of couples. One of the women told me that the five were like adik beradik (siblings). She later married a man from the group.

When they arrived at my hotel, I asked where they wanted to go. After some politeness about my choosing a place (because I had invited them and was paying for whatever entertainment we would have), the urban man suggested The Tin Mine, the disco at the Hilton. They had been there once, as a group, and greatly enjoyed it. We went. My guests appeared completely at home in the place, and performed the latest dance steps, but they drank fruit juices and soft drinks as proper Muslims should (whether for my benefit or not, I am unsure). They told me about other places where they sometimes went dancing, beach parties they had, and day trips facilitated by the urban male student's owning a car. They obviously enjoyed many

good times together. Such unchaperoned parties and picnics would
be impossible in the village milieu, however innocent the activities.

I know the parents of the Rusila man would have been shocked
by his going to a disco, despite his 22 years, for whether or not one
drinks alcoholic beverages, they are served; some women are
dressed in suggestive or revealing clothes; and men and women,
married or not, touch one another with an improper familiarity—
totally unacceptable if they are not married, and inappropriate in a
public place if they are spouses. The parents of the young women
would likely have similar or stronger reactions.

The point is, these young people spent a great deal of their
free time together and knew each other far better than an average
couple know one another when they are wed following traditional
mate selection patterns. There are dangers, for women, in such
close relationships with men. Even in a city the size of Kuala
Lumpur, relatives or friends from the village might be encountered
and information transmitted back to parents, creating problems between them and their daughter. If marriage does not result from
the friendship, but a woman is known to have been keeping company
with a man, even within a group, her reputation can be damaged or
completely ruined, and other men will judge her unacceptable as a
wife. A woman also gets different ideas about men, female-male
interactions, and the type of marriage relationship she wants than
she has from her village experience. Thus she may be the one to do
the rejecting when marriage proposals are made.

In 1979 there were 24 normal Rusila women between the ages
of 20 and 26 who were not yet married. Some were still in school.
Economic independence had allowed others to be assertive about
prospective mates, although no one wants to create a rift between
herself and her parents. Unlike Ali and the women who have made
their own choice, all of them live with parents and commute to jobs
near the village. Thus far their assertiveness is essentially negative: refusal to marry a particular man. For them to act positively,
suggesting a prospect to parents, is more difficult. Not only are
contacts with eligible men very limited, but young Malay women are
not expected to be thinking about men in general or evaluating particular men as likely husbands. Some courage is needed for such
boldness.

At 26, Rogayah was the oldest anak dara in Rusila in 1979.
She laughed when she told me that her parents had already suggested four men to her, none of whom was satisfactory. She had
eventually suggested someone for their consideration. They rejected him. She confided a degree of concern about her situation:
she wants to marry and have children; she also wants a husband with
whom she will feel contented (senang). She knows a man through her

work who appeals to her, although he is almost two years her junior.
He is intelligent and personable, and has other qualities that Rogayah
finds attractive. She is sure that he is interested in her. Rogayah
has spoken about him to her mother, who agreed to approach the
father about the matter. When I left the village, Rogayah was hope-
ful. The parents and the daughter are aware that very soon Rogayah's
options will be limited to men who are divorced, widowed, or already
married.

There is no doubt that women have more to lose than men by
agreeing to unacceptable liaisons; males can divorce easily, while
women cannot. Thus a man who bows to parental pressure and re-
grets it can end the marriage, although he forfeits the bridewealth
that he or his family paid to his wife and may still incur his parents'
wrath. A woman who finds herself trapped in an intolerable union
has no simple recourse, a matter discussed in Chapter 6. However,
a woman who is divorced can be approached directly about another
marriage, and keeps a high degree of control over the male selection process.

MARRIAGE ARRANGEMENTS

Formalization of an engagement takes place once the marriage
agreement is finalized. Sirih leaves, a traditional symbol of friendship and hospitality, and one or more personal gifts, including a
piece of gold jewelry (probably a ring) are sent to the young woman
by her fiancé. If she later breaks the engagement the gifts are returned to the man; if he breaks it, the woman keeps the gifts. A
broken engagement is uncommon, but it may occur if either tries
to renege on the agreement—for instance, by postponing the wedding
date or wanting to pay bridewealth in installments after a lump-sum
payment was agreed upon. Bad feelings between the families can
result, but embarrassment rather than scandal is involved.

One 1965 situation was defined as scandalous: the woman's
parents had allowed her to go about unchaperoned with her fiancé, a
practice still rare in Rusila and environs in 1979, although not uncommon among upper-class Malays (and others) in urban areas
(Roose 1965:287). Nevertheless, even engaged Muslim couples are
"not free to date," according to a syariah court official (NST
12/28/78).

A great deal of gossip was generated by the local couple's behavior, but the onus was upon the woman and her parents. When the
man broke the engagement, it was consensus among the villagers
that the woman was no longer a virgin, and thus would have difficulty
finding a husband. Several people said that the man should have

married his fiancée and then divorced her, so that she would not have been stigmatized. But they added that such a course would have resulted in a financial burden (the bridewealth payment) for the man and his family.

Economic arrangements associated with marriage rites and other events require the families of the bride and groom to mobilize cash and credit resources and activate reciprocal obligations to an extent uncalled for at any other time during the life cycle. Both men and women can be involved in raising cash and obtaining credit, but the reciprocal relationships involved are mainly those between women. It is women who make gifts of sugar, eggs, and other food-stuffs to one another and gather to bake hundreds of cakes and pre-pare other foods; it is women who decorate the bride's home, select and prepare gifts and special finery, and arrange ceremonial para-phernalia.

The period of time between formalization of an engagement and the wedding ceremonies varies, but a few weeks or months is most common. About a week before the round of wedding festivities begins, the home of the bride is decorated. Newspapers or sheets of plain white paper are pasted to inner walls if they are roughly finished. Bright cotton fabric is used to make curtains for the win-dows, hangings for the bridal bed, and, if the family can afford it, a matching cover for the bridal throne used in the bersanding cere-mony, although this can be borrowed. Dozens of crepe-paper flowers are fashioned to decorate the furnishings.

A few days prior to the wedding ceremonies, more gifts are sent to the bride by the groom's family. The number and quality of the gifts depend on the socioeconomic status of both. A piece of gold jewelry, cloth arranged in the form of a flower, perfume and other cosmetics, a pair of ornate sandals, and a parasol, all with price tags attached, may be included along with sirih leaves, cakes, and raw husked rice arranged on trays decorated with fragrant blossoms. The bridewealth money may be sent with the gifts, which are carried in procession by women of the bridegroom's kindred and their friends, each dressed in her best clothing, to the home of the bride.

The gifts are presented to the bride's mother, who has as-sembled her female kin and friends, and an elaborate but brief ritual, involving counting the bridewealth, is performed by Mariam, the tukang bersanding ("wedding expert"). Mariam has been in charge of marriage rites at the homes of brides in Rusila and nearby villages since the early 1960s, and was still performing them in 1979. Cakes and beverages are served to the guests, who enjoy a pleasant hour or two with their hostesses and then depart with their empty trays. The gifts will be displayed throughout the wedding festivities. Mariam receives cakes and husked rice for conducting this ceremony. When the last marriage ceremony of the several at which she officiates has been performed, she receives more food and a fine sarong or enough cloth to make a formal outfit.

Relatives and friends, particularly those who have come great distances for the round of festivities, attend a small feast at the home of the groom prior to akhad nikah, the legally prescribed Muslim marriage ceremony. Local guests bring gifts of sugar to the bridegroom's mother and receive some little cakes in return. The sugar is used for cakes needed on future occasions in the marriage round, or is given to neighbors in partial repayment for cakes they have prepared.

Akhad nikah always takes place at the home of the groom, although the ritual can be held at the bride's home, on a Thursday night (Friday night by Malay reckoning). The room where the ceremony is performed is decorated simply; the floors are covered with pandanus mats and the place where the active participants sit is spread with a carpet from Mecca, flanked by candelabra. Only men are involved in the ceremony. Some women are present, sitting behind screens in back of the men. The bride is not among them. When I took photographs at an akhad nikah in 1966, with the permission of the groom and his family, some of the older women were shocked and upset by my intrusion into the masculine gathering.

The registrar, flanked by the guardian of the bride and official witnesses, presides. Facing them are the formally dressed groom and two close friends, who sit near him. The groom wears dark glasses because he is malu and they boost his self-confidence. The male guests sit behind the groom and his friends.

Muslim laws pertaining to marriage and divorce are intoned by the registrar, who also announces the bridewealth arrangements. If the money was previously sent to the bride, it is now displayed. If not, it is paid to her guardian (her father, if he is living), but the money belongs to the bride. The bridegroom and the bride's guardian agree to the terms of the marriage, a benediction is given, and the necessary papers are signed. The young couple are now officially wed in the eyes of the law, but they have no contact with one another—do not even see each other—until the bersanding ceremony, which is usually scheduled for the following night, but may sometimes be held a week later.

Refreshments are served to the men by male friends of the groom. Only after the men have been served and had their fill do the women eat, but young children of both sexes join groups of men to get tidbits passed to them.

Following the akhad nikah an entertainment of some sort, sponsored by the bride's parents, is presented near their home.

Everyone is welcome to attend such events, and people without vehicular transportation will walk from villages three or four miles away to do so. The groom makes a brief appearance, but the bride is closeted in her home, probably watching from behind a curtain or window shutter. The entertainment preferred in Rusila is rodat, a singing-dancing style indigenous to the east coast of Malaysia. Rodat troupes are not found locally; they are engaged through contacts in villages nearer the town. Three distinct groups of performers, one composed of males and two made up of females, sing while doing line dances to the accompaniment of percussion music played by a group of men.

Performances begin around 11 P.M. and continue as late as 4 or 5 A.M. The men, a dozen or more, begin the entertainment. When they tire, a group of several young girls about six to eight years of age replaces them. Members of the audience show appreciation for these two performances by tossing coins and cigarettes on the ground near the musicians.

The third group of performers is composed of young divorcées wearing very tight clothing and lots of makeup. Their appearance evokes the freest public expression of sexuality by village bachelors. Much of the male behavior is obviously hostile. The men whoop, holler, and compete with one another in shouting things that range from witty to obscene. Perhaps only five or six young men behave wildly, but many more shout encouragement to them. Now they throw the cigarettes like missiles, aiming them at the women's low-cut necklines. This part of the performance is provocative, with the women moving sinuously and singing songs fraught with double en-tendre, but even so the reaction is extreme.

In dress and behavior the adult female performers exemplify the opposite of the ideal for Malay women in public. They look and act like the stereotype of the young divorcée who is also an outsider, an unknown quality—sexually knowledgeable and possibly available, a vamp to men and a threat to other women. Because of the reactions, women never perform in their own or nearby villages.

Later the villagers will discuss the most rambunctious of the young men and say that their parents should arrange marriages for them before they get into trouble. Does this performance also serve as a reminder to the bride about the ambivalent position of the at-tractive young divorcée in Malay society?

Rodat, although it is preferred, is not always performed prior to a wedding. In one instance the bride's home was close to that of the imam. It would be an insult to present a boisterous, provocative entertainment near his home because, as a pious man, he would not attend that type of social function; nor would his family members be allowed to go to it. No pious adults go to such events, nor will they

sponsor them. Such a decision by anyone whose piety is a normal
aspect of behavior is highly respected by fellow villagers; those who
develop a pious leaning when a child's marriage is planned may find
the sharp yet subtle humor of their peers focusing on the interrela-
tionship between piety and stinginess.

In the instance mentioned, the bride's family held only the
Quran recitation that gives the bride an opportunity to demonstrate
her knowledge of holy Scripture. It may be part of the marriage activities for any bride who has the skill. About 20 men are invited
to the bride's home one evening. They sit in the main room of the
house; the woman is behind a partition or in an adjoining room.
Each man recites a section from the Quran, and she responds with
the same passage. A benediction ends the ritual, and refreshments
are served to the male guests.

Friday afternoon, the marriage feast (jamuan) is held at the
home of the bride. Almost everyone in the village, as well as relatives and friends from other places, has been invited verbally, by
handwritten announcements, or, increasingly, by printed invitations.
Neither the bride nor the groom attends the feast. The focus of attention is the bride's parents.

Some of the feast preparations are usually undertaken by two
local men, who supervise the cooking of the meat in huge pots over
fire pits dug behind the bride's home. They render their services
in return for generous gifts of the cooked food. The spicy sauce in
which the meat is cooked is prepared beforehand by the women of
the household, kinswomen, and friends under the direction of Kulsum,
an admired expert, who is paid a few dollars for coordinating everyone's efforts and seeing that the proper amounts of each ingredient
are used. Women also cook the plain boiled rice for the feast and
glutinous rice to be given as gifts to the female guests.

The cost of a feast depends both on the number of guests who
are invited and on which meat is served. If 500 people or fewer are
expected to dine, the meat from one large cow is adequate to serve
them. Meat from a water buffalo will be needed for more guests.
Buffalo meat is a more expensive and more prestigious meat to offer
them. One gantang (a measure of quantity, not weight, but equal to
approximately eight pounds of milled rice) of rice must be prepared
for every 20 guests, and a gantang of glutinous rice is needed for
every ten gifts.

Men go to a local feast after midday prayers at the mosque or
later in the day. If the weather is fine, rented trestle tables and
chairs are set for them under awnings. The food is served by young
kinsmen of the bride. Women and children go later in the afternoon
and eat inside the house. Each woman greets the bride's mother
and surreptitiously gives her money, receiving a gift of glutinous

rice wrapped in leaves from her. The men follow the same custom
with the host, but they receive no rice. In 1966 $1 was expected
from a male villager; a woman gave $.50. The amounts had doubled
by 1975. Relatives and close friends are expected to be more generous, if they are able.

Red-dyed hard-boiled eggs, symbols of fertility, are presented to some of the guests at the feast. Tiny plastic baskets purchased in the town are used as containers, or baskets woven from
pandanus strands can be ordered from village women. In some
families the women fashion elaborate gift eggs called bunga telor
(flower egg) by gluing eggs into the centers of crepe-paper flowers
attached to sticks from which leaves and buds protrude. The number of eggs given varies considerably, poorer families preparing
them only for a few special guests. Regardless of who receives
them, they invariably are in the possession of delighted small children before the day is out.

During the lunar calendar months preferred for marriages—
the month during which the Prophet Muhammad's birthday falls and
the month of the pilgrimage to Mecca—a family may be invited to
several wedding feasts on one day, though not in the same village.
Depending on kinship and friendship ties, they may want to attend
all of them, however briefly. One Friday some of my neighbors
attended three feasts in different villages, which, when transportation costs were included, meant a considerable financial outlay.
However, the entire family ate well and no food except snacks had
to be prepared at home.

Villagers say that the costs of the bridal feast are rarely covered by the gifts of money given by guests. In a 1966 instance the
feast expenses for one family were $576. A total of $328 was received in guest gifts, leaving a deficit of $248, an amount greater
than two months' income. No wonder some parents must borrow a
daughter's bridewealth to pay for wedding expenses. The money
must be repaid, however, or the parents are guilty of a sin.

As soon as the feast guests have departed, preparations begin
for another event at the bride's home, the bersanding. The ceremony, of Hindu origin (Winstedt 1961:38), is the first occasion when
the bride and groom appear together, and it may be the first occasion when they see one another if they are from different villages.
Although the akhad nikah legalized the marriage, it is the bersanding
that makes a woman's first marriage official in the eyes of the villagers. A woman experiences only one bersanding in her lifetime;
a man may have several if he weds a series of anak dara.

The custom of filing the bride's teeth (to make them even)
prior to the ceremony was not normally carried out in Rusila in 1966,
and was no longer practiced in 1979. However, cutting her fine

temple hair and, sometimes, staining her finger tips and palms with henna—both to enhance her beauty—are done by Mariam. Then the bride is dressed and helped to apply her cosmetics. The groom is at his home, where male kin and friends help him to don his wedding outfit. Bersanding attire for both is elegant and elaborate, usually patterned after the court dress of Malay royalty.

The throne where the couple will sit, atop a two-step platform, is the focal point of the initial rite. Two large bowls of nasi semangat—"the rice of the spirit of life" (Wira undated:41)—decorated with paper flowers, red eggs, and tinsel, are placed on either side of the second step and candelabra on the bottom one. A table covered with fine cloth and two chairs are placed nearby for the second part of the ceremony. When everything is ready and a large number of women, as well as preadolescent children of both sexes, are present, a messenger is sent to the groom's house to inform him. If he is not a Rusila man, he and his entourage are accommodated in a home near that of the bride.

The bridegroom's escort is composed of two groups: his female relatives, who lead him into the bride's home, pushing their way through a cordon of her resisting female kin (we cherish her and refuse to give her up to you easily), and his male friends, who sing along the way but do not enter the house. Men stay outside but make their presence known, whooping and shouting ribald comments in an attempt to shake the bridegroom's composure. The comments are acknowledged by appreciative chuckles and retorts from some of the older female guests, but the bride and groom are expected to remain solemn and unresponsive, their heads bowed. They are shy (malu) and, ideally, the bride at least should be innocently uncomprehending. She ". . . is expected . . . in all patience and dignity, to bear the brunt of the slanted and pointed remarks . . ." (Mohd. Din undated, b:35).

The bride is already seated on the throne when the groom arrives. Two women lead him to his seat on the bride's right while his female relatives find places amid the guests sitting on the floor. Young married women stand, one on each side of the throne, to fan the bride and groom during the ceremony and possibly to cover any lapses in their serious demeanor.

The tukang bersanding, Mariam, conducts the brief ceremony. When she finishes, she sits, covers her head with a handkerchief, and recites a benediction, thus incorporating an Islamic element into the ancient Hindu ritual. Then she leads the couple to the table and seats them. The groom is given a bit of cake or some rice to eat, a sip of coffee, and one puff on a cigarette, all symbolizing that his wife will tend to his needs and comfort. The bride sits limply with head bowed, eyes downcast, shy. They rise, and the bride is led behind a curtained area at the foot of the nearby bridal bed, while the groom goes to a curtained area at its head. Everyone departs except kin, who wait while he changes into a complete set of new clothing provided by his wife's family. When he is dressed, he reappears, is escorted to the door by Mariam, and leaves for his home, accompanied by his relatives and male friends. The bersanding is a women's event, yet the main focus of attention is the bridegroom.

I have suggested that the bersanding may disappear from the villages (Strange 1976). In Rusila today the ceremony is held for some couples but others refuse to have it, a trend that began in the early 1970s. As Muslim fundamentalism grows in Malaysia, the bersanding is openly criticized by some because of its Hindu origins. Others accept it as part of their rich and varied cultural heritage, and it continues to be an important part of upper-class weddings. For example, "Thousands Turn out for Royal Bersanding" (NST 4/15/79) for the daughter of the Sultan and Tengku Ampuan of Selangor and the son of the Raja and Raja Perempuan of Perlis, a ceremony attended by men as well as women, a notable class difference.

In the village the groom returns to the bride's home later and spends the night there. The newlyweds, ideally, are expected to sleep apart for at least one or two nights—a time for becoming acquainted with one another, but older villagers doubt that the ideal is realized. Nevertheless, when asked their reactions to Judith Djamour's observation that Singaporean Malay women bragged about the length of time they or their daughters spent with a husband before engaging in sexual intercourse (1965:77), Rusila women found the practice peculiar. Sexual relations are normal, and should be pleasurable to both persons; both have sexual needs. However a couple work out their first-night relationship, the bride is purified by ritual bathing the following day, with her female kin in attendance and Mariam officiating. In some places both the bride and groom are purified through lustration.

The couple stays at the bride's home, the length of time depending on various family circumstances. Then they go to the home of the groom for the bride to be welcomed by his family. If she is from another village, her mother and several female relatives accompany her, and stay at the groom's home until she feels at ease in the strange surroundings. The young wife is presented with gifts, including a mattress, pillows, kitchen utensils, and other useful household equipment, by her husband's parents.

The people of the groom's village are invited "to look at the daughter-in-law" (tengok menantu). The formally dressed bride sits in state with a cloth-covered dish before her. As they arrive,

the women greet her and put small amounts of money into the dish.
The bride returns their greetings but otherwise sits quietly with her
head bowed, isolated from social intercourse and apparently oblivi-
ous to the chatter about her. Male visitors also give small gifts of
money through her father-in-law, but do not greet the bride. The
money gifts belong to the bride. Guests talk, examine the daughter-
in-law closely but rather covertly, eat the provided refreshments,
and take their leave.

With the tengok menantu the round of rites and special activities associated with marriage comes to an end, but many of the
debts incurred may remain to be paid. The financial burden of wedding expenses is borne by both the bride's and bridegroom's families,
but relatives and friends, especially the women, also make contributions in time and effort as well as foodstuffs.

One Rusila woman organized a 1,000-guest feast for her
daughter Aminah's wedding in 1973. There was scarcely an adult
woman in the village who did not owe her a return for foodstuffs
given to them for marriages or other events, and there were other
women who gave, knowing they would get reciprocal treatment in
the future. She is still proud to recall that nothing except the meat
(one water buffalo and one cow) and some beverage ingredients had
to be purchased. Total expenditures were almost equaled by the
guest gifts. Generous portions were served; 300 packets of glutinous
rice and 12 dozen red eggs were distributed. The feast was a magnificent success. Aminah's mother had been very generous with her
time, efforts, and food gifts through the years, and her generosity
was recalled and repaid.

The activities pertaining to marriage have religious, social,
economic, and legal aspects. A rodat performance or other public
entertainment adds a recreational aspect that can also be seen in
the gatherings for the wedding feast and other ceremonies. The villagers look forward to the festivities and enjoy participating in them.
At the same time they may feel an obligation to participate and to
assist in preparations. Mauss (1967:37-41) wrote of "the three obligations: giving, receiving and repaying." All are expressed in
daily life in the village but emphasized in ceremonial activity. Assistance, attendance, and gifts are given and received, and will be
repaid in the future when the giver is involved in similar preparations, or are repayment for past assistance.

Reciprocal behavior is embedded in the Malay value system
and is summed up in the concept gotong royong (cooperation or mutual assistance), which finds expression when women work together
preparing feast foods or when men participate in a house raising.
The person who is generous is admired and referred to as a good
person, while the individual who regularly fails to reciprocate is

labeled as stingy or lazy. In a village the size of Rusila, everyone knows from personal experience or gossip who is cooperative and who is difficult, who is generous and who is mean, although there is not always 100 percent consensus about who merits which designation.

It was shown that mate selection patterns are changing. The same holds true for some marriage events and rituals.

The bride's home is decorated, with plastic flowers and other purchased things sometimes replacing the traditional handmade crepe-paper ornaments. Strings of tiny colored lights have become popular as a greater number of homes have been wired for electricity.

The procession of a groom's kinswomen bearing gifts to his fiancée's home is usually held when the families live near one another. When they do not, gifts are delivered informally. And it is becoming common for the young couple to receive wedding presents, such as sets of tumblers, vases, and the like, from their friends.

The akhad nikah is unchanged, and may well become the sole wedding ceremony if the bersanding continues to fall into disfavor. When the bersanding is held, it may differ from the traditional in some way. One bride showed me photographs of her 1978 ceremony: she was attired in a white satin gown and Western-style bridal veil, although her husband wore the customary male garb.

Photographers, professionals or local amateurs, are now active at all of the events, and wedding albums are popular.

The wedding feast is still important to villagers, and an avenue of prestige for the bride's parents when it is exceptionally well prepared and well attended.

An entertainment event is no longer considered mandatory, although it is expected if the bride's parents are affluent. It is said that there are fewer rodat troupes available today, and that they are expensive to hire and to transport. Films have been shown in two villages nearer the town, but no one in Rusila has yet sponsored a cinema.

Quran reading by the bride is held when the young woman can perform creditably.

Since the early 1970s honeymoon trips to other parts of Malaysia, Singapore, and Indonesia have become the norm among the educated and others who hold wage-paying jobs, but are not universal.

The traditional viewing of the bride in the groom's village is usually held in one form or another. Among the educated the bride is no longer set apart, but she is still expected to act demurely. Women who have wage-paying or salaried jobs, or whose husbands are regularly employed, find it incongruous to accept money from the visitors, so the cloth-covered dish may be absent.

In the middle 1960s parents and children followed long-established traditions, and everyone knew what to expect. Today there is a range of alternatives and the young have more influence in making choices from among them. One thing has not changed: a woman keeps her own (her father's) name, regardless of marital status.

FAMILIES

Marriage legitimizes sexual relations between a married pair and establishes a new family of procreation, but does not necessarily herald the beginning of a new household. In the 1950s and 1960s newlyweds always lived with the parents of bride or groom for at least one or two years, and sometimes as long as a dozen years, before they were able to set up a separate household. They were very young and without economic resources; parents were reluctant to help finance a separate home until they thought the marriage was stable. Parents also could exert more influence on children living with them, sometimes using the child and in-law as underpaid or unpaid workers on family landholdings. Today some couples follow the pattern of residing with parents, but a few are building homes even before they marry.

When newlyweds do live with parents, choice of family tends to be expedient, based on a husband's economic opportunities and the personal preferences of those concerned, a pattern referred to as ambilocal residence. Because of the close affective ties between mothers and daughters, a young wife usually prefers to live with her parents because she and her mother have well-established cooperative patterns and the daughter can be incorporated into her mother's mutual-aid network, taking her place among women she already knows. Such an uxorilocal bias was found in five of eight 1966 examples. But perhaps a young woman's in-laws are alone while her parents have younger children still at home, or her father-in-law in another village owns a fishing boat and her husband is part of the crew. Then they will more likely live with his parents.

The most common residence form is still ambilocal, in the broad sense that the average newly married couple locates its home in the natal village of one or the other, normally in the same neighborhood where parents are living. But the lineally extended family created when a married couple joins the household of parents has become an interlude, existing for shorter and shorter periods of time, if at all. The extended bilateral kinship network known as the kindred continues to be important to villagers. Young married couples want to have their own homes, but they prefer to settle

where they have parents and other relatives nearby. Independence
is combined with social security in its most basic form, the underlying assumption being that close kin are concerned about an individual's welfare.

Ambilocality is also seen in the movement of some families
within the village. Hasnah and Amin, for example, began married
life in the home of his father and stepmother in 1950. They had
several children before they were able to afford to buy a small
house that they moved to her mother's land. When his father died
in 1969, they inherited the house where they had lived as newlyweds,
and shortly afterward had the opportunity to rent their own home to
a teacher from another state. Hasnah and Amin moved back to the
neighborhood where his brother and two sisters have their homes,
on land that originally belonged to their father. In 1976 the couple
sold that house (but not the house land) and returned to the one on
Hasnah's mother's land, land that Hasnah will eventually inherit.
When Hasnah and Amin's children are ready to build their homes,
one or two will be able to locate near patri-kin and others near their
parents' present home and matri-kin.

Looking at the points of origin of married persons living in
Rusila in 1966 and 1979, some changes are notable (see Table 5.1).
In 1966 there were 120 married couples and 58 examples (48 percent) where both husband and wife were from Rusila. By 1979, of
165 married couples, 56 (34 percent) were both from Rusila. Among
persons who are under 40 years of age (98 couples), 27 percent of
the couples are both from the village.

There has been an increase in the local men marrying women
from other places but settling in Rusila, from 28 percent in 1966 to
35 percent in 1979. The percentage of Rusila women with husbands
from other places has changed little (18 percent in 1966; 19 percent
in 1979), although the number of women with husbands who are not
from Rusila rose from 22 to 32. The great majority of spouses who
"married in" are from villages within ten miles of Rusila, and most
come from places not more than five miles away. Similarly, the
women and men who settle in other places after marriage are mostly
located in half a dozen villages near Rusila.

When it was typical for newlyweds to live with the parents of
one or the other, a slight uxorilocal bias was noted. Where separate
households are established, a virilocal bias is evident. It existed
in 1966 and gained strength by 1979, although some men from other
places did settle uxorilocally. The availability of house land appears
to be the basic determinant of who settles where.

In one Rusila hamlet, for example, there are now six houses
in a section where in 1966 there had been three. The original house
and a sizable piece of land belong to Abdul Razak. His eldest son

TABLE 5.1

Points of Origin of Married Persons: Rusila, 1966 and 1979

	Rusila				Within 10 Miles				Beyond 10 Miles				Total			
	1966		1979		1966		1979		1966		1979		1966		1979	
	No.	%	No.	%	No.	%	No.	%	No.	%	No.	%	No.	%	No.	%
Wife	22*	18	32	19	25*	21	49	30	9*	8	13	8	56	47	94	57
Husband	34*	28	58	35	8	7	20	12	14*	12	16	10				
Both	58*	48	56*	34	2	2	10	6	4	3	5	3	64	53	71	43
Total													120	100	165	100

*Polygynous unions with both wives residents of Rusila; each * equals one union. Thus, in 1966, there were 120 married couples and 120 married women, but only 116 married men; in 1979 there were 165 couples and married women, but only 163 married men.

and daughter built their homes on his land prior to 1966. By 1979 three more children—two sons and a daughter—had married and accepted their father's offer to loan them house land, with the understanding that each will inherit the plots on which they built. The eldest son and daughter married other Rusila people; the next two sons wed women from nearby villages and brought their wives to Rusila; one daughter "married out" and now lives in a contiguous village; a third daughter married a local man and settled near her parents. In all cases one spouse had immediate access to land because Abdul Razak was willing to parcel his land and to agree that the child who built on it would inherit it. The husband of the daughter who "married out" already owned suitable land in his village. Abdul Razak and his wife have one daughter who is not yet married. There appears to be no room for an additional house. Where will the youngest daughter live? They will be content if she lives with them after marriage, but they recognize that such an arrangement is unlikely. Abdul Razak says that after he and his wife die, the two daughters who have not built nearby will inherit the parental home and the plot on which it stands, because the other children already have homes and house land. Either daughter might live there. Even when a woman appears to be nicely settled in her husband's village, life is unpredictable. The husband might divorce her or he might die. It is good if she has a place near her siblings in case she needs it. If she does not need it, she can loan it to a niece or nephew or, later, one of her children can live there.

Generation by generation land fragmentation occurs because partible inheritance is the Islamic rule, with all children having rights to the property of both mother and father. Men are defined as the supporters of their families, so under Islamic law a son receives twice the amount due to a daughter. Malay adat modifies the law. In the example of Abdul Razak and his children, the three sons and four daughters have been (or will be) treated more or less equitably with regard to house land. Productive land is another matter, but accommodations among heirs are common and involve consideration for the needs of a widowed mother and siblings as well as the location and type of property.

Table 5.1 also shows 15 instances (9 percent) where both spouses were born outside of Rusila. Notably, in 11 cases one spouse has a parent (or grandparent) who was born in Rusila and inherited land there, land on which a child can build or work. Among those who marry out of Rusila, it is not unusual for a person to return to a grandparent's natal village where there is access to land now owned by a parent.

Increasingly, young couples with above-average education are settling neolocally as more persons get jobs outside the village and

the state. There are now people from Rusila working in almost
every state in the Federation, a majority in the Federal Territory
of Kuala Lumpur, Pahang, and Kelantan. Some of them are content
in their new milieus, but others look forward to returning to
Trengganu and several have bought house land in the village. Two
male teachers, after working in other states, have secured transfers to local schools and have built homes near those of parents.
Similarly, three young women (two police officers and one teacher)
from other states who were assigned to posts in Trengganu told me
they would apply for transfers to their home areas as soon as they
qualified to do so.

There were 134 households in Rusila in 1965 and 192 in 1979.
Each household can be seen as comprising a family of some type.
A nuclear family is defined as a married couple with or without unmarried children, while a subnuclear family is a fragment of a former nuclear family. An extended family is one composed of three
generations related by consanguineal ties: parents, their unmarried
children, a married child, and his or her spouse and their children.
A supplement to a family is any unmarried household member who
is not a child of the married couple or couples, such as an unmarried sibling or a grandchild. A polygynous family is one in which a
wife shares her husband with a co-wife although each woman is separately domiciled. Individuals who live alone are single-person
families (Freed and Freed 1969; Murdock 1960).

Utilizing the basic categories of nuclear, subnuclear, and extended, plus the qualifications of supplements and polygynous unions,
nine family types can be distinguished in the village.

Nuclear families accounted for 59.7 percent (N = 80) of the
total families in 1965-66 and for 75.5 percent (N = 145) in 1979 (see
Table 5.2). The significant increase is due to several changes.

Greater affluence has allowed newly married couples to move
into their own homes immediately or within a brief period of time,
making the lineally extended family less common. There has also
been a decrease in the number of polygynous unions (see Chapter 6).
The remarriage of several women who, with their children, were
subnuclear families in 1966 has shifted them back into the nuclear
family category.

An examination of family types alone does not reveal that all
single-person families are female (older widows or divorcées whose
children have established their own households), or that a majority
of the families with a single adult (subnuclear and supplemented subnuclear) are headed by women (18 of the 21 instances). The latter,
too, are widows or divorcées, but with children still living at home
and grandchildren or other kin as part of the household. The persons who supplement a family, in the order of decreasing frequency,

are grandchildren (most often granddaughters, because they can
assume more household duties), an aging mother or grandmother
(usually the wife's kin, because she has the most responsibility for
their care), a divorced daughter, a younger sibling, or, in two examples, a combination. Widowers remarry, taking younger wives,
and are therefore rarely found as members of a child's or grandchild's household. There was one male elder living as part of a
son's family in 1965; there was no instance in 1979.

TABLE 5.2

Rusila Family Types: 1965/66, 1979

Family Type	1965-66		1979	
	No.	Percent	No.	Percent
Nuclear	80	59.7	145	75.5
Supplemented nuclear	16	11.9	11	5.7
Subnuclear	7	5.2	4	2.1
Supplemented subnuclear	9	6.7	17	8.9
Lineal extended	5	3.8	1	0.5
Supplemented lineal extended	3	2.2	1	0.5
Polygynous	5	3.8	4	2.1
Supplemented polygynous	3	2.2	1	0.5
Single-person	6	4.5	8	4.2
Total	134	100.0	192	100.0

Families are dynamic. At different points in a diachronic
sequence, any family changes, gaining or losing members. Hindun
and Husein, for example, marry and join the household of Hindun's
parents for an indefinite period of time, creating a lineally extended
family. After a few years they and their two children move to their
own home, establishing a separate household and a new nuclear family. Then Husein's parents decide to move to another village where
the husband has recently inherited property. Their teenage son
joins his older brother's household/family on a semipermanent basis
so as to continue his secondary education in the area. The family
can be defined as supplemented nuclear until the younger brother
leaves the household a few years later. Husein takes a second wife,
and his family becomes redefined as polygynous. Husein dies;

Hindun and her children now are a subnuclear family. Each change requires some readjustment of existing relationships, creates different sets of rights and obligations, and has other social as well as economic repercussions.

From Hindun's perspective she begins married life in a familiar milieu, her parents' home, under the direction of her mother, sharing a food budget and cooperating in household chores. Everyone in the household must accommodate to the presence of Husein and his relationship with Hindun, as well as to her new status as a married woman. Then Hindun becomes the mistress of an independent household, and her decision-making role is enormously expanded; she is juggling finances and taking full responsibility for the daily welfare and care of children and husband. Her brother-in-law's incorporation into the household and family requires further changes. Hindun's relationship with her husband becomes outwardly more formal because it is less private. The young man can be helpful in many ways, but his presence also adds to Hindun's chores. Husein must act in loco parentis, which sometimes leads to conflict between him and his brother. Hindun has the role of subtle mediator, not openly involved in the difficulties but building bridges of understanding between opposing viewpoints and maintaining a harmonious home.

When Husein takes a second wife, Hindun has a half-time husband, their children have a half-time father, and the household must be run on half of the previous income. The economic and parental burden increases when Husein dies and Hindun must assume total responsibility for her children's welfare. If Hindun's parents are still living, she may return to their home with her children or expect her father (or a brother) to perform some aspects of the paternal role vis-à-vis her children even if she maintains a separate household. And if she is under 40 years of age, she will probably marry again within a year or two.

The labels give clues to the social realities of different types of family configurations that affect the lives of the individuals who function within them. Living as part of an extended family is not the same as running one's own home; living with a husband who is monogamous is different from being a co-wife. But the labels only give clues about any family and the individual lives of its members, and then only at specific points in time.

One way of examining a woman's position in the family is through her basic familial roles: daughter, sister, wife, and mother. Each role exists in relation to others: as daughter to mother, daughter to father, and daughter to parents as a couple. Is a daughter the first child or the sixth? Her birth order can determine many aspects of her life. In some families, for example, eldest daughters

receive no education beyond the primary level because they are
needed at home to care for younger siblings and to take other household responsibilities; younger sisters go on to secondary school. Is
a female the first daughter when there are already several sons, or
the fourth daughter when there are no sons? Children of both sexes
are wanted and loved by the average Malay parent but a sexual mix
is preferred, so the third or fourth daughter in a row may generate
much less enthusiasm than the first or second.

A daughter's public behavior is judged more stringently than
a son's actions. If a teenage girl and boy who are not close kin are
observed chatting together, both may be criticized by parents (and
others) for behaving in an unseemly manner but "she is not malu"
(has no sense of shame, of what is appropriate) or "she is bodoh"
(foolish), while "he is budak kacau" (a bad boy in the semijocular
sense that is accompanied by a smile and a what–can–one–do? ges-
ture). It is a mother's duty to train all of her children to behave
properly, but she is most concerned with how her daughters act.
A family's women bear its honor.

Ideal behavior for her potential roles as wife and mother is
inculcated in a girl during her early years. She learns, through
being daughter and sister, attitudes and behavior patterns for a lifetime. She is taught to be dutiful, self-effacing, and modest; to have
a strong sense of the proper way to comport herself, particularly in
the presence of men; and to know that her behavior reflects on her
parents and other family members.

A daughter learns child care through looking after younger
siblings or cousins, and to perform household chores through doing
them. She will have those responsibilities as wife and mother, so
she should be trained for them from an early age. Simultaneously
she learns that a woman's primary goal is to be a wife and mother,
and that whatever else she might be is secondary. If a young woman
is a hard worker, her mother will be credited; if she is lazy or
slovenly, it is assumed that her mother was remiss in training her.
Or one might hear a statement such as "Her mother died when she
was small and her grandmother spoiled her." Or "She behaves that
way because her stepmother had no interest in her." A daughter
also learns to be immediately responsive to her father's requests
and to try to please him. If she does not, her mother is at fault.
When villagers criticize the behavior of a child, they may see both
parents as responsible, but the mother invariably bears more of the
brunt than the father.

Young women who do not continue their education beyond primary school learn to be economically productive outside the home
as well as to make their contributions within it. Some girls of 12
or 14 are proficient mat and basket weavers who can earn money for

their wares as well as produce things needed for household use.
Girls in their late teens may take the full responsibility of care for
younger siblings to free a mother for work outside the home, or
take their places side by side with a mother transplanting or harvesting rice. They are trained not only to run a household but also
to help support it through agricultural and other labor (paid and unpaid) and through remunerative work of various kinds.

This is an important point. Married women are expected to
be obedient to their husbands and to continue being modest and self-
effacing. At the same time they assume the responsibility for managing their households, including serving as the treasurers, and
also earn money in their own right. Thus the ideal of obedience to
husband is balanced by the real responsibilities that encourage independence of action on the wife's part. Both women and men talk
about a wife's obedience more than they expect or practice it in the
family milieu.

A wife is supposed to obtain her husband's permission to absent herself from the home, but she usually goes about her work in
the fields, visits kin and friends, shops in the town, or takes produce to market without permission being sought or given. The average husband has a fairly good idea of what his wife's plans and
obligations are, and he does not want to be bothered with details.
If he does want to know, she should account for herself. He, on the
other hand, does not have to account for himself. But he also has a
routine known to his wife, and should he deviate from it without explanation, he may find himself eating yesterday's leftover rice.

In terms of accountability ideals, the family can be viewed as
a pyramid composed of levels, lower levels being accountable to the
ones above, with the father/husband at the apex, the mother/wife
below him, and the children at the bottom, accountable to mother
and father, with mother often playing a mediating role between the
levels. The pyramid image will not take us further because there
is a triple standard of behavior for children. Preschool-age children of either sex are not accountable for many of the things they do,
and can make demands on parents that an older child cannot. Among
older children there is a double standard of behavior by sex, with
boys being far less accountable than girls. A son of 17 or 18 may
absent himself from home for a day (or more) without informing his
parents. Such behavior on the part of a daughter is unthinkable.
She must return home directly after her classes end; she does not
even visit a friend in the village without her mother's permission.
Her virginity must be protected, from her own sexual urges as well
as the seduction of men, for sexual desire is normal to both.

There is, however, a category of sexual behavior that is not
normal: incest. The forbidden relationships are explicitly stated
in the Quran:

> Forbidden unto you are your mothers, and your daugh-
> ters, and your sisters, and your father's sisters, and
> your mother's sisters, and your brother's daughters
> and your sister's daughters, and your foster-mothers,
> and your foster-sisters, and your mothers-in-law, and
> your stepdaughters who are under your protection (born)
> of your women unto whom ye have gone in—but if ye
> have not gone in unto them, then it is no sin for you (to
> marry their daughters)—and the wives of your sons who
> (spring) from your own loins. And (it is forbidden unto
> you) that ye shall have two sisters together, except
> what hath already happened (of that nature) in the past.
> Lo! Allah is ever Forgiving, Merciful (Pickthall
> 1959:81-82).

In Rusila only a few people, both women and men, were asked in 1966 for information about incest. Most denied the possibility of such sinful behavior; a few admitted to knowing of one incident that had happened before World War II. A man, now deceased, allegedly seduced his wife's unmarried, younger sister while she was living in his home and, therefore, under his protection. When these lim-ited discussions took place, I was struck by the general nervousness of informants: they first looked outside to see if anyone was nearby, and then lowered their voices to whispers. Initially I thought that incest must be a terrible, unthinkable relationship to them. That certainly was the reaction of everyone to the idea of incest within the nuclear family. They were not shocked by the relationship in the example given me, although it is forbidden, but by the fact that the man had betrayed a trust by taking advantage of a virgin woman who had the right to his protection. Their nervousness was engen-dered by fear of being overheard by kin of the persons involved, for any of them would feel shamed to have the incident recalled.

My discussion thus far makes family relationships appear very serious: members are accountable, have obligations, responsibili-ties, and duties. Husbands and wives also develop deep and strong affective feelings (I hesitate to use the word "love" only because of its possible romantic connotation, a connotation that lacks reality among older Rusila villagers), cooperate in many ways that indicate a full sharing of responsibility, and enjoy joking with and teasing one another. There is often a relaxed and joyful aspect to family life, a flexibility that accepts the unexpected, and a more-the-merrier ac-commodation of kin and friends. A daughter, her husband, their three children, the husband's parents, and a younger sibling arrive unexpectedly for a three-day holiday, to give one example. Every-one is delighted and goes into action: buying food, borrowing bedding, rearranging use of space, sending some of the children to spend the night with grandmother or other kin. The spontaneous nature of the visit is accepted and enjoyed to the utmost.

The same flexibility normally prevails where there are supplements to a family, accommodation occurring without any indication that it is burdensome. That families can and do expand for a few days or a few years is a function of the use of household space and the perception of what constitutes privacy.

Privacy in a village home is more a state of mind than access to unshared space. A need for solitude can be met by taking a walk, appearing to nap, performing a chore outdoors when everyone else is inside, or going to the well to bathe when no one else is about. The need for private space to which no one else has access suggests the possibility of unacceptable behavior. If one is not behaving in an unacceptable way, why should others be excluded? If no one has an exclusive right to any particular space, then use of what is available can be rearranged as needed without anyone feeling displaced. This is not to suggest lack of patterning: parents usually have a double bed where they sleep; prepubescent children may sleep together with an older sister; older brothers sleep in another part of the house. In one family the eldest son has claimed a narrow single bed as his own; two of his younger brothers sleep on the floor nearby. But when the eldest goes squid fishing at night, the bed does not remain empty. Older brother's claim to the bed is good only while he is in it. And during the day anyone uses the sleeping areas for other activities—playing, doing homework, making something, performing prayers.

The concept of privacy and use of space is changing. During the 1960s everyone bathed publicly and urinated or defecated on the beach or in the bush, albeit with extreme decorum and modesty. Today outhouse toilets are common, and bathing rooms and toilets inside the home are preferred. A few of the more affluent villagers have built large houses with interior space divided by permanent walls (rather than cloth or woven partitions), creating rooms with doors that close. Exclusivity in the use of space still is not the norm, but privacy is assuming a spatial dimension. The long-term result may well be a diminished flexibility in accommodating kin who now are readily accepted as family supplements.

Like the preindustrial family in the West, the traditional rural Malay family incorporated a variety of functions and continues to control some of them. Marriage legitimizes a sexual relationship between a man and woman; their children are born into a family of one type or another. The parents assume the major responsibility for early socialization of their children, but the secular government schools provide formal education from age six. Religious teachers were active before secular schooling was available, and they continue

Figure 4. Family Cooperation (Rusila, 1966). Awang re-placing palm trunk sections with cement house support blocks while Selamah, his wife, and three of their children provide leverage.

to take part in the educational process. The family was, and for many still is, the basic unit of production, with wider kinship and friendship networks making some productive contributions. Homes, for example, can be built from local materials, with village men working collectively at house raising and women preparing food for all of the workers. But today professional carpenters, plumbers, and other experts are much in evidence. They are paid in cash rather than kind. Social welfare functions in the care of the aged, the ill, the handicapped, and the mentally disturbed once resided in the family, with some assistance from the kindred and possibly the entire village community. Now hospitalization, government training programs for the handicapped, and state welfare assistance programs take full responsibility or at least supplement family efforts.

Family functions have decreased as more of them have been as-sumed by state agencies and influenced by an expanding market econ-omy. Thus two results of development have been increasing interac-tion between villagers and nonvillagers, and the dependency of vil-lagers on nonvillagers and the government bureaucratic structure. The family as a unit has become less self-sufficient.

6
POLYGYNY AND DIVORCE

Two practices have far-reaching effects on many Malaysian families: polygyny and divorce. The latter is far more common than the former, but both practices are ones over which a woman has had very little, if any, control, and either usually imposes an economic burden on her.

The two legal systems—Muslim and civil—that regulate marriage (whether monogamous or polygynous) and some family matters also delineate divorce rights and processes. Within the civil system the law has been liberalized, although not yet implemented, in favor of women's rights; the fundamentalist Muslim influence has effected a much stricter application of the Islamic code, with its pro-male bias.

That the two legal systems exist side by side is a function of the government's attempt to maintain the delicate balance among the several ethnic communities, upholding Islamic norms for Muslims while trying not to alienate the non-Muslim Chinese, Indians, and native peoples who account for approximately half of the nation's population.

National statistics show that divorce and polygyny are more common among Muslims than non-Muslims in Malaysia. But the numbers and percentages are less important than the effect that either practice can have on individual lives and families, whatever their religious affiliation.

In Rusila, despite differences between and among married couples, every woman is aware of the possibility that her husband can take another wife, just as she knows that he can easily repudiate her. This awareness can affect the way in which a married woman relates to her husband and to other women, and fosters her

perception of young divorcées as dangerous competition. The threat
of both practices is always present, implicitly if not explicitly.
Thus it is the possibilities, the potentials, as much as local instances of divorce and polygyny that affect a woman's thinking and
behavior.

POLYGYNY

The Law Reform (Marriage and Divorce) Act, 1975, makes
polygyny illegal in Malaysia—except for Muslims, among whom the
practice is most widespread. Polygynous unions contracted by non-
Muslims before the law went into effect are recognized as valid.

The Johore Legislative Assembly approved the Administration
of Islamic Law Enactment, 1978 on December 13 of that year.
Among the provisions is one allowing a Muslim male to take a second wife without the first wife's consent. Prior to the enactment
Johore was one state where the first wife's agreement was needed.
The law went into effect on February 2, 1979, although women's organizations had urged the government not to enact it. A spokesman
for the Johore government discounted the women's pleas as "based
on emotion" rather than the teachings of Islam (NST 11/21/78).

Under the enactment a Muslim male in Johore who wishes to
take a second (or third or fourth) wife must apply to the Chief Kadi
of the Syariah Court in the state for permission, showing that he
has the financial means to support more than one wife. There is a
further provision that wives must be treated equally. A man who
fails to do so is liable to as much as three months in jail and a
$500 fine.

In the state of Kedah, the Chief Kadi reported receiving letters from women requesting that their husbands not be allowed to
take second wives. He said that the State Religious Council would
not consider restricting Muslim males to one wife, but would issue
permission only after careful study of an application (NST 11/28/78).

Datin Paduka Hajjah Aishah Ghani, Minister of Welfare Services, supported the idea that Muslim men could take more than one
wife without the first wife's consent (NST 12/22/78). She might
have remained mute on the subject, but had she made a negative
statement, it could have affected her political career. She did,
however, emphasize the circumstances in which such action was acceptable: A man should have to obtain written permission from the
syariah court, permission that would be based on his financial situation, commitments, and responsibilities, including the number of
dependents he would have following the marriage. The Welfare Minister said that men should have valid reasons, such as barrenness

of the first wife, her incapacity to have sexual relations, or her refusal of conjugal rights to her husband (Ibid.).

A woman's physical incapacity to have a sexual relationship
may be established fairly easily—for example, if she has a prolonged and debilitating illness or suffers permanent disability from
an accident. Barrenness is assumed if a woman does not produce
offspring. She—or her husband—is barren, but the likely assumption (among villagers at least) is that it is she who is physically
flawed. Whoever has the problem, it can be shown that the union
has produced no children. The claim that a wife has refused her
husband his conjugal "rights" is the reason most open to abuse, for
how can it be proved that a woman denies her husband's "rights"?
To take a hypothetical example, a man requests permission from
syariah court to take another wife because his present wife, whom
he does not wish to divorce, refuses to have sexual intercourse
with him. How can the Chief Kadi make a judgment that this is in
fact the case? The two people who know about this intimate relationship are husband and wife: one of them claims that there is no
sexual relationship. And the one making the claim is also the one
who is acknowledged as guardian of wife and home; he is in a super-
ordinate position to her, and has the right (not shared by the wife)
to a very easy divorce. The husband's claim is likely to be accepted.
However, the first wife can bring the case to court "if she believes
that by marrying another woman her husband sought to injure her"
(Shaltout 1958:121).

Many Muslims speak against polygyny when they are among
friends, but would be reluctant to make a public statement against
the practice as individuals because it is allowed by Islam, and therefore opposition could be construed as anti-Islamic. With open opposition to polygyny thus precluded, women can only work to encourage
the adoption of stricter control of the practice by the syariah courts
and State Religious Councils, although any form of permission system is obviously open to abuse.

Many would agree that

[where] polygamy . . . is legalized in the marriage institution, a woman's position is automatically relegated
below that of the man. Her subordinate position becomes
both socially and legally recognized. To abolish . . .
polygamy is therefore one of the first steps to upgrade
a woman's status before the law . . . (Chung and Meng
1977:9).

The Law Reform (Marriage and Divorce Act, 1975, making
polygyny illegal among non-Muslims, should eventually serve to

decrease polygynous unions, particularly in those areas of the country where non-Muslims are concentrated (the cities). But another factor must be taken into consideration: there has been a growing interest in and adherence to Muslim fundamentalism since the early 1970s. Fundamentalism promotes "letter of the law" interpretations of the Islamic legal code, and thus affects all Muslims. One example, mentioned above, is the provision in the Administration of Islamic Law Enactment, 1978, passed by the Johore State Legislative Assembly, which allows a man to take a second wife without his first wife's consent.

The overall statistical picture thus may change very little during the 1980s as one trend or change in the law balances another. However, within religious categories legal polygyny will lessen and finally disappear among non-Muslims, while fundamentalism could encourage the proliferation of polygynous unions among Muslims.

POLYGYNY IN RUSILA

The population of Rusila is 100 percent Muslim; of the 120 married men in Rusila in 1965, only six (5 percent) were polygynists. None had the four wives allowed by Islam. One man had three wives; the others had two each. None of the co-wives shared living quarters. Three men admitted to prior polygynous unions, but they had divorced second wives and remained married to their first wives.

By 1979 four of the six polygynists had died, leaving two men in their seventies, each married to the same women who had been their wives in 1965. Another villager had married a second wife and one newcomer to the village, a middle-aged townsman, is also a polygynist. The total number of married men had increased to 170, while the number of polygynists was reduced by one-third. However, during the 14-year interim several other men had brief polygynous unions before divorcing one of the wives, usually the second.

Where details of these divorces are known, there is one common factor: strong disapproval of his second marriage by a man's kin—parents, siblings, and adult children. Younger siblings and children have no right to be critical of elder brother or parent, but if they are strong-minded, they may speak. One young man, when he learned of his father's second marriage, took leave from work and returned to his home village from another part of the country, in order to give his mother moral support. He went so far as to tell his father that should he remain married to the second wife, he (the son) would have no further contact with him. The father eventually divorced the second wife and remained married to the youth's mother, but it is unclear how much influence was exerted on him and by whom.

Polygyny alters existing family structure because the husband-father becomes a part-time member of the unit. Among Malays it is usual for each wife to be separately domiciled with her children. The male, constrained by law to treat his wives equally, is expected to divide his time between them. He is also expected to divide his income, his concern, his attentions, and affections. "Islam stipulates that [a man] may have not more than one wife unless he is able to discharge the rights of each wife and maintain absolute equity between them" (Shaltout 1958:121). Absolute equity is impossible. That this is so was used by educated Singaporean Malays to argue that "the Prophet indirectly banned polygyny" (Djamour 1965:83, 87). No one in Rusila ever suggested that explanation, but all recognize the great difficulty, if not the impossibility, of a man's treating co-wives equally.

In 1965, Haji Mohammed, recently divorced from his first wife, lived with his third and visited his second wife in another village only one afternoon per week. His behavior was criticized covertly by both women and men, who said he would be condemned to a grim, lopsided existence in the next world because he had not treated his wives equally in this one.

Other examples were not so obvious, and therefore fostered less gossip. Ismail was punctilious with his time, spending three days and nights with each of his three wives and then beginning the cycle over again. But one of his sons felt that he was unfair with his money, spending a disproportionate amount on his most recent and youngest wife and leaving his first wife, the youth's mother, heavily reliant on what she could earn from mat weaving, copra production, and rice planting. A man's most recent wife usually holds a privileged position vis-à-vis his other spouse(s), at least for a few months.

The only woman who ever spoke positively about polygyny to me had once been the youngest and most recent wife of a prosperous man who lived in a town about 50 miles south of Rusila. She sometimes reminisced about the nice home she had had and the leisurely days when there was little to do except housekeeping and visiting her neighbors—far different from her present situation, supporting a husband who hasn't earned more than a few dollars in any given month for the past five years. The contrast between the two situations made the earlier one sound even better in 1979 than when she talked about it in 1965. Regardless, she still acknowledges that the polygynous marriage might not have been so pleasant if her husband had been less prosperous or if she had been the first wife.

There is only one case of polygyny known to me in Rusila and nearby villages where a man informed his first wife of his intent to take a second one. Usually she finds out afterward. If circumstances allow, the tendency is for a man to keep the second or subsequent union secret for as long as possible. The first wife may be among the last people in the village to hear the news, because friends avoid telling her for fear of being perceived as troublemakers.

Aishah had been married for almost 22 years and had borne six children when she learned that her husband, Mahmoud, had taken a second wife, a young divorcée living in another village, almost two months previously. Mahmoud kept his secret so long because his work took him out of Rusila at different times, day and night, and occasionally for several days at a time. Aishah's suspicions developed because he was away from home more frequently, apparently working, yet he was giving her less money with which to run the household. At first she believed his explanation that he had not yet been paid for the work done, but as the weeks passed, that excuse wore thin. She probably had other clues to the new reality but was loath to accept them. She confronted him and learned the truth.

During the months that followed, Aishah literally made herself ill from worrying about finances. There were five children living at home, four of them attending school and one below primary school age. Even before Mahmoud's second marriage Aishah—like most village women—had been juggling finances to meet the family's needs while trying to save a few dollars for unanticipated expenses or emergencies, but the financial situation was stable enough that she had been able to reduce her own remunerative work after the birth of her youngest child and devote more time to the family and home. After Mahmoud's second marriage, household income dropped drastically and the problems of significantly supplementing it once again fell to Aishah. She was soon convinced that Mahmoud was not giving her a fair share of his income, but there was no way for her to prove her contention because he, like a majority of village men, receives earnings on an irregular basis.

Aishah felt angry toward Mahmoud, but most of her negative feelings were for the other wife, whom she strongly suspected of using magical means to get a husband, another woman's husband— her husband. The "blame the other woman" reaction is not unique to Rusila. Western readers will recognize it as having validity in their own societies. Aishah was constrained to find mitigating circumstances for Mahmoud's behavior, circumstances that allowed her to see him as victimized and thus to maintain her own self-respect. Magic that pulls a man to another woman can be ranked very high among mitigating circumstances.

Aishah had worked hard for 20 years, and was finally enjoying reduced responsibilities for household support when she was thrust back into the financial situation of her younger years because of a "wicked woman" (perempuan jahat). On one occasion Aishah encountered her co-wife while shopping in the Kuala Trengganu market, and publicly denounced her as an evil husband stealer. The younger woman fled, followed by laughter and catcalls from some of the market women, who had been dealing with Aishah for years and sympathized with her feelings and to whom the younger woman was an outsider.

As well as Aishah's anger, Mahmoud had to deal with a wall of disapproval, mostly unstated but nevertheless obvious, from his mother, mother-in-law, other in-laws, siblings, and older children. All of these reactions apparently pushed him into spending more time with his second wife, but she began pressuring him to divorce Aishah. He refused, knowing his kin would be outraged and fearful of what Aishah might do. She had already told him that should he divorce her, she would take the children and secretly move to another part of the country where he would never find them.

Mahmoud divorced the second wife after about eight months of living polygynously. Among the villagers who knew the details of the triangle, some women as well as men were critical of Aishah, pointing out that a man has the right to take more than one wife and that it is his first wife's duty to accept it. Other women admired her. Aishah ignored the gossip; she had gotten her husband back as a full-time member of the family and his income, however variable, was no longer split between two households. Aishah is an unusual woman. Most women whose husbands have taken other wives have accepted the situation stoically and worked harder to compensate for the decreased financial support.

"If a man takes a second wife, it is better if neither wife knows about the other." A village woman made this remark after a neighbor had been teasing her about her husband's prolonged absence from the village and suggesting that perhaps he had met someone else. If so, she felt there was nothing she could do about it, and she did not want to know about it. In 1965 only a few men had jobs that took them away from the village for fairly long periods of time, a situation that would enable them to have secret marriages to women in other places. Today mobility has increased through improved transportation facilities, and more men have jobs that take them outside the village. But if any of them have contracted second marriages elsewhere, they have kept their secrets better than Mahmoud was able to do. In most cases lessened income over a period of more than a couple of months would alert a wife to the possibility of a husband's changed marital status, in spite of the common problem of fluctuating household finances.

Polygynous marriages are labeled by many women with monogamous husbands as <u>susah</u>, a term that covers a multitude of difficult,
worrisome, or unhappy situations. Many feel that their children
would suffer from not having a father's full interest and affection.
And if there were a co-wife who had children, the first wife's children would inherit a smaller portion of whatever a father owns. All
women know polygyny would increase their own financial burden because of the division of a husband's income. And, whatever the
reason for taking another wife, the first suffers some degree of
public humiliation because of his action.

Young Rusila villagers who have secondary school or higher
education were almost unanimously negative about polygyny in 1965
and continue to express the same attitudes today, viewing the practice as typical of the uneducated. Yet uneducated women and many
men share their negative attitudes, condoning polygyny only in exceptional circumstances, such as barrenness of a wife. A favorite
male response to the idea that polygyny is a village practice is that
only a rajah can afford more than one wife. Certainly more than
one member of Malay royalty is polygynous, as are some elite com-
moners.

Other researchers have reported on how few Malay men were
polygynous in the areas where they worked, giving poverty and the
difficulty of maintaining harmonious relationships with first wives
as the most common explanations (Djamour 1965:83-86; Rosemary
Firth 1966:48).

In Rusila the desire for harmonious relationships is a basic
value among the villagers. As a reason for monogamy it usually
emerges in half-joking/half-serious statements by men: "I am not
brave enough for two wives." or "Zaitun [his wife] would no longer
cook my rice." Still, some men are polygynous and the threat of
polygyny is ever-present.

Economically, even in 1965, some men who were monogamous
could have afforded two wives, assuming that both were partly self-
supporting, as is typically the case. Since then, economic conditions
in the village have improved generally, but not evenly, and fewer
men have more than one wife. There is a correlation between increasing urbanization, in the broad sense of urban values seeping
inexorably into the village, and a decrease in the number and percentage of polygynists. Had there been a very high number of polygynous men in 1965 and a great decrease by 1979, the urbanization-
modernization argument for the change would be an obvious one.

Some villagers think there have been few polygynous marriages
through the years because of the influence of the former imam. He
disapproved of polygyny unless there was compelling need, as in the
case of a barren wife whom a man did not want to divorce. Recount-

ing the good things he had done, one woman credited him with having influenced her husband against taking a second wife, and thought
that he had done the same for others. There is no doubt that he was
a devout, learned, and strong-willed person who never hesitated to
speak his mind to anyone or to act on his principles. And he set an
example: he married only once, and he remained married until his
death. His behavior contrasts with the stereotypic and possibly
accurate view of some well-educated Malays who think that village
religious leaders are the most likely men to be polygynous. It is
idle to speculate whether the polygyny rate in the area would have
been higher had the imam been a polygynist, but it would be interesting to compare polygyny rates in villages where the acknowledged
leaders, secular as well as religious, are polygynous with those
where they are monogamous. Unfortunately, such data are not
presently available.

The reasons why some men seek second wives are probably
diverse. I have already mentioned that barrenness of a wife is an
acceptable reason, but of the polygynists in the village, only one
took a second wife for this reason. She bore several children; the
first wife never became pregnant. The two women had what appeared to be a warm and friendly relationship. If the husband became ill in the home of one, the other was always called. When the
man died, both women were at his bedside and they cooperated fully
in funeral arrangements and afterward in holding commemoration
feasts. This is the only example known to me in Rusila and nearby
villages where co-wives had a harmonious relationship. Avoidance
is more usual. Other first wives had already borne between two and
ten children when their husbands became polygynists.

Another reason for a village man to take a second wife might
be increased prestige in the eyes of his peers, but this does not
seem to be the case. If polygynists expected to gain prestige, it is
unlikely that any of them would try to keep second marriages secret,
yet most of them do try. Also, if polygyny conferred prestige,
there should be a larger number of polygynous unions—whatever the
influence of the imam. I see no indication that marital status in and
of itself either enhances or detracts from a person's prestige.
Rather, it is the manner in which an individual establishes and maintains relationships, of whatever type, with others that can lead to
enhanced prestige.

Unlike some societies where the number of a man's wives reflects his importance and wealth (Hammond and Jablow 1976:108-09),
polygyny does not correlate with wealth among Malays in Rusila.
One polygynist had a higher-than-average income in 1965; the others
did not. In 1979 the men with the highest incomes were school-
teachers, who verbally reject polygyny. Certainly none of them

were known as polygynists and, considering their lifestyles and consumption patterns—fine homes, automobiles, and other expensive
goods—it is extremely unlikely that any of them could have maintained secret second wives. Both in 1965 and in 1979, it was not
polygyny, but the possession of expensive consumer goods locally
defined as modern, that was the means of indicating an elevated
financial position in the community.

If the rewards of polygyny are not social, and I see no evidence that they are, then they would seem to be personal: physical
and/or psychological. There is no local instance of a man's taking
a second wife because the first was physically incapacitated and
therefore unable to engage in sexual relations. And were a physically normal woman habitually to refuse to have sexual relations
with her husband, he would probably divorce her rather than take a
second wife. But polygyny as a "further sex outlet" (Rosemary
Firth 1966:55) is likely, especially when a man takes a much younger
woman as the second wife. More than a third of the polygynous
unions contracted by Rusila men have ended in divorce—most of a
subsequent wife rather than of the first wife. It seems that whatever the attraction of having two wives, and however sexually or
psychologically satisfying the experience may be, it is often short-
lived—it cannot stand up to the pressures, both overt and covert,
that polygyny engenders.

With the exception of the barren woman mentioned above, I
know of no woman who was agreeable to her husband's taking a second wife. But normally the woman who becomes a second or subsequent wife is a widow or divorcée, and she does have a choice.
Why does she agree?

It will be recalled that the one woman who spoke positively
about polygyny had been the second wife of a prosperous townsman
in another area; she remembers the period as the most leisurely of
her life. Her economic position was very good and, because the
husband was prosperous, the first wife did not suffer financially.
Polygyny usually increases the economic burden of the first wife
whose husband has an average income, but a second wife gains economically because she receives some income where previously she
was self-supporting. Moreover, in a society where marriage is the
normal concomitant of adulthood, it can be better to be married
polygynously than not at all: half of a husband (or less) is better
than none. Sexual appetite is viewed as normal, but illicit unions
are classed as both sinful and illegal. A woman may elect polygyny
as a legal, sinfree means of satisfying sexual needs when no other
marital options are available.

The second or subsequent wife is sometimes said to have used
magical means to get a man to marry her. Aishah believed this was

the explanation for Mahmoud's other marriage. Rosemary Firth points out that "in non-magical terms" this is the explanation when it is the woman who wants a sexual outlet and takes "the initiative" (1966:55). The magical interpretation removes some of the onus and humiliation from the first wife because her husband was helpless. If he was entrapped by magic, his taking a second wife is not due to any inadequacies of the first.

Magic can also be used by a man to influence a woman to become a second wife. Malays in Singapore believed that "no woman in her right mind would agree to being a co-wife and earning a living as well unless she were bewitched into doing so" (Djamour 1965:86). Locally there is no case of a second wife who does not have to make a substantial contribution to the support of her household or, in the case of the older triads, didn't have to do so at the time of the marriage. Magic has been suggested in some instances, foolishness in others, but only where the woman is thought to have made a bad bargain in more than just the economic sense.

It would seem that attributing use of magic to a woman's getting a husband would preclude the interpretation that the man had used magic to get a wife. However, the tendency of men to contract second or subsequent marriages with women living in villages where the first wife is not resident allows for the two interpretations simultaneously in different places.

Whatever their individual reasons, some women can accept being a co-wife while others would find the status intolerable. Some divorcées and widows have refused to become co-wives. A few women whose husbands are monogamous have volunteered the view that they would prefer to be divorced rather than endure a polygynous marriage, and Djamour reports the same reaction (1965:85). But polygyny is not grounds for a woman to get a divorce, and a husband can simply refuse to grant one. It is he who has the right to an easy divorce.

DIVORCE

The northeast coast states have the highest Muslim divorce rates found on the peninsula. The figures in Table 6.1 show Muslim marriage and divorce patterns in the 11 peninsular states and Singapore from the late 1940s until 1957. Trengganu, with 59.91 absolute (irrevocable) divorces against marriages, is second only to Kelantan (70.96 percent). The four states that exceeded the 50 percent mark—Trengganu, Kelantan, and Pahang on the east coast and Perlis in the northwest—and Kedah (46.81 percent) shared two interrelated features: they were the least modernized states, and their Malay populations were highly tradition-oriented.

TABLE 6.1

Muslim Marriage and Divorce in the States of Malaya

State	Years	No. of Years	Marriages	Divorces	Revocation of Divorces	Absolute Divorces	Percent of Divorces against Marriages	Percent of Absolute Divorces against Marriages
Johore	1948–57	10	49,543	14,825	N.A.	N.A.	29.92	N.A.
Malacca	1947–57	11	22,292	7,326	767	6,559	32.86	29.42
Selangor	1948–57	10	28,719	10,422	1,230	9,192	36.29	32.01
Perak	1948–57	10	54,471	24,846	4,143	20,703	45.61	38.01
Penang	1945–57	13	30,056	13,911	2,497	11,414	46.28	37.98
Negri Sembilan	1950–57	8	13,346	6,335	367	5,968	47.47	44.72
Pahang	1952–57	6	11,543	6,640	312	6,328	57.52	54.82
Kedah	1948–57	10	64,157	39,324	9,291	30,033	61.29	46.81
Perlis	1948–58	10	10,836	7,386	992	6,394	67.33	58.18
Trengganu	1948–57	10	54,791	39,052	6,225	32,827	71.27	59.91
Kelantan	1948–57	10	116,767	90,296	7,442	82,854	77.33	70.96

N.A. = not available.

Source: Gordon undated (circa 1965).

Analyzing the statistics by year, Douglas Raybeck found a decrease in the divorce rate, from 6 to 30 percent, between the first year (varying from 1947 to 1952) and the last year (1957) for which information is given, the greatest decrease being in those states where economic development was most pronounced. He then examined data showing percentages of the Malay work force engaged in traditional and industrial occupations. Raybeck found a significant correlation between the average divorce rates in the 11 peninsular states and participation in traditional occupations. He concluded that ". . . Malay divorce rates are directly proportional to participation in traditional economic pursuits and inversely proportional to participation in an industrializing economy . . . ," thus supporting his previously stated hypothesis: ". . . modernization should reduce the [Malay] divorce rate rather than increase it" (Raybeck 1975:11-12).

Many men involved in the industrializing sector of the economy are wage earners. One financial feature that sets them apart from men with traditional occupations is regular income. A man with a regular income, in village or town, is more likely to have to pay child support than a man whose income from traditional forms of work is irregular, and therefore difficult to assess accurately. This may be an underlying reason for fewer divorces among those working in the industrial sector. In either case a wife would have to seek a syariah court judgment.

Statistics from 1974 to 1978 support the hypothesis that development (modernization/industrialization) leads to decreasing Malay (Muslim) divorce rates. The percentage of absolute (irrevocable) divorced to marriages among Muslims is lower for all states during the 1970s (Table 6.2) than in the earlier decades shown in Table 6.1—a range from approximately 11 percent in Penang to 26 percent in Perlis. The four states that had the lowest per capita income in 1977 (Star 3/30/79) also had the highest divorce rates in 1976 and 1978: the east coast states of Kelantan and Trengganu, and the northwest states of Perlis and Kedah. Per capita income was the lowest in Kelantan, which was also the only state where the percentage of divorces to marriages continued to top the 50 percent mark during the 1970s although there had been a 17 percent reduction since the earlier decades. Despite the decrease in divorces everywhere, the highest percentages are still found in the areas most dependent on agriculture.

Judith Djamour lists several factors that she sees as congruent with the high frequency of divorce among Malay Muslims in Singapore: divorce is facilitated by law and tolerated by general morality; strong economic deterrents are lacking; remarriage is easy and inexpensive for both sexes; practical and moral support by kin for a divorced woman exists; access to children for both parents and their kin is possible; and adoption is possible if neither parent wants or is able to keep the children (1965:139).

TABLE 6.2

Percentage of Muslim Absolute Divorces against Marriages
for the States of Peninsular Malaysia: 1974-78

State	1974	1975	1976	1978
Perlis	29.0	29.0	30.2	34.0
Kedah	33.9	28.8	36.0	35.8
Penang	25.0	24.4	27.0	26.5
Perak	16.0	16.7	15.8	14.8
Selangor	17.2	16.3	17.5	14.9
Negri Sembilan	14.3	13.1	13.4	12.6
Malacca	10.1	10.0	10.1	6.9
Johore	13.4	13.7	15.0	9.5
Pahang	22.5	25.5	27.3	23.8
Trengganu	41.1	43.1	44.2	38.9
Kelantan	53.2	56.0	52.2	51.5

Source: Unit Pertukaran Maklumat, Pusat Penyelidikan Islam, Jabatan Perdana Menteri. (Statistics for 1977 not available.) Information provided by Michael Peletz, personal correspondence, 1980.

The six factors are operant among Malays elsewhere, especially in rural areas where adherence to traditional cultural values is strongest. And Malays do place high value on harmony in their personal relationships. Raybeck considers the values of interpersonal and village harmony to be important ideological contributors to divorce: although bad feelings result from the divorce, they are short-lived, while bad feelings between married persons continue to promote tension among their kin and in the village generally (1975:8).

Also common in rural areas is the tendency to marry at a young age, which T. E. Smith argues increases ". . . the likelihood of a Malay marriage ending in divorce" (1961:304). Hence the modernizing trend toward increased education and the concomitant postponement of marriage should contribute to a decreasing divorce rate.

Despite the high divorce rate in some states, at any given time there are relatively few individuals who are not married, because Malays tend to remarry within a year or less of a divorce.

The 1970 census data for Trengganu show that of all Malay females in the state, only 3.16 percent were categorized as divorced or permanently separated at the time of the census, while men accounted for 1.30 percent. An examination of numbers of persons rather than percentages shows that there are far more women than men who are divorced and not yet remarried. Of all persons in the divorced/separated category (N = 5,769), women numbered 4,158 (72.0 percent of the total), while there were 1,611 men (less than 30 percent of the total).

The 1970 Trengganu census figures do not list number of times married beyond a "four or more" category. There is no way to determine from these data how many polygynists are included, nor is it possible to distinguish between persons remarrying after a divorce and those who did so after the death of a spouse. Nevertheless, several patterns can be seen from the figures in Table 6.3 for Malays and Chinese, of both sexes, in areas of Trengganu that have a population of 999 or less, and Table 6.4, which has the same categories for the entire state.

Both tables show that a far larger percentage of Malay men than women have been married more than one time: almost 44 percent as opposed to nearly 35 percent for the entire state, and approximately 50 percent males to 37 percent females in the villages. The percentage of men in each category—two, three, and four or more times—is also greater than the percentage of women, with the widest gap found in the "four or more times" category. However, the number of women in all categories in both tables is greater—except the "four or more," where men outnumber women and account for a larger percentage of the total.

The Chinese show a very different pattern. More than 90 percent of Chinese men and over 95 percent of Chinese women in Trengganu as a whole and in small communities have been married only once. Less than 0.50 percent of Chinese of either sex have had four or more marriages.

In part, the difference between the Chinese and the Malay patterns reflects different cultural value systems. But it is also a reflection of the fact that two entirely different legal codes pertaining to marriage, divorce, and family matters are in effect: an Islamic legal code for Malays and other Muslims, and a civil code for all non-Muslims, a category that includes the vast majority of Chinese despite some recent conversions.

As part of the civil code, the Law Reform (Marriage and Divorce) Act, 1975, when it is implemented, will liberalize grounds

TABLE 6.3

Numbers of Times Married, Malays and Chinese, by Sex:
All Areas of Trengganu with a Population of 999 or Less

| | Number of Times Married | | | | | | | | | |
| | One | | Two | | Three | | Four or More | | Total Ever Married | |
	Number	Percent	Number	Percent	Number	Percent	Number	Percent	Number	Percent
Malays										
Males	20,003	49.9	9,859	24.6	4,951	12.4	5,261	13.1	40,074	100.0
Females	37,124	62.8	11,403	19.3	5,707	9.7	4,840	8.2	59,074	100.0
Total	57,127		21,262		10,658		10,101		99,148	
Chinese										
Males	1,555	92.5	105	6.2	14	0.8	8	0.5	1,682	100.0
Females	1,111	96.0	39	3.4	5	0.4	2	0.2	1,157	100.0
Total	2,666		144		19		10		2,839	

Note: Percentages calculated by the author.
Source: Federation of Malaysia, 1977b, Table 2.27, p. 310.

TABLE 6.4

Number of Times Married, Malays and Chinese, by Sex:
All Areas of Trengganu

| | Number of Times Married | | | | | | | | Total Ever Married | |
| | One | | Two | | Three | | Four or More | | | |
	Number	Percent	Number	Percent	Number	Percent	Number	Percent	Number	Percent
Malays										
Males	36,050	56.1	14,049	21.9	6,908	10.7	7,269	11.3	64,276	100.0
Females	59,142	64.5	17,097	18.7	8,407	9.2	6,971	7.6	91,617	100.0
Total	95,192		31,146		15,315		14,240		155,893	
Chinese										
Males	4,310	94.4	221	4.8	25	0.5	12	0.3	4,568	100.0
Females	4,345	97.5	102	2.3	9	0.2	4	0.09	4,460	100.0
Total	8,655		323		34		16		9,028	

Note: Percentages calculated by the author.
Source: Federation of Malaysia 1977b, Table 2.28, p. 315.

for divorce among non-Muslims. It provides for divorce by mutual consent, or by judicial decree on a variety of grounds, with either party petitioning. A marriage must have been in effect for two or more years before a petition is heard, and the parties must have made attempts to reconcile their differences before resorting to divorce (Chung and Meng 1977:19-20). Other changes that will benefit women pertain to property:

> Under the present law, property is divided according to how much each party has contributed in terms of cash and the woman . . . who has worked hard at housekeeping and child rearing finds her equally important contribution not considered (NST 8/15/79).

Further, women tend to earn less than men, so wives working outside the home probably contributed less cash to purchases, and therefore would get a smaller portion from a division under the old system. The new law will give a woman full ownership of a house and half of all other property acquired during the marriage.

Regardless of these changes, a divorce in the civil courts will continue to be relatively expensive—from a minimum of $500 to $1,000 or more (NST 8/15/79). Muslims, subject to an entirely different legal system, usually pay a total legal fee of $20 for having a divorce registered—usually, because the majority of Muslim divorces are initiated by men, who are required only to inform their wives and register a divorce for it to be legal. Muslim women are in a very different position.

A Muslim woman who wants a divorce has three possibilities: taklik, tebus talak (also referred to as khul'), and fasah (faskh). Taklik, allowed in most states, is a conditional divorce in the form of a written statement granted to the woman at the time of marriage. It gives her the right to a divorce if it is proven that her husband has either deserted her or failed to support her for a given period of time. Her proofs must be presented to the syariah court, which has the power to grant or withhold a divorce (Ahmad Ibrahim 1965:34). Under the Trengganu Administration of Islamic Law Enactment, 1955, taklik is mandatory in that state and allows a woman a divorce "if her husband should abandon her or fail to maintain her for a stated period or assault her" (Ahmad Ibrahim, undated:58).

Fasah divorce is granted if a wife can prove to the syariah court that her husband has a major physical or mental defect—impotence, leprosy, elephantiasis, or insanity—or that he is unable to support her (Abdul Kadir bin Yusof 1975:4).

To obtain a tebus talak divorce, a wife pays her husband to divorce her. The amount may be equivalent to the bridewealth given

at the time of marriage, but with initiation of the divorce resting
with the husband, he can demand more, including transfer of property to his name. If he is unreasonable and the wife is knowledgeable and determined, she can petition the syariah court, which then
should appoint arbitrators to try to settle the case (Ahmad Ibrahim
1965:37-39).

> If ill feelings gain such a hold on the married couple
> that their union is endangered . . . indeed is almost
> hell, then in such a situation, and only in such a situ-
> ation, the husband is allowed by Islam, against its
> better judgement, to seek the remedy of divorce.
> Strictly speaking, divorce is a right bestowed on the
> husband in view of his ability to shoulder the marriage
> obligations and because of his aptitude for better self-
> restraint than the wife can display (Shaltout 1958:121).

The "obligations" refer to the ideal that a husband supports
and protects his wife and children, but the statement also implies a
lack of "marriage obligations" for a woman, or at least the idea
that her "obligations" are of a lower order than those of the husband.
That women are characterized by a "worse" self-restraint suggests
that, given ease of divorce, their actions would result from emo-
tionalism—as when a husband takes a second wife?—while men can
be expected to behave more rationally.

Regardless of the implications of the statement, the orthodox
Muslim position opposes divorce except in extreme situations. As
is the case within any religious system, the orthodox position is not
always reflected in the behavior of adherents. A Muslim husband
can divorce his wife simply by stating or writing to her the formula,
"I divorce you," which is called talak, and registering it. He may
do so after careful consideration, but it is not unusual for a divorce
to occur as the result of an argument, a talak—or even three talak—
being pronounced during a moment of rage. Neither the first nor
the second talak is irrevocable; there is a period of three months
during which the husband is permitted to change his mind and resume cohabiting with his wife, and legally she cannot refuse to resume the marriage. Once a third talak has been registered with
the official registrar, the divorce is absolute.

Rojok (return) following a divorce is quite common, but after
the second talak/rojok, the idea of irrevocable or absolute divorce,
if there is a third talak, hangs over both wife and husband, and may
exert restraint on a man. It also leaves a woman in a more tenuous
situation, for she has no control over another unwanted pronouncement except to become a "better" wife. If she wants a divorce, she

now has two examples of what will goad her husband into a pronouncement and can use that knowledge to her own advantage.

The contrasts between divorce forms allowed to women and
to men are obvious. A husband need only pronounce or write the
formula to his wife in order to repudiate her—for whatever reason.
A wife either has to bribe her husband to make the pronouncement,
or to petition the syariah court and prove abandonment, lack of
financial support, or a major mental or physical incapacity in the
husband. The implication is that, for a woman, "marriage should
only be considered in utilitarian terms" (Chung and Meng 1977:19),
because those are the only bases from which she can petition for
divorce. Assuming that she has the needed proofs, she must still
make trips to court, get witnesses to testify on her behalf, and go
through at least one hearing. She also must have enough knowledge
about the system to initiate the process. And, as has been suggested elsewhere (Razman 1975:16), the judge may be far more
sympathetic to the husband than to the wife.

DIVORCE IN RUSILA

There were 120 married couples in Rusila in 1965. Only 57
of them (47.5 percent) had never been irrevocably divorced. In
addition, 8 men were never divorced but married divorcées; 15
women were married to their original spouses, men who had prior
divorces.

The divorce rate is high, but a diachronic perspective indicates a concomitant high degree of marital stability for Rusila
couples. In 1979 I found that 111 (92.5 percent) of the 120 married
couples in the 1965-66 household survey were still married or had
been married at the time when one died. Three couples had moved
from the area and their marital status could not be determined.

The majority of divorces take place during the early years of
first, arranged marriages. The pattern largely fits Smith's observation of a correlation between youth at the time of marriage and
the likelihood of divorce. However, the fact that first marriages
are usually arranged by the parents may also be a factor. If a marriage survives for a few years, it has a very good chance of lasting
until the death of one of the partners. And second marriages are
more stable than first marriages. Data from the 1965 and 1979
surveys support this conclusion. While there were only 57 instances
among the 120 couples where both individuals were married to their
original spouse in 1965, 111 of the 120 couples were still married
14 years later or had been separated by death rather than divorce.

TABLE 6.5

1979 Marital Status of Couples in the 1965-66 Survey

Marital Status	Number	Percent
Couples still married	87	72.5
Widows and widowers ⎫ married to same spouse	19	15.8
Both deceased ⎬ at time of death	5	4.2
Subtotal	111	92.5
Irrevocably divorced	6	5.0
No longer living in Rusila	3	2.5
Total	120	100.0

When divorce does occur, it is likely that both partners will remarry within a brief period of time, with the woman as well as the man having an active role in mate selection. The tendency to remarry is reflected by the 1970 census data for Trengganu (Tables 6.3 and 6.4).

A factor that does not appear in the statistics is the inability of a few individuals to establish a lasting marital relationship. There are two Rusila men who, by 1979, accounted for 45 irrevocable divorces—28 for one and 17 for the other. The highest number of divorces for a local woman is seven. The two men have married and divorced an amazing number of women, the majority of whom were already divorcées. But as their reputations have spread, they have had increasing difficulty finding wives, and must seek their brides further and further from Rusila. Even in a society where divorce is considered preferable to an unhappy union, the behavior of these men is viewed as aberrant.

The reason most often given for divorce after a brief marriage is incompatibility, while a variety of reasons are stated by those who have been married longer, including jealousy, a wife's lack of concern about her husband's welfare, laziness, nagging or arguing, desire to marry someone else, and barrenness of the wife (see Firth 1966:37; Djamour 1965:118-19).

One man divorced three women because they were barren. When they married other men and became pregnant, he had to face the reality of his own sterility. He remained married to his fourth wife and they adopted two children. Because of the relative ease of "adoption," a divorce does not usually occur for barrenness alone: a couple have no children after four years of marriage and they have

frequent arguments about financial matters or something else; she
is flirtatious or a slovenly housekeeper; he is lazy, and therefore a
poor provider, or bad-tempered. If they are compatible and feel
contented with one another, the lack of children will not lead to
divorce but will be met through borrowing, buying, or adopting them.

Almost all divorces between Rusila couples have been initiated
by men, although some (almost 20 percent) were of the tebus talak
type where bridewealth was returned by the wife or her family or
other property was given to the husband as compensation. No village woman has obtained a divorce because her husband is mentally
or physically impaired (faskh), although one woman has clear
grounds for doing so because her husband has been institutionalized
for years. And one young woman has obtained a conditional divorce
(taklik) since 1970.

The villagers say that although it is not good, any smart
woman can push her husband into divorcing her by embarrassing
him publicly and making his life generally unpleasant in other ways.
The other ways often involve food: she may prepare meals late,
cook dishes she knows he dislikes, make them too spicy or too
bland. She might nag or be aloof, or do other things that she knows
will annoy him. Whatever the case, he is being hit on two fronts:
in public he is made to feel malu, an unpleasant state, and at home
he is at least subject to discomfort and annoyances. ". . . That a
woman has to resort to guile to obtain her freedom from a union she
finds insufferable is . . . an indication of the unfair state of things"
(Chung and Meng 1977:18). It may also strike one as demeaning to
the woman, but some villagers express admiration for a wife who
has manipulated her husband into divorcing her. The psychological
cost to both parties is a subject that needs careful examination and
analysis.

A woman may believe she is divorced and then discover that
she is not. When Safiah, a woman in her forties, received a marriage proposal in 1965, she went to the local registrar for a statement of divorce, and found that she was still legally married to
Omar, the man whom she and others in the village thought was her
ex-husband. He had pronounced a third talak almost four years
earlier; she assumed that he had registered it but she never sub-
stantiated that he had done so. Omar, who came from another part
of the country, no longer lived in Rusila. Although she made several attempts to locate him, Safiah was unsuccessful. She could
have petitioned the syariah court for a divorce on grounds of deser-
tion and nonsupport, but the procedure would have been lengthy and
costly for her. While she was trying to decide whether to take that
step, the man she had expected to marry tired of waiting and took
another wife. Safiah dropped the matter rather than cope with the
problems and expenses of a divorce for no immediate reason.

In 1979, Safiah was still married to Omar, although she had neither seen him nor heard from him for 17 years. Omar could have taken a second wife elsewhere. It is impossible to know whether Omar's failure to register the divorce was done with intent or was just carelessness; either way, Safiah has suffered the consequences.

Whatever the case, should Safiah predecease him, Omar has inheritance rights with regard to her property—a house, some coconut palms, and a small piece of padi land. Safiah has two sons by a former marriage, but Omar's share would still be one-fourth. Should he die first and leave children, she would be entitled to share one-eighth of his property with any co-wives. Given the lack of communication between Safiah and Omar for such a long period of time, it is likely that the death of one would never be known to the other, although attempts to find legal heirs and heiresses are made.

According to Muslim law, a divorced woman must wait for "three periods of purity after menstruation" (Ahmad Ibrahim undated:59) or, by Malay custom, for three months and ten days before she can remarry. The time span is _idda_ (formerly, _eddah_), and is enforced in order to assign paternity to the former husband if the woman is pregnant. If she is, the father is expected to assume some financial responsibility for the child, and the child's right to inherit property from him is guaranteed by Islamic law.

Following a first or second talak, a husband has the entire idda period to change his mind about divorce and request his wife to resume living with him. Legally she cannot refuse; in fact, a few women do refuse and try to exert pressure on husbands to make divorces final. No village man has resorted to the law to force an unwilling wife to resume living with him. The usual pressure is economic. An example can be seen in the situation of Mak Mah, a woman now in her sixties.

She had been married for more than 30 years and had borne her husband six children, five of whom lived to adulthood, were married, and living in their own homes at the time of the divorce. She went to the home of her eldest son and, during several weeks, convinced all of her children that she was unhappy living with their father since he had taken a second wife, and that she would not go back to him. She asked them for financial help. Her husband requested that she return, and told her that he would give her no funds nor property, although he was considered a wealthy man by local standards, if she refused. Legally she was in the wrong because her husband was willing to take her back and to support her. None of the children confronted the father in support of the mother, but when he finally recognized, after about six months, that Mak Mah

would not return to him and agreed to make the divorce final, the
children contributed enough for her to buy a small house. They
continue to support her today. As a divorcée she got nothing when
her former husband died, although she had worked with him for
more than 30 years, significantly contributing to his financial success. Her children did benefit, sharing all of his property among
themselves because he had no children by his second wife.

A man is supposed to support his former wife during idda—if
she subjects herself to his control ". . . with regard to her place
of residence and her behaviour, and . . . if the cause for the divorce
was no fault of hers" (Chung and Meng 1977:22), which thus excludes
most divorces of the talak type.

In Rusila divorce–decision reversals usually take place following a first or second talak stated in anger and within one or two
weeks of the pronouncement. In those cases where the husband
does not intend to reverse his decision, financial assistance is usually nil, although the wife may continue to reside in a home purchased during the marriage. Property division will be made at the
end of idda.

If a divorce is by three talak, spoken either on the same oc-
cation or at three different times, a woman cannot remarry her
previous husband unless she has consummated a marriage with
another man and then been divorced from him. The requirement
". . . reflects the detestation with which Islam views divorce and
is intended to deter a man from abusing the power or right to divorce
given to him" (Abdul Kadir bin Yusof 1975:4).

Considering the high divorce rates through the years, the requirement does not seem to act as a deterrent, but it is rare for
irrevocably divorced spouses to remarry each other. Only three
Rusila couples still living in the village had done so prior to 1965;
one couple remarried during 1966, as did a pair in a contiguous village. All of them were still married in 1979. During the interim
only one couple had remarried following a three-talak divorce.

A man who becomes an interim husband is a muhallil or, more
commonly, China buta (literally, "blind Chinese"). China buta is a
peculiar term, because a Muslim woman can marry only a Muslim
man and the designation dates back to a time when there were few
Chinese Muslims. It also is widely used. Djamour found it popularly used in Singapore in 1949 and noted, "Only destitute men with
very little dignity consent to play the muhallil, a role which is considered degrading" (1965:113-14). Rusila villagers agree with her
statement. Because of the degradation a muhallil will act only in a
village far from his own residence, attempting to keep his role
secret from those who know him.

A muhallil is a man who, for a fee, marries a woman and divorces her after the marriage is consummated. The "marriage" may last for an hour or less. The legal requirement has been met and the spirit of the law flouted, for if a marriage is arranged with "the intention of divorce . . . the contract for the second marriage was unlawful" (Shaltout 1958;122). Any man who acts as muhallil is the butt of many jokes, as are the couple who use him. Everyone involved is seen as shamed (malu). Because of this element of shame, the subject is never discussed in the company of anyone who has had recourse to a muhallil. The persons involved are aware, nevertheless, of being subjects of jokes and comments, for they have made similar remarks about others before finding themselves in the same situation. Their neighbors see them as demeaned by the experience, and they are fully aware of the judgment.

I, too, was malu and could not bring myself to raise the subject except with women who had not experienced it, and none of them had discussed the matter with women who had. Their views were largely in agreement, along the following lines: the woman's experience is unpleasant as well as degrading; the woman has to agree to it—she cannot be forced into it, but pressures are brought to bear, usually financial along with arguments about the children; the woman is paying for her ex-husband's actions because he was the one who spoke the three talak; while it is not pleasant for the man to know that his ex-wife is having sexual intercourse with another, it is she who has to go through the act with a man who is a stranger, just as a prostitute would do.

Because two couples in the area had recourse to muhallil during 1965-66, the subject was discussed often and at length, and stories were told about people in other villages as well as Rusila who had done the same. Whether or not the stories are true, they are believed.

The stories have common elements. First, the focus is invariably the ex-husband. He is outside the house where the former wife is with the muhallil, but he is nearby, usually on the porch or verandah. He makes his presence known—doing something bold (berani) and, very likely, crude (kasar) that is later discussed with amusement and, perhaps, admiration by men and some women. In one often-repeated tale, the most extreme of those told, the exhusband sat on the ground beneath the house and made loud comments. As the consummation neared its climax, he reached through a wide crack in the floor and pinched the muhallil on his buttocks. Very crude but very bold.

Second, the muhallil is almost always said to be ugly, malformed, or both. (Thus a popular interpretation of China buta as meaning such a person. But blindness is defined by Malays as an extremely pitiable rather than a repulsive state and Rusila Malays consider some Chinese physically attractive, especially those with fair skin color. The suggestion of sexual relations with a non-Muslim might be the repugnant or defiling element.)

Third, the woman's situation is acknowledged to be susah (miserable, in this context), and her reactions to it described as anything from stolid to hysterical. But as the stories are told, she is not the principal. Her ex-husband is.

I interpret the ex-husbands' behaviors as attempts to neutralize their shame by treating the situation contemptuously. They may be criticized for crudity, but the boldness is admired.

What can a woman do to deflect her shame? Very little. One woman tried to avoid the negative labeling of other villagers by keeping secret her agreement to remarry her former husband. She waited beyond the idda period to arrange an interim marriage with a man of her own choice, and remained married to him for more than a month. Speculation was widespread in the village anyway, and many people referred to her China buta marriage, confirmed to all when she later re-wed her former husband. Nevertheless, the fact that she chose the man herself and stayed with him for a while lessened the shame element and added to her reputation as a very clever woman.

A final example illustrates that the unexpected can happen: one muhallil and his bride found one another so attractive and compatible that they decided not to divorce, leaving the former husband complaining and regretful. This story was told, with some relish, in 1965. Interestingly, an identical tale is reported by M. G. Swift (1963:273), whose research was carried out on the western side of the peninsula. It is possible, despite the infrequency of China buta marriages, that the unexpected has actually occurred more than once or, equally possible, the idea of such an outcome appeals to Malay humor. It is the only example in which the husband is the butt of the story, which thus serves as a cautionary tale to the quick-tempered.

Under Islamic law a divorced woman retains any property she owned prior to her marriage (unless she transferred it to her husband in order to obtain a tebus talak divorce). Property acquired during the marriage is supposed to be divided. For example, if a couple owns padi land on which both of them have worked, the wife is entitled to half. If it can be proved that she did not work on the land, she receives less. Today married women in the village are careful to have their names along with their husbands' names registered on property deeds, so that there can be no misunderstanding if divorce occurs. But this was not always the case, and there are elderly women in the village who were left with little or nothing following a divorce because husbands had deeds only in their names and the women did not know their legal rights. It will be recalled that Mak Mah received nothing because she refused to resume cohabiting with her husband after he changed his mind about divorcing her.

In urban areas the question of a wife's property rights becomes more problematic:

> Most urban Malay men are wage-earners with a fixed
> salary and the wife is usually not in employment. In
> this case the husband can argue that whatever property
> he purchased or whatever goods he acquired are paid
> for from his own earnings and that the non-working wife
> has not contributed in monetary terms to the purchase
> of such goods. Hence very often the wife is not entitled
> to a share (Chung and Meng 1977:22).

There are many village couples who own little or no productive land, so there is nothing to divide at the time of divorce. This is especially true of young couples whose parents are still living. They have inherited nothing, and have not yet been able to save enough to buy land. It is among this category that a majority of divorces occur.

Even if a divorcée receives some land, she has a more difficult time economically than a man if there are children from the marriage, because they usually stay with her. The Shafi'aite code of Muslim law gives a mother custody of a daughter until puberty and a son until he is seven. Then custody of both reverts to the father. A child of either sex "who has reached the age of discernment" is allowed a choice between parents. By custom "girls are expected to follow their mother and boys their father" (Ibid. :23-24).

In Rusila customary practice is for all children to stay with their mother following a divorce. Exceptions occur, with children going to live with grandparents or other kin. And there is one instance of a man keeping his infant daughter—which worried almost every woman in the village, because they were convinced that the father could not care for the child properly.

The economic burden of supporting the children normally falls on the mother and those of her kin who are able to help. Ideally a father should contribute to his children's support, but I could not find one instance in which he did so in any regular manner either in 1965 or in 1979. Both Djamour (1965:125) and Rosemary Firth (1966:34-35) found similar patterns. Some men provide financial assistance occasionally or buy clothing or toys for their children, especially at holiday time. Others do nothing. There is no case locally where a woman petitioned the syariah court to order an ex-husband to pay child support. A majority of men still engage in village work, which provides an irregular income, so a ruling would be difficult to enforce. If a man earns a salary or weekly wages, the court can arrange to have a sum paid directly to the former wife. But the village men in that category are either still married to their original spouses or were divorced from a first wife before any children were born to them.

Despite the financial problems, villagers think it is better for children to stay with their mother. Young children are more dependent on her, and older children often have stronger emotional attachments to her than to their father. An older child's relationship with the father becomes more formal and bound by respect behavior, although it is the mother who is more deserving of respect, a view reflected in the adage "Heaven lies under the sole of mother's foot."

It is common for young divorcées to return with their children to their families of orientation, if the parents are still living, or to take up residence in the home of a married sibling. The addition of two or three more people to the average village household is accomplished fairly easily, especially if the divorcée is economically productive (as most women are). Older women are more likely to stay in the homes they own outright or that they have helped to buy during a marriage, and to support their children through their own remunerative work, with assistance from older children or other kin.

Most individuals who are not categorized as old will probably contract another marriage within a year or two of being divorced. As is true in many other societies, an older man is more likely to marry again or sooner than a woman in the same age cohort, because he can seek someone younger than himself as well as a woman who is approximately his age. A woman's choice is generally confined to men in her cohort or older, so she has fewer opportunities.

Most women in their fifties who have their own homes, a piece of productive land, and/or children who can give periodic financial assistance opt against remarriage when they do have the opportunity. They are content to be answerable only to themselves. Men rarely remain single. They may remarry primarily for socioemotional reasons, but the practical aspects of the division of labor between a married couple are also important. The home is a woman's domain, and most men, while capable of doing household chores, will do them only in unusual or emergency situations.

Some social difficulties, usually temporary, result from divorce because marriages tend to be contracted between persons within the village or with residents of nearby villages. Individuals try to avoid contact with former spouses as much as possible. If they meet unexpectedly, they are polite or ignore one another.

Avoidance is strongest when one or both have recently married again, because current spouses may be jealous of former spouses. However, some people remain on friendly, cooperative terms with their former in-laws.

Divorce among Malays has not been stigmatized in any general way. Whether or not a divorced individual is stigmatized in Rusila depends on other villagers' perceptions of the person. Everyone's marital situation is fairly well known—the hard-working mother and loving wife whose husband is lazy and uncaring and the good husband whose wife flirts with every tradesman who comes into the village are two hypothetical extremes.

A divorce between the first couple would find sympathy directed to the wife, while the husband of the second couple would be seen as justified if he divorced his wife. Behavior of both the wife and the husband will be judged, and one may be found wanting. Focusing on the stereotypic women of the hypothetical cases, the "good" wife poses no threat to her peers because her energies are devoted to her family and she does not look at other women's husbands with interest. The "bad" wife is a threat because she is flirtatious and her peers may worry that now she is free, she will be casting her glances at their husbands. The divorcée is not stigmatized because she is a divorcée. She must also be perceived as a threat by other women for them to define her status negatively. Most divorcées who are also outsiders, especially if they are young and attractive, are assumed to be threatening simply because they are an unknown quantity, potential rivals. The assumption may be correct.

For example, a young married Rusila woman took her two children and went to visit relatives in another village for a few days. When they got on the bus to return home, she encountered her husband with a divorcée from a nearby village whom he had taken to the cinema in the town. He had never taken his wife to the cinema. Angry words were exchanged on the bus, and the married couple resorted to blows when they descended from the vehicle. Several other couples had similar quarrels. One woman thought it was very bad that the married women had fought with their husbands. They should have directed their anger toward the divorcée, who might then learn to stay away from married men, especially those with young children. The typical wife's response is to direct anger toward her husband, but to blame the divorcée for his behavior.

A divorcée has great freedom compared with that enjoyed by a woman who has never married, and she will make her own decision about any subsequent union, while the unmarried woman is largely subject to her parents' wishes. The divorcée is assumed to be sexually knowledgeable, while her never-married peer is supposed to be totally ignorant, an unreal ideal. The stereotype of the sexy, free divorcée is nourished by the behavior of a few women, such as those who participate in rodat performances.

Young divorcées are also the women who become prostitutes in Kuala Trengganu—or so the villagers believe. I have personally interviewed only one Malay prostitute there. She was not a village woman, but came from another part of the state. She claimed that she received nothing when her husband divorced her and that she had no family to whom she could turn for help. With only a primary school education, she could not qualify for the jobs she had tried to get. So she had become a prostitute in order to support herself and a three-year-old daughter. Whether the story is true or not, the woman's described situation is certainly possible. It highlights again a major difference between town and village women. A village woman may be left in an equally bad situation following a divorce, but she can support herself and her children more easily because she can continue doing the same kinds of village work that she most likely performed as a married woman—planting and harvesting padi, tapping rubber, making copra, and so on. And there are usually relatives who will help her.

What happens to a non-Muslim woman if her husband converts to Islam and then decides to end their marriage? There may be a number of possibilities for resolution, depending on the persons involved. But one case, reported from London, is suggestive.

The newspaper account (NST 3/16/79) focused on a Malaysian doctor, a former Hindu who converted to Islam in 1976 without informing his wife of 24 years, Sarojini, the mother of their three children and a Christian. His marriage to Sarojini was "deemed null by a Muslim jurist," and he married another woman. Sarojini, now living in England, sued for divorce in the British High Court and was granted a decree nisi as well as a lump sum of approximately U.S.$60,000. A smaller sum was awarded immediately, and the right of the husband to appeal was acknowledged. The presiding justice read a ruling by an Islamic official in Kuala Lumpur that stated, "Under Muslim law, the marriage to Sarojini no longer existed since the doctor had embraced Islam but his wife had not." The judge pointed out that Sarojini was entitled to a decree under English law and that the High Court "was not bound to recognize happenings in Malaysia as putting an end to the marriage," but he noted that he was not "criticizing the laws of Malaysia nor the precepts of the Islamic law or religion."

According to canon law, Muslim males are allowed to have non-Muslim wives if they are Christians or Jews, while Muslim women can marry only Muslim men. In Malaysia, however, a woman must "confess the faith before she can be wed to a Muslim" (Rauf 1964:102).

In both Malaysia and England, Sarojini is no longer married. Under English law she was awarded a cash settlement to support herself and the three children. Under Islamic law she, a non-Muslim, has no legal rights, but she could have sued her husband/former husband under the civil code in Malaysia. In an instance of conflicting decisions reached by the syariah courts (which deemed the marriage null) and the civil courts, "that of the civil court prevails . . . but the civil court may apply to the Kathi [syariah court official] for guidance" (Ibid.:96). Speculation about possible outcomes if Sarojini had sued her husband in the Malaysian civil courts are idle because she took legal action elsewhere. But one question is obvious: If the civil court does ask for guidance from the syariah court, will the decision reflect the Islamic viewpoint?

Muslim fundamentalists would like to replace the present Malaysian civil and criminal codes with the Islamic code and bring all Malaysian citizens, non-Muslim and Muslim alike, under its jurisdiction. Such an extreme change is unlikely within the foreseeable future. Former Prime Minister Tunku Abdul Rahman is quoted as saying "there might be bloodshed and chaos" if non-Muslim Malaysians "had Muslim law forced down their throats," and other Muslim moderates, such as the Lord President of the Federal Court, Tun Mohamed Suffian, have spoken against further extension of the Islamic code (Das 1979b:23).

It is clear, however, that within the realm where Muslim law applies, to family and inheritance matters as well as to aspects of personal conduct, the Islamic code is being interpreted and applied more strictly. The new provision in Johore, allowing men to take second wives without a first wife's permission, is one example. The 1975 Law Reform (Marriage and Divorce) Act for non-Muslims shows an opposing trend, significantly liberalizing the rights of women. Thus there are not only two legal codes pertaining to marriage and family matters, but one is being developed to give women greater equality while the other is becoming more restrictive and allowing women less equality.

7

THE ECONOMY

Malaysia is one of the fastest-growing developing countries in the world. Development within the nation has been geographically uneven for historical, political, and ecological reasons, and the members of the several ethnic categories that make up the population have traditionally participated in different sectors of the economy.

In Chapter 1, I discussed the ethnic categories that make up Malaysian society. Socioeconomic classes that cut horizontally across ethnic categories also exist in Malaysia. But the growth of a "class consciousness" overriding broad ethnic divisions and encompassing recognition of common problems and interests has been slow, except among the elite.

Rural Malays in Trengganu are aware of the vast differences in wealth and lifestyle between themselves and the Malay Rulers and, thus far, think of the differences as part of the basic life scheme. There is also a stereotype, new in Rusila since the early 1970s, that Chinese are rich, or at least better off financially, than the average local person—and there is growing resentment about it. Acceptance of this stereotype works against the generation of feelings of shared problems or common cause among ethnic groups.

Nevertheless, some observers report:

. . . there are increasing signs of peasant willingness to participate in class-based actions. Recently urbanized Malay peasants returning to rural life are among the leaders in this direction. . . . It is too early to tell how fast the trend toward class-based action and the decline of ethnic conflict will go. The history of racial antagonism goes so far back that

class relations often are expressed—albeit in distorted fashion—in ethnic terms. More important,
although the government officially condemns racial
conflict and calls for national unity, it continues to
drive the peoples of Malaysia further apart by making race the focus of concerns about inequality
(SEAC 1980:23).

THE NATION

Nationwide, the poor are found among all of the ethnic categories, particularly in rural areas, where the poverty incidence in
1975 was 54 percent (compared with 19 percent in urban areas).
However, rural population is largely composed of Malays. The
poverty line is vaguely defined by the government as monthly income below that "necessary to cover minimum nutritional requirements and essential non-food expenses to sustain a decent standard
of living" (Federation of Malaysia 1976a:73).

Despite the poverty incidence, Malaysia ranks above all other
Southeast Asian nations except Singapore on the Physical Quality of
Life Index (PQLI) published by the Population Reference Bureau.
The PQLI is a social indicator of development based on a composite
of life expectancy, infant mortality, and literacy rates. Southeast
Asia as an area has a PQLI of 56, Singapore has 86, and Malaysia
is rated 73 (Kane 1979).

Malaysia had had a favorable annual balance of trade since
1961, although unemployment stood at 6.8 percent by 1976 and no
marked improvement was predicted during the remainder of the
decade. The per capita income had reached $1,600 by early 1979
(Star 3/20/79) and the per capita Gross National Product (GNP),
estimated for 1978 by the World Bank at U.S.$1,090, is the third
highest in Southeast Asia, after the oil-rich Sultanate of Brunei and
Singapore (Haub and Heisler 1980). In one analysis of economic development, Malaysia was classified as "lower-middle," the median
category among seven ranging from "rich" to "poor III," based on
per capita Gross Domestic Product (GDP). A "lower-middle" rank
means that GDP, "the output produced within the country," ranges
from U.S.$1,425 to U.S.$2,500. In Southeast Asia only Singapore
("near-rich") ranked higher (Dadzie 1980:60-61).

Malaysia is the world's largest exporter of tropical hardwoods
and rubber. In the order of their export value, five major commodity groups—rubber, sawn logs and sawn timber, crude and partly
refined petroleum, palm oil/palm kernels, and tin—accounted for
73.3 percent of Malaysia's total export earnings in 1978. Their

contribution to government revenues through export duties, indirect taxes, and corporate income taxes was also considerable (Das et al. 9/79:64).

Smallholder rubber is seen by the government as the most important form of agriculture in Peninsular Malaysia. There were some 350,000 smallholders, mainly Malays, in 1970, and 90 percent were working holdings less than ten acres in size, with 45 percent owning less than five acres of trees. The average smallholder produces about 650 pounds of rubber per acre, compared with 1,020 pounds per acre produced on large estates (Federation of Malaysia 1976a:164), only 66 percent of average estate production.

The government is helping smallholders improve production practices and replant holdings with high-yield trees, and will encourage out-migration to new development schemes by those whose present holdings are too small to allow an income above poverty level (Ibid. :46).

The second most important smallholder crop is rice (padi), involving 300,000 farmers. In this sector 80 percent of the holdings are less than five acres. The government estimates poverty among padi farmers to be around 88 percent because of "small size of holdings, prevalence of tenancy, lack of drainage and low yields" (Ibid.: 164).

The government is committed to expanding acreage under double-cropping where feasible, encouraging more use of high-yield varieties of rice, and otherwise promoting the planting of off-season crops such as tobacco and groundnuts (Ibid. :46). Malaysia is not self-sufficient in rice production and remains dependent on imports, mostly from neighboring Thailand, to meet domestic demands.

Prices of some foods—among them rice, sugar, meat, and sweetened condensed milk (an indispensable ingredient in the type of café au lait preferred by Malays)—and of nonedibles such as petrol and kerosene are government-controlled. For those things that are produced in Malaysia, government controls go hand in hand with government subsidies: rice producers are ". . . the most subsidized and government-supported . . ." of any of the ASEAN nations (Peyman and Das 1980:33). Yet thousands of rice farmers in the Muda agricultural scheme, a "showpiece project" in the state of Kedah, protested during January 1980 against an automatic savings plan that deprived them of a percentage of expected cash income, a savings they felt they could not afford.

Politicians blamed extremists and the political opposition for the protest, but falling real incomes are seen by some observers as the underlying cause for discontent. Although new facilities and double-cropping have reduced the numbers of agriculturalists living in poverty and, at today's prices, Muda farmers' incomes have more than doubled in one decade, a rice farmer earned 20-25 percent less in real income in 1980 than in 1975 (Ibid.:37). If the government allows rice farmers to sell the basic diet staple at higher prices, consumers—including landless villagers—throughout the country will suffer; if the government does nothing to assist the farmers, their real incomes will continue to decline and the gains made will be entirely lost. In Peyman's phrase, "The government is caught in a cleft stick" (Ibid.:38).

The state governments' policy of restricting the alienation of new land to non-Malay agricultural producers, using the argument that such land should be reserved for landless bumiputras, is seen by some as preventing Malaysia from exploiting its full agricultural potential. Land under agriculture was 11.9 percent of total land area in 1978 and, while much of the total is not suitable for agriculture, the possibilities for further exploitation are great (Das et al. 1979:68).

Exploitation of oil and natural gas is relatively recent, and exports continue to rise. By 1978 they accounted for 13.3 percent of export values. The international oil crisis has aided Malaysia by elevating the value of oil earnings as well as making substitutes for natural rubber and timber more costly (Ibid.:61). It is forecast that by 1985, Malaysia will become a net importer of oil because of increased domestic demand. The government hopes to compensate through export of natural gas from fields off Sarawak by 1983 (Ibid.:64). Malaysia's energy position has earned the old but accurate "embarrassment of riches" cliché: as well as oil and natural gas reserves, there is coal, and great hydroelectric and solar energy potential. The nuclear energy option has been rejected, but there are plans to open a nuclear research center (Peyson 1980:40-41).

Manufacturing accounted for approximately 21 percent of total exports in 1978. Diversification in the manufacturing sector of the economy is viewed by local economists as particularly important for continued development. Malaysia also needs to control the international marketing of what is produced in all sectors in order to exploit world markets for its own benefit. Currently marketing is largely dominated by U.S., European, and Japanese interests (Das et al. 1979:64).

The Third Malaysia Plan (TMP), covering 1976-80, is an integral part of the New Economic Policy (NEP) and the means for implementing it to the benefit of "all the races, and all the socioeconomic groups," according to P. M. Datuk Hussein Onn (Das 1979a:20).

> The overriding objective [of the NEP] is that of national unity with implementation to be so effected that no one

> racial group should feel deprived in the process. . . .
> [The 1990 target] is ownership and management by
> Malays and other indigenous people [bumiputras] of
> at least 30% of commercial and industrial activities
> in the economy [from 2.4 percent in 1970] and an em-
> ployment structure at all levels of operation and man-
> agement that reflects the composition of the nation. . . .
> Since restructuring is planned to result from growth,
> Government policy [is] directed towards assisting the
> Malays and other indigenous people to participate
> fully (Federation of Malaysia 1976a:30).

Changes would not apply to every enterprise, but to commerce
and industry as a sector of the economy, and would be implemented
from anticipated growth, thus assuring that no particular "race"
(the Chinese) suffered during the process. Ideally, identification
of "race" with geographical location and economic function would be
eliminated. Should growth falter as a result of international reces-
sion, it is questionable whether implementation could proceed without causing deprivation to some segments of the population.

The NEP did not focus on the distribution of income within
"racial groups." The elite have taken advantage of the policy, while
most of the rural poor lack the skills, knowledge, and economic resources to do so. One effect has probably been to increase inequality of income distribution within the Malay community. However,
this has been denied by Dr. Mahatir Mohamed, the Deputy Prime
Minister (Kraar and Blank 1980:9).

Increased government involvement in the economy through
direct investment in commerce and industry was necessitated by
the NEP provisions. For example, State Economic Development
Corporations, assisted by federal funding, have been formed in all
states and charged with local economic development, especially
through encouragement of Malay and other bumiputra participation
in commercial and industrial enterprises. A shortage of skilled
personnel to implement these programs is a basic problem, and
raises the question of whether

> . . . an educational policy oriented largely towards
> improving the lot of the Malays is likely to damage
> the economy by limiting the supply of managers, scien-
> tists and technologists available from other racial
> groups in Malaysia. . . . The economic need for
> Malaysia to square its racial contradictions and to
> unite all ethnic groups behind a common development
> strategy is obvious enough in the light of the threats

which external economic forces pose (Das et al.
1979:62, 63).

Malaysia's fourth five-year plan (1981-85) will be officially
unveiled in March 1981, but an interview with Finance Minister
Tunku Razaleigh Hamzah by Hugh Peyman (1980:50) suggests some
of the priorities:

Major Differences with Third Malaysia Plan (TMP):
—There is even more emphasis on the eradication of
poverty.
—There is more concern with narrowing the income
gap between the poor and those people who have
benefited from government development efforts.
—There is control of inflation to maintain the real
incomes of the low income group.

Other concerns are not new, and include raising rural living
standards; encouraging diversification in the industrial sector of
the economy; development or improvement of infrastructural features—roads, power, water, and other amenities, ports and air-
ports, and upgrading manpower skills—in less-developed areas of
the country as a means to encouraging internal and foreign investment; emphasis on housing construction; an increase in expenditures
for defense; creation of a Cabinet committee to cut red tape; stem-
ming inflation through government controls, with a free-market
economy as a long-range goal. "Labour—Will continue to be a big
problem" (Ibid.): There is already a shortage of plantation workers; management has requested permission to bring them from
Indonesia on five-year contracts. Other questions pertaining to
labor, such as the role of unions, were not addressed in the article.
One example of Malaysia's "racial contradictions" can be seen
through contrasting the present status of the labor movement with
that of the cooperative movement.
The labor movement is politically weak and subject to numerous legal restrictions, two features that are strongly interrelated.
Union membership is approximately 70 percent Indian and, because
Indians are a small minority in the nation's population, the unions
can be largely ignored by the Malay leaders of UMNO, who take a pro-
management stance and favor restraints on labor. Union executives
are legally excluded from being employees or officers of political
parties, effectively restricting their development of a power base
from which to push for legislation favorable to labor. Only 10 to 14
percent of the Malaysian work force is unionized (anon. 1977:130-38).
Legislation by Parliament in 1980 gave the labor minister greater
power, and is expected to result in a number of unions being dissolved.

The cooperative movement is gaining strength because of liberal funding of two government agencies, Majuikan and the Farmer's Organization Authority (FOA). They are charged with coordinating and integrating development in their respective spheres, fishing and agriculture, the sectors of the economy where poor Malays are concentrated. Both agencies have encouraged and subsidized the development of cooperatives, as well as instituting training programs to teach fishermen and farmers new techniques and arranging loans for the purchase of equipment or for farmers to shift from subsistence agriculture to cash crops. A major problem is securing capable staff to manage village-based cooperatives (Das et al. 1979:66-68).

A Malaysian cooperative is characterized by "open membership, democratic management and limited interest on capital, [with a] . . . proportionate distribution of any gains." The purpose is "to provide a service, not to make money" (Ibid.:66). The Quran forbids usury, which leads some Malays to reject the idea that fixed interest earned from investments is legitimate.

Fishermen's cooperatives existed before the 1970s, but many of them were unsuccessful because members lacked the skills needed to run them. The government formed Majuikan in 1971, with the goals of elevating the socioeconomic status of fishermen and expanding and developing the fisheries sector of the economy. Cooperatives are viewed as an alternative to the traditional dependence of many Malay fishermen on patrons, Chinese entrepreneurs (towkay) who owned the boats and other capital equipment and controlled the marketing of catches. There are now 100 fishing cooperatives and associations with a combined membership of over 35,000, about 43 percent of all fishermen. Members can purchase ice and boat fuel, spare parts, and household supplies at discount rates through some co-op complexes, and also process and market catches collectively (Ibid.).

The agricultural counterpart of Majuikan, the FOA, was established in 1973. Its goal is to raise income of smallholder farmers through increased productivity and by making the cooperative a means for distributing farm supplies, processing crops, and selling them. There are over 1,000 "agro-based cooperative societies" in Malaysia today with a total membership of more than 300,000 people (Ibid.:68).

Farmers have also been encouraged to pool lands and to farm cooperatively as a means of compensating for land fragmentation resulting from bilateral partible inheritance practices. The idea of cooperative farming seems to accord well with the value of gotong royong (mutual aid and cooperation), but often that value is offset by individualism. People who own better or larger pieces of land are reluctant to join with those owning less productive or smaller sections; those who consider themselves to be hard and careful workers believe that combining with others who are not, will add to their own work burden. Farmers do cooperate in arranging to bring equipment, such as government-owned disk plows, into their villages to prepare many small sections of land at one time. And they have accepted various innovations on their own land.

The growth of the cooperative movement is supported by federal and state governments as a means to raise the living standards of rural Malays and make them independent of Chinese patrons. The political aspect of this support cannot be overlooked: rural Malays form the largest part of UMNO's constituency; a disillusioned electorate might seek political alternatives among the opposition parties, with PAS (the Muslim Party) the most likely beneficiary. With Islamic fundamentalism growing in Malaysia, UMNO leaders must increasingly demonstrate their concern about the socioeconomic position of rural Malays with more than words.

On the other hand, the union movement is largely supported by Indians, a minority with little political clout, although Malay membership is increasing. Further, a fairly docile work force and a pro-management stance by the government can be a positive draw to potential investors in the commerce and industry sector, where further development and diversification are desired by the government.

Space does not allow discussion of the many government programs and agencies, aside from FOA and Majuikan, that are involved with development. MARA (Majlis Amanah Rakyat) is mentioned here essentially because it has had impact on women's lives in Rusila.

MARA, originally the Rural Industrial Development Authority (RIDA), has undergone several complete reorganizations as well as the name change through the years. As of May 1979, "two holding companies to supervise different groups of activities had been formed to promote greater efficiency" (SunMail 5/13/79), a common explanation for reorganizing government agencies. What the effects will be and how the changes articulate with plans announced in 1978 to raise one subsidiary "to a corporation by an act of Parliament" (NST 8/29/78) are unclear. In the past MARA has promoted local handicrafts, made loans enabling villagers to open small businesses, and developed transportation companies to serve rural populations.

This brief overview would be incomplete without another reference to the growth of Islamic fundamentalism and the revitalization movement. Some fundamentalist leaders have expressed anti-modernization views and are thought to have political ambitions.

Their influence may not be widespread, but its impact is being felt. There were, for example, university students who dropped out of science and medicine faculties during 1978-79 when they became convinced that the courses of study were anti-Islamic. And there is increasing demand for the imposition of Islamic law as the only code of law in the nation by members of the Muslim Youth Movement (ABIM) and others who may be using the issue for their own political purposes.

> Malaysia's antidote to extremism . . . is material prosperity. If it can, it will take religion out of political life. But as it stands, the government's solution is to create its own missionary movement on the one hand and raise living standards as quickly as possible on the other (Das et al. 1979:60).

By creating its own missionary movement, the government allies itself firmly with Islam but can simultaneously promote a moderate viewpoint. That material prosperity is acceptable within Islam, and that balance between religious fervor and material striving is needed, was pointed out by the Yang di Pertuan Agong when he opened an exhibition of Islamic artifacts. He quoted the Prophet Muhammad: "Strive for material benefits as if you are going to live for a thousand years. On the other hand, prepare for the next world as if you are going to die tomorrow" (Ibid.).

TRENGGANU

The population in Trengganu is overwhelmingly Malay and Muslim, and a large percentage of it is characterized by poverty. People try to fulfill their religious obligations, and they also want a better standard of living.

Labor force participation by persons between 15 and 64 years of age was 61 percent in 1970, very close to the national figure of 59.8 percent (Federation of Malaysia 1977:23), but the sectors of the economy in which people labor are mostly rural-based. The cooperative movement is growing among fishermen and agriculturalists, who form the majority of the state's workers; union membership is almost nil.

Diversification of cash crops has occurred during the 1960s and 1970s, with oil palm and tobacco taking their place alongside rubber. Padi is also widely grown in the state, mostly by smallholders who produce for their own consumption. Trengganu and Kelantan have "a long history" as rice importers, although they comprise "the second most important rice-growing region [after Kedah] in the peninsula" (Jackson 1972:83).

The poverty incidence is estimated to be as high as 99 percent in some communities where low-yield stock (rubber) and single-cropping (padi) are characteristic (Federation of Malaysia 1976a: 165). Per capita income in Trengganu for 1977 was $1,005.50, well below the national average but slightly greater than income in Kedah and Perlis, where drought caused drastic reduction of padi yields, and well above the per capita income in Kelantan. Trengganu and the other three low-income states are targets for accelerated development, with Trengganu judged as having the best potential for rapid improvement because of extensive forestry resources and offshore oil fields (Star 3/30/79).

Large-scale exploitation of the forestry sector is just beginning, but income to the state from offshore oil is already significant. Oil production was "80,000 barrels a day from 40 wells" (NST 3/5/79) early in 1979. Although the state receives only 5 percent of the oil revenues, the amount comes "off the top" before company profits and taxes are reckoned. Petronas, the federal organization that controls oil exploration and production, and Exxon are working with the state government to develop petroleum-related projects, such as a housing complex with supporting services for Exxon employees, a helicopter base, warehouses, and a research and training center. People living along the coast near Kuala Trengganu are well aware of the oil resource, and concerned about whether they will benefit from it. Local men were hired as laborers at $29.50 per 12-hour day, very high wages for the area, to build a jetty and other facilities related to the petroleum industry on Pulau Kapas, an island a few miles offshore. Others are working on the rigs in the South China Sea.

There were rumors in 1978 that the state government planned to use some of the revenues to pave all dirt roads in the state, a considerable undertaking, and to widen the coastal highway from two to four lanes. For people living in the interior, the establishment of a network of paved roads will have many advantages, making it easier to get cash crops to market and to reach health, educational, and other facilities. By mid-1979 work on the coastal highway had begun. Villagers whose homes are located near that major transportation artery were frightened and worried about how near the traffic would be to their homes.

Kuala Trengganu appeared to be experiencing a boom by mid-1979 and was looking more and more like a city. New government buildings, several banks, and other multistory structures lined the main street through town, a street recently widened to four lanes. Construction of housing in, around, and for several miles north and south of the urban center was proceeding rapidly.

Marang district, which comprises 23 villages, including Rusila, and the minitown of Marang, will have its share of the funds for development, according to Encik Zahid bin Muda, the district officer.

Ground was already being cleared for a multimillion-dollar telecommunications center and training facility on a hilltop near the coast. A low-income housing project of 450 units for fishermen will be built on land nearby, along with roads, a school, a mosque, other public buildings, and shops. Villagers who owned land in that area, mostly planed with old, low-yield rubber trees, sold it to the government for good prices, some becoming wealthy by local standards. The government has allocated $70,000 to build a 30-unit project for healthy aged persons with no means of support. Garden land will be included with each house plot. The project is to be located near an established village so that the elders are not isolated. Also, a match factory may be built in the district, although the location has yet to be agreed upon. Finally, interior roads will be paved, and electricity lines and water mains are scheduled to follow. Large-scale hydroelectric development will be needed first, because periodic water shortages and electricity failures are already a problem in Kuala Trengganu and environs.

Many villagers are aware that development is not a completely positive process. For example, the improvement of transportation routes offers many advantages. At the same time, traffic increases and poses new dangers: children and adults are killed or injured, mobile thieves rob houses, and marijuana and other drugs—once an urban problem—find their way into the villages. It is the latter changes upon which some of the Islamic fundamentalists in other parts of the country have focused when urging Muslims to live like the Prophet Muhammad.

WOMEN AND THE ECONOMY

Women will be more affected than men if fundamentalism in an extreme form becomes established in Malaysia. Tun Mohamed Suffian, Lord President of the Federal Court of Malaysia, outlined some of the effects of replacing the present criminal and civil legal codes with Islamic law in its entirety during a lecture at Manila in March 1978:

> . . . all non-Muslim and women judges who have rendered distinguished service could be dismissed . . . non-Muslim lawyers [many of whom are women] would be disqualified; and outside the legal system, Muslim

women would be denied education and the opportunity
to secure economic independence (Das 1979b:23).

One result of fundamentalist influence can be observed in
Kuala Lumpur and other urban areas, where some Muslim women
wear veils and all-enveloping garments, usually a black cloak or
full-length green coat. Others have adopted the telekong, a hood
that covers head and neck but leaves the face exposed; still others
use kerchiefs wrapped to cover their hair. These head coverings
are worn with the traditional and modest baju kurung-type "blouse"
and ankle-length skirt. In the 1960s no Malay woman used a veil;
only girls attending Islamic secondary schools wore the telekong,
and then only during school hours. In Rusila and environs it is still
only schoolgirls who wear it. The more extreme forms of attire
have been criticized by Muslim moderates. Prime Minister Datuk
Hussein Onn, for example, was quoted as saying that "Women 'going
about with a lot of curtains around them' is alien to the Malaysian
scene" (Das et al. 1979:60).

Full veiling and covering could never be adopted by rural
women as long as they plant and harvest crops, nor could women
factory and office workers adopt that mode of dress. But such
clothing could become a sign not only of piety but also of affluence,
as is true in parts of the Muslim world where the mode is found
among the upper class (Cohen 1967:42) or is "the privilege of women
married to rich men" (Mernissi 1975:84)—women who labor neither
in factory nor in field. Acceptance or imposition of such a dress
code would effectively remove Malay and other Muslim women from
many occupations. The term "imposition" is not inaccurate, because there are students at the University of Malaya who wear the
telekong in response to peer pressure, although others now accept
that a good Muslim woman should cover herself to greater or lesser
extent. The adoption of coverings sends a clear social message to
others and establishes social distance between the wearer and others—
the more the coverings, the greater the distance—which is very re-
assuring to some women in a rapidly changing society where the
norms are no longer clear-cut. Little is known about the organizational affiliations of these women, except that the more extreme
forms of dress (black cloak, green coat) apparently denote adherence
to the prescriptions of one or another of the dakwah associations.
Thus far, few women have donned the extreme dress forms.

All Muslim women are affected by Islamic law and its economic repercussions. Children have the right to inherit from a
parent, with female children receiving half of the amount that male
children get. The argument is made that a woman will be supported
by her husband, so receipt of half of a brother's share is really

"equitable" (Abdul Kadir 1975:6), a view that ignores the economic realities of life in the villages and among the urban poor. When survivors include a widow, she receives "one-quarter of her deceased husband's estate if there was no issue, and one-eighth if there was" (Foo et al. 1976:35), the assumption being that children will provide for an aged mother. A widower receives two times more of a deceased wife's property than a widow receives of a deceased husband's estate. When other kin have inheritance rights, the rule of one share for the woman and two for the man also holds. Muslims are allowed to make wills "with regard to one-third of their property only" (Ibid.).

Non-Muslims of either sex, regardless of marital status, may will their property under the provisions of the Wills Ordinance of 1959, but under the Inheritance (Family Provision) Act the court has power to make reasonable provision for the surviving spouse(s) or dependent children of a deceased person if the court finds the will has inadequate provisions. If a non-Muslim woman dies intestate and is survived by her husband, he receives all of her property. If a non-Muslim man dies intestate, leaving a wife and children, one-third of his estate goes to his wife or is divided between his wives, and the remaining two-thirds goes to his children "in equal shares irrespective of their sex." If there are no children, his widow receives half of his estate and "the other half shall go to his closest relatives" (Ibid.).

Men obviously benefit more than women under either the civil or the Islamic code, while the civil code seems to benefit non-Muslim women more than the Islamic code benefits Muslim women. Certainly this is the case where a man dies intestate. A non-Muslim widow with no children receives half of her husband's estate, compared with the one-quarter due to a Muslim woman. And, where there are children, the non-Muslim widow receives one-third of the estate, while the Muslim woman gets only one-eighth. Further, children of an intestate non-Muslim father share equally in the two-thirds remaining after the widow's share is apportioned, while the three-quarters remaining in a Muslim father's estate are divided unequally between the surviving sons and daughters. But a Muslim man or woman can will only one-third of an estate, while a non-Muslim, after making provision for spouse and dependent children, can will the entire remainder. Where patri-bias is strong and primogeniture common, as among the Chinese, one or more male children are likely to benefit.

The influence of adat upon Muslim inheritance arrangements cannot be overlooked. Accommodation among heirs continues to be the norm, at least in rural Trengganu; and where adat perpateh prevails, in parts of Malacca and Negri Sembilan, "ancestral property vested in the tribe" can be passed only from female to female (Chung and Meng 1977:34).

> The legal status of an unmarried woman is similar to that of a man regarding her rights, duties and liabilities concerning property.
>
> The law relating to the status, rights and obligations of married women in Peninsular Malaysia is contained in the Married Women Ordinance 1957, which applies to all married women.
>
> This Ordinance provides that a married woman shall be capable of acquiring, holding and disposing of property as if she were a single woman.
>
> Under this Ordinance,
> —a woman can enter into contracts, debts and obligations as if she were a single woman;
> —a husband is not responsible for his wife's contracts, torts, debts or obligations unless his wife is assumed to be his agent;
> —a married woman can sue and be sued over a tort (civil wrong) although she may not sue her own husband or be sued by him over a tort;
> —a woman may take criminal proceedings against her husband for personal injuries inflicted upon her, but she may not take criminal proceedings against her husband regarding any property unless he wrongfully took the property while separating from her or deserting (Foo 1976:34-35).

The Married Women and Children (Maintenance) Ordinance 1950 and (Enforcement of Maintenance) Act 1968 provide financial protection for non-Muslim women whose husbands fail to support them. Under the former a woman can obtain a court order for support, and under the latter the court can order the husband's employer to make payments directly to the wife if the husband fails to do so (Ibid. :32-33), provisions that can benefit women whose husbands work for wages and salaries but are difficult to enforce when such is not the case, as among rural men whose income is from agriculture or fishing.

Among Muslims a married woman is entitled to maintenance (nafkah) from her husband, even if she earns money in her own right, unless "she unreasonably refuses to obey [his] lawful wishes or commands" (Ibid. :32). (Problem: where is the line between reasonable and unreasonable drawn?) Many men, particularly those engaged in traditional rural occupations, cannot support their families alone: the economic contribution of a wife is needed. Thus nafkah is an ideal that is far from universally realized. A woman can claim suitable housing during the idda period following a divorce, but she is not entitled to maintenance after dissolution of her marriage.

The economic situation of divorcées and widows is reflected in national employment patterns:

> The participation rate amongst employed women is highest for those who are divorced and secondly, for those who are widowed. In the case of divorced or widowed women, it is imperative that they work in order to support themselves and their families (Ibid.:11).

The ultimate socioeconomic goals for the nation during the Third Malaysia Plan (1976-80) include "ensuring national security, eradicating poverty and restructuring society . . . commitment of the people to the triple goals . . . development or strengthening of qualities needed to achieve the goals. . . ." The role of women was noted in a focus on "parental responsibility for good socialization" (Federation of Malaysia 1976a:104-05) and, more specifically:

> Fifthly, the role of women in society has become an increasingly important factor in both the developed and developing countries. The active participation and contribution of women in development outside the family circle are no longer saddled by prejudice and traditional conservatism. This is manifest by their leadership potentials in the fight for individual rights and freedom in society, equal treatment and respect for individuals irrespective of sex, race, culture and religion and the acceptance of human individual worth and capability in all walks of life. These are significant factors in a nation's search for character and identity. The contribution of women to the evolution of a strong and self-reliant society in Malaysia needs to be appreciated and taken into consideration in the agenda for rapid development and progress (Ibid.:105).

The idea that women are no longer "saddled by prejudice and traditional conservatism" owes more to idealism than to reality, as many women, particularly in rural areas, could attest. The TMP casts women as the humanists in development, but does not directly address the question of their economic role in that process.

In which occupations are women now employed? Women are represented more in agricultural occupations, characterized by low wages and low status, than any others. Of all employed women 56 percent are working in agriculture, one-third of them as "unpaid family workers" (Foo 1976:14). Mavis Puthucheary, a social scientist, has shown that 41.4 percent of Malay women are "unpaid family workers," compared with 19.6 percent of Chinese women and 9.8 percent of Indian and other women (1975:4).

Outside of agricultural employment, women are concentrated in a few occupations. Initially it is impressive to learn that they are 64.35 percent of the census category "medical, dental, veterinary and related workers." When the figure is apportioned by subcategory, it is found that women are mostly nurses, midwives, and dentists in charge of small government clinics. There are few women doctors and almost no women surgeons, dental specialists, or veterinarians. Women are 37.95 percent of all teachers, but the number of headmistresses is infinitesimal. Among administrative and managerial workers, women were only 3.37 percent of the total, but they accounted for 81.52 percent of stenographers, typists, and key-punch machine operators (". . . the standard new occupations everywhere for women are elementary school teaching, nursing and clerical . . . which have significant continuity with traditional women's roles" [Boserup 1970:26]). In the service occupations, women are 92.23 percent of the maids and related housekeeping workers; they are less than 10 percent of managers of catering and lodging services. Among production workers they are two-thirds or more of the spinners, weavers, knitters, and dyers, tobacco preparers, and tobacco product makers. And they are assembly-line workers in the electronics industry. Altogether women were 36.54 percent of the paid work force in Peninsular Malaysia in 1974, a decrease from 43.14 percent in 1967 (NACIWID 1978:35-45, 7; Foo 1976:17).

That women were almost 7 percent less of the paid work force in 1974 than in 1967 is surprising. The rapid development taking place in Malaysia during those years created a demand for workers in many fields, irrespective of sex. Industrialization has continued since 1974, with young women being actively recruited for factory work, so the 1980 census may show an increase in the percentage of women in the paid work force. Nevertheless, the decrease between 1967 and 1974 could support the view that as modernization proceeds, women lose some of their traditional occupations to mechanization and to men (Boserup 1970). Other women have been able to leave the paid work force as their husbands have obtained full-time or better-paying jobs. The two propositions are not incongruous. While development pushes some women out of their traditional occupations and deprives them of work because they are replaced by men, other women are quite content to leave the paid work force once their husbands are able to support them and their families.

In Trengganu women are a significant percentage of the workers in very few of the 101 census categories: nurses and midwives (100 percent), primary school teachers (25.7 percent), secondary school teachers (20.4 percent), stenographers, typists, and teletypists (53.9 percent), working proprietors—usually of very small village shops—(30.8 percent), street vendors and hawkers (36.53 percent), salespersons and shop assistants (50.95 percent), and service workers, particularly maids, cleaners, launderers, hairdressers, and beauticians (34.4 percent). More than 8,600 women (33.55 percent) are employed in production jobs of some sort, most in the "not elsewhere classified" category. By far the greatest number of women in the state are agricultural workers. The 1970 census shows a total of 25,390 women (32.2 percent) employed in that sector, with more than 10,000 in the "rice farm employee" category. Women who labor as "unpaid family workers" are not shown as a category (Federation of Malaysia 1977:Table 2.20; percentages calculated by the author).

In urban areas women pursue an enormous variety of careers, run their businesses or run for elective office, engage in charitable or organizational work, knowing that chores and children are being tended by at least one amah—maid, cook, laundrywoman, and childsitter. I know no "middle-class" woman who cleans her own house, washes and irons clothes, cooks meals on a regular basis, or is at the constant call of her children.

At a meeting of University of Malaya professional women, everyone was asked to fill out a questionnaire about her educational/ occupational situation. One question provided a checklist for each person to show who had been most-to-least important in helping her to achieve her career goals—husband, parents, friends, colleagues, other. Looking at the list, a professor said "My amah was by far the most important!" The women around her laughed and agreed. But when the amah has her day off, it is normally the wife who does any household chores.

Servant "woes" are a regular topic of conversation among friends and at social gatherings. In some parts of the country, factories and shops are competing with households for available female labor, a situation that was practically unknown in the 1960s. But enough women prefer the more intimate surroundings of a home over the impersonal factory to assure that servants can be found, albeit for higher wages. The situation should favor the woman who works as a servant, guaranteeing her better working conditions and better pay. The woman who needs a servant to lessen her own housework burden is faced with the problems of being able to find, afford, and keep one. It takes little imagination to envision a future situation, like the one already existing for women in the West, where middle-class Malaysian women will work outside the home and also have the responsibility for household chores or share them with a husband. Women laborers have always had the responsibility for two full-time jobs:

> . . . not all women can afford to employ domestic servants. In the rubber estates, for example, it is not possible for women to employ paid help. So the elder daughters are forced to help look after the younger children while mother is at work. This results in a vicious circle of poverty. The Indian girl on the estate is never able to do better than her mother as she is deprived of the necessary education to give her occupational mobility. . . . To a large extent domestic chores can be reduced by having an understanding and enlightened husband. But not all of us are lucky in this respect and it takes time to change men's attitudes toward child-rearing and household chores (Puthucheary 1975:7, 10).

A widespread assumption by men and many women regarding the household is that it is the woman's province. During a tutorial discussion about women's roles that I held with University of Malaya students, the men—Malays, Chinese, Indians, and others—were united in this view. It was the one subject of all those discussed during the year for which there was unanimity among them.

An alternative to full-time servants is provided by "odd-job maids" (SunEcho 12/10/78), but they usually are directed by the woman for whom they are working. They are a "new breed" of household workers who find they can earn more by working part-time in several households and have a greater degree of independence than would be possible working for one family. One woman does laundry and ironing in four homes on a daily basis, beginning her rounds after finishing the chores in her own home. Others do cleaning indoors or outside, and some specialize in making preparations for the evening meal.

Jobs for servants are among those advertised in the classified sections of newspapers under "Appointments," but demand is not adequately reflected because many women hire only through agencies.

The same discrepancy between positions advertised and actual demand probably holds for many other jobs.

Advertised positions (NST 2/7/79, 3/20/79) that specify female applicants fall mainly into two categories: office personnel and food or beverage service workers. Office personnel include confidential secretaries, accounts clerks, file clerks, receptionist-typists, stenographers, and ticketing clerks. In the second category there are numerous listings for waitresses and some for barmaids and bar hostesses ("you only serve, sit and talk 5 hours per day and earn $1,500 per month") and household cooks. Additional jobs for women are as teachers in private schools or programs, trainee supervisors (for what, was not revealed), insurance saleswomen, cashiers, hairdressers, manager for a luggage shop, public relations officers, nurses and midwives, doctor for a group practice, saleswomen, live-in baby-sitter, technical assistant with a mechanical engineering diploma, and factory workers.

Approximately half of the ads specify the sex of the person wanted for a job, with a majority seeking males. Of the other half, most positions are in occupations that are unlikely to attract female applicants because they are in fields where women will have had no opportunity to gain experience (die supervisor with foundry experience) or where the requisite degrees are most likely to be held by men (civil engineering and animal husbandry are two examples).

The ads are placed by local firms and multinational corporations. Most of the positions are in Malaysia or Singapore, but jobs in Saudi Arabia (English-speaking hostesses for Saudi Arabian Airlines; various household servants) appear occasionally. Few of the ads list wages or salaries. One that did was for female production technicians in a food manufacturing company at $280 per month.

The income gap between the rural and urban sectors of the nation is wide; employment opportunities in rural areas are not expanding as fast as the population is increasing. Prior to 1970 male migration from rural to urban areas slightly exceeded that of females. Today there is a massive influx of female migrants who gain employment mainly in the industrial sector. In part this is a result of NEP provisions requiring employers to hire a specific percentage of Malays, which has led to their recruitment from rural areas. Women migrate to improve their standard of living and, in many cases, to achieve individual freedom, a response to shifting norms in the society (Jamillah Ariffin 1978).

There is increasing demand by multinational corporations and local businesses for factory workers, especially females, as Malaysia continues to industrialize by attracting employers in search of low-cost labor. The demand is geographically uneven, as the following news report indicates.

3,000 jobs . . . at Bayan Lepas for female production
operators in electronics were unfilled due to a labor
shortage in Penang. Recruiting teams had been sent
to the East Coast [probably to Kelantan and Trengganu,
where development has been slower than in Pahang]
but . . . responses from outstation girls have been
rather slow . . . because they are reluctant to leave
home, do not want to work shifts, and there is also
competition from factories being built in some of their
home areas. In Penang, local supermarkets and shopping complexes are competing with the factories for
labor but there is no labor drain from the state. Most
of the girls who resign from their factory jobs, do so
to get married. . . (NST 8/17/78).

Women workers are preferred by multinational corporations,
many of them U.S.-based, because they can be paid less and are
easier to control. (See SEAC 1979 for Rachael Grossman's study
of the manipulation of women assembly-line workers in Asia, including Malaysia.)

The general tenor of many 1978-79 newspaper articles about
"factory girls"—female factory workers are always referred to as
"girls," just as female university students are designated "ladies"
in the English-language press—indicated that more public concern
was devoted to their personal behavior and morals than to their
working conditions and pay rates. Young women were exhorted
against abusing their independence and about their "duty to guard
and uplift their public image" (NST 2/12/79). Many families, equat-
ing factory work with the loss of traditional values and norms of
behavior, refused to allow their daughters to seek such employment. An alternative was to permit daughters to get jobs in factories while living in kampung homes with adult supervision, as
shown in an article by Anna Cheah, who interviewed some of the
Bayan Lepas workers in their "Home Away from Home" (Star
2/18/79) in Kampung Perlis.

"It's not fair to associate ALL factory girls with immorality. The outstation girls lodging in Kampung
Perlis . . . have to observe a strict code of behavior.
No boys are allowed to visit the girls at the kampung
houses unless . . . they are relatives." Even kinsmen are not allowed to spend a night in the same house.
If a girl does have a date with a boy friend, she meets
him outside the village, secretly.

Haji Abdul Razak bin Yunus, a member of the kampung committee and the mosque committee, expressed the community viewpoint: "In other kampungs, there have been cases of young innocents associating with undesirable men—and getting pregnant. We don't want this to happen to the girls living in our kampung. We don't want our kampung to get a bad name." [Concern for the reputation of their kampungs is commonplace among Malays, and frequently leads to dealing with problems locally rather than referring them to outside authorities, such as the police or the Department of Religious Affairs.]

Faulizah binti Mat Yatin, 21, a production operator who shares a house with her sister and three other girls, says: "We all live here like one happy family, doing our own marketing and cooking, our own washing, and spending a lot of time knitting, crocheting, sewing, reading and simply chit-chatting. . . . We don't go to town very often because we are trying to save as much as we can. Most of us send some money back to our families. . . . But we can't save a lot because our salary is low and we have to pay for our food and other needs. Thank goodness our rent is cheap."

Four other girls pay $11 each, for two rooms which they share, to landlord Encik Babji, 69, a retired Telecoms clerk, and his wife, who are very strict with them. The young women have lived "as part of the family" for about a year. "We like it here because we have someone elderly to keep an eye on us all the time. . . . We are less likely to go astray," Rodzian Murad, 24, from Alor Star says. Her parents are very religious and strict. "They like me to stay with a family rather than in a hostel or house with no one to supervise me."

Thus far, few Rusila women or those from contiguous villages have been attracted to the cities for factory work—or, if they were attracted, their families have discouraged them from leaving the kampung. Most of the migrants from Rusila are women employed by the government as teachers or in other professional capacities, or they have accompanied husbands who are employed in urban areas.

Whether they are rural or urban, a majority of Peninsular Malaysia's women workers are in the sectors of the economy where income is lowest. In 1972, 64 percent of paid women workers

earned less than $100 per month; 24 percent of employed men
earned less than $100. Approximately 35 percent of the men
earned $200 or more per month, while only 5 percent of women
earned that much (Foo 1976:19-20). Most countries fail to include
the economic contribution of women in household work and child
care when they are reckoning GNP or other economic indexes
(Boserup 1970), and Malaysia is no exception. Yet the vast majority of women who work outside the home also have the responsibility for cooking, cleaning, and other housework, as well as caring
for their children during hours spent at home. In other words, they
are performing two full-time jobs. And it is the unpaid job that
they are often exhorted not to slight.

Speaking at the Seventh Asian Regional Conference of the Associated Country Women of the World, Deputy Prime Minister Datuk
Seri Dr. Mahatir Mohamad said there was an urgent need to high-
light the problems of rural women in the country. These women
form about 58 percent of the female work force, and for them to
contribute effectively to the development of the country, their intelligence, skills, abilities, and potentials need to be developed
and applied right through to the highest level. However, he reminded women that in their pursuit of increasing their income-
generating capacity, they should not neglect their moral duties as
homemakers, wives, and mothers (NST 3/27/79).

The Deputy Prime Minister seems to be suggesting that rural
women work outside their homes from choice rather than necessity,
whereas the vast majority engage in remunerative work because
they must. And they still carry the full burden of home and child
care because the home and children are defined as a woman's responsibility. An example can be seen in an article about Indian
women estate workers by Cristel Kraal.

> "Can There Be a Better Way to Live?" (NST 10/3/70)
> deals with a seminar given for the women members of
> the National Union of Plantation Workers. The title of
> the article was taken from a statement by one of the
> participants, ". . . women in the plantations [mostly
> Indians] work hard from dawn to afternoon. They
> then rush home to cook, tend to their children and
> their husband's needs. They have been doing that for
> 100 years. Can there be a better way to live?" Other
> participants made it clear that while both husband and
> wife are wage earners, each getting a fixed daily wage
> of $5.65, it is the woman who is left with the extra
> burden of home and child care, many suffering from
> "miscarriages, anaemia and loss of weight" as a

result of the extra strain. Suggestions made by some
of the seminar speakers included establishing better
communication between husbands and wives and educating both in family planning. One speaker thought
that husbands should be "brainwashed" to rid them of
the idea that it is "unmanly" to do household chores.

The article and the earlier quote from Puthucheary might suggest that Malaysian men, except those working on plantations, take
routine responsibility for household chores and child care. A few
do. They are unusual individuals, or else they are acting under unusual circumstances, as when a wife is ill.

An examination of rural development undertaken by one agency,
FELDA (Federal Land Development Authority), and the participation
of women in its resettlement schemes shows a clear emphasis on the
wife/mother role almost to the exclusion of a direct economic role
outside of the home.

FELDA has transformed thousands of acres of land into resettlement schemes for landless families since it began in 1956.
Some of the schemes are being funded by Arab aid: the Kuwait Fund
provided U.S.$28 million in long-term, low-interest loans to meet
part of the costs of one scheme, and the Saudi Fund has helped to
open two others through a similar loan (Lawton 1979:36). Development of a scheme includes creation of an economic base for each
community—rubber or oil palm supplemented by coconuts, pine-
apples, vegetables, and other crops—through extensive land clear-
ing and planting, and the provision of housing, shops, roads, electricity, water mains, school, and mosque. In other words, total
communities are being fashioned out of the forest. Each family accepted for a scheme is allotted a home and ten acres of land, and is
subsidized until the crops reach the productive stage; then repayment to the government, in small monthly increments, begins.

Three types of training programs have been instituted for
settlers: technical, managerial, and leadership. Technical training for men focuses on the best ways to grow and exploit rubber or
oil palm, depending on the economic base of the scheme. "Settlers
wives . . . attend home economics courses." Women are taught
nutrition, child care, and budgeting among a variety of subjects;
the "objective . . . is to increase income of settlers through planned
healthy families." Vocational training, encouragement of subsidiary
agricultural enterprises, and other programs "involve token participation" of the women, especially by "the more adventurous and mentally liberated," thus adding overall to "the opportunities for women
in acquiring income generating skills" (NACIWID 1978:123-25). But
providing income-generating skills for women is not integral to the
programs.

An All-Girls Youth Land Development Scheme, patterned after
the FELDA schemes except that participants own land cooperatively
instead of individually, was instituted at Bukit Mambai in Johore in
response to pressure from Wanita UMNO after two all-male schemes
were set up in 1968. Land was not cleared properly and there were
many other problems—for instance, the decision to base the scheme
on oil palm and then accepting women who were unfamiliar with that
crop although many had experience with some aspect of rubber production, and provision of inadequate amounts of fertilizer and pesti-
cides for the scheme. More important from the personal point of
view, the dormitories provided for the women were supposed to be
replaced with individual housing that never materialized. Thus
women who married had to find housing outside the scheme. In
their evaluation of the scheme, Mazidah Zakaria and Nik Safiah
Karim conclude that on the positive side, it was shown that women
are as capable as men of participating fully in a land development
scheme. They also found that

> . . . the government has been rather shortsighted. . . .
> In other words, a more meaningful way of improving the
> position of women is to provide changes within the exist-
> ing structure of the society, eradicating practices which
> have proven detrimental to them, introducing new ones
> which will be of benefit to both men and women. One way
> is to ensure equal rights to land that has been developed
> through direct participation of husband and wife, rather
> than treating the husband as sole beneficiary. Perhaps
> one viable [alternative] is a land development scheme
> jointly owned and operated by newly-married couples
> rather than separate schemes for young men and women
> (1978:29-30).

There has been some spin-off effect on women from the cooperative movement although they have not been a target category
for co-op organization. As in the land development schemes, their
role generally appears to be defined as ancillary. Deputy Agriculture Minister Haji Zakaria Haji Abdul Rahman, discussing Majuikan,
emphasized the need to diversify the livelihood of fishermen's families. The wives and children of fishermen could be encouraged to
participate in processing catches or in unrelated economic activities,
such as raising poultry, producing handicrafts, or operating small
businesses (NST 10/10/78:1).

Tengku Maziedah Khaulah Ahmad, Director of Women's Activities at FOA, says women's participation has increased steadily since
the department was founded in 1975. The FOA distributes guidebooks

describing recommended projects for rural women. "But the women must take the initiative to begin a project," she says. If they need money to start it, they can submit a proposal to the FOA, which decides whether the project is feasible. Most of those funded become self-sustaining. Women have undertaken individual and cooperative ventures, such as poultry rearing, as well as establishing cottage industries, such as tailoring and producing prawn chips (Das et al. 1979:68).

The projects suggested are ones that village women have organized on an individual basis for more years than anyone can remember: processing fish for family consumption and sale; making handicrafts, women's clothing, and foodstuffs for sale; raising chickens and ducks and selling them or their eggs; and operating small shops. Because all have been among women's traditional economic activities, they are projects that are the easiest for women to undertake on a larger scale if they are given financial assistance, but they do not widen the scope of women's participation in the economy.

Other government programs have concentrated on mothering and on women's welfare needs such as health and family planning. Certainly these are worthy concerns. Women do want to know about proper nutrition for their children; they want to improve their own health and to produce healthy children; and many want to have fewer children and to space those they do have. But it is critical that government programs to develop productive skills among women be based on economic rather than welfare principles. Such has rarely been the case thus far.

> . . . more often than not, [programs] have not been
> based on sound economic planning (craft projects have
> been developed without thorough market research) and
> have involved "make work" projects that produce un-
> marketable items and skills which are sold at subsidized
> rates, if at all. These programmes tend therefore to
> promote the very dependency they were meant to allevi-
> ate (NACIWID 1978:130).

The need for education and training programs to assure development with equity for women is emphasized in the NACIWID report. But NACIWID is an advisory group that has no power to implement its recommendations, however sound they may be. It remains for the government and the private sector to act.

PEASANTS AND SEXUAL EQUALITY

The people of Rusila relied on fishing and agricultural production (particularly of rice, but vegetables, yams, fruit, and coconuts
were also important) for their subsistence prior to World War II.
All primary remunerative occupations were tied to one or the other.
Most of the women active in marketing sold their own garden produce; some men were fish hawkers but they, like many of the fishermen, were also seasonally engaged in preparing the fields where
their wives cultivated rice. Other occupations were secondary, involving individuals or families periodically—for instance, copra
(dried coconut) production or, on a spare-time basis, sewing, mattress making, the weaving of pandanus mats and basketry, or midwifery (for women) and production of thatching for roofs or car-
pentry (for men).

Raymond Firth considered similar villages to the north as
peasant communities despite the high reliance on fishing.

> . . . we can speak not only of peasant agriculturalists
> but also of peasant fishermen, peasant craftsmen and
> peasant marketers, if they are part of the same social
> system. In any case, such people are often in fact
> part-time cultivators as well. If the concept "peasant"
> be viewed as indicating a set of structural or social re-
> lations rather than a technological category of persons
> engaged in the same employment, then this unconven-
> tional inclusive usage seems justified (1964:17-18).

By definition, however "etymologically scandalous" (Leeds
1977:228) it might be to include fishermen as peasants, Rusila was
a peasant community in 1965. A majority of fishermen were part-
time cultivators; full-time and some part-time agricultural producers owned the land that they cultivated or worked for local owners, usually kin (as opposed to absentee landlords); they produced
for their own subsistence (rice and other crops) and for exchange
(rubber, coconuts, and vegetables); and they were part of a state-
organized political system, a subsociety within a large, stratified
society.

The influences of development were being felt in the 1960s:
there had been a primary school in the village for more than a
decade and the first young village women were enrolled in secondary
schools; the dirt road through the village had recently been paved;
villagers had voted in state and national elections; the first mechanized plows in the area had already prepared land for wet rice

cultivation, a step toward the replacement of the hoe and the buffalo-drawn plow; and a few people held wage-paying jobs. Today the out-side influences have markedly increased: more young people are continuing education beyond the primary level; occupational speciali-zation in the village has increased, and more people hold wage-paying or salaried positions in the towns; use of mass media, in-cluding television, is becoming commonplace; new patterns of mate selection and other challenges to tradition and the status quo are observable; and, gradually, the villages near Kuala Trengganu are assuming the appearance of suburbs. Thus, in Rusila and nearby areas many people are being "depeasantized" or moving into a "postpeasant" phase (Gamst 1974:64). Nevertheless, the trend is uneven, very recent, and far from universal in Trengganu or in Malaysia. Hence some questions about peasants are of interest.

Strong male dominance is a usual feature of peasant societies, but it is not characteristic of those in Southeast Asia, which are "bilateral with respect to inheritance, nonrigid with respect to rule of residence, and . . . unlike most peasant communities . . . ac-cord rather high social status to women" (Goldschmidt and Kunkel 1971:1069). Walter Goldschmidt and Evelyn Kunkel included six Southeast Asian examples (one each from Burma and Vietnam and four from Thailand) among the 29 peasant societies in their cross-cultural study. None from Malaysia was listed, although they refer to M. G. Swift's 1965 study of Jelebu in their text. The authors state that they cannot fully account for "the distinctive character of peasants in Southeast Asia," but suggest two features of the region that may be explanatory: the existence of large frontier areas that only recently were brought under cultivation, "so that the area is not one of a long-established, traditional peasantry," and, until recent times, the absence of strong central governments. Else-where the state influenced the structure of peasant families and promoted male dominance of farming by depriving men of their former pursuits—warfare and hunting (Ibid.:1061-70). Strong cen-tral governments and the contemporary states of Southeast Asia were molded during the colonial era.

In response to the Goldschmidt and Kunkel interpretation, Mick Moore (1973) proposed that the preponderance of wet rice cultivation in Southeast Asia required approximately equal labor contributions from women and men, creating a sexual interdepen-dence that led to relative equality between them. It is notable that Muslim wet rice cultivators in Southeast Asia, such as Javanese, Minangkabau, and Malays, "are, perhaps, when compared to their Islamic counterparts elsewhere in the world, among the most im-pressive examples of relative sexual equality" (Winzeler 1974:564).

In parts of Southeast Asia, the expansion of wet rice agriculture at the expense of swidden (slash and burn) cultivation occurred during the colonial period and is well documented. Most of Java, for example, was under ladang (a form of swidden) when the Dutch arrived. There followed "successive changes in some areas from long fallow to short fallow to annual and multiple cropping" (Boserup 1965:60) due to "the great pressure on land that arose from excessive increase in the population" (H. H. Bartlett, quoted in ibid.).

Population pressure does not appear to have pushed Malays from ladang to wet rice agriculture, but migrants from Sumatra and from Thailand introduced some rice-farming practices (Jackson 1972) and the British colonial government also played a part. Wet rice production (sawah) was encouraged during the early 1900s, in an attempt to eliminate dependency on imports, and was facilitated through the building of irrigation works, distribution of seed, a system of loans to wet rice growers for the purchase of buffaloes (to pull plows), and exemption of wet rice land from taxes (Cooke 1961: 3-9). The impact of these programs was felt most keenly in Kedah, today commonly referred to as "the ricebowl of Malaysia," and other parts of the country where plains are extensive. In Trengganu and Kelantan, wet rice was grown in the major valleys, but on "the higher alluvial terraces" people continued to plant hill rice and to rely on rainfall rather than irrigation; this northeastern region ". . . account[s] for over half the total dry rice acreage in West Malaysia" (Jackson 1972:84).

That Muslim women in Southeast Asia enjoy relative equality with men, compared with Muslim women elsewhere, suggests that such equality was an established cultural pattern before Islam gained strength in the area during the fourteenth century. Extensive dependence on wet rice by many Southeast Asian peoples has occurred rather recently, and relative equality between the sexes predates such dependency. Actually, relative sex-role equality appears to be a general feature of Southeast Asian social organization, regardless of subsistence type—wet rice agriculture, swidden cultivation, or foraging—thus suggesting that the causes should be sought "in circumstances more general than those which concern only state-level or peasant societies" or in dependence on wet rice agriculture (Winzeler 1974:565-66).

Increased interest by social scientists during the 1970s in the social position of women has resulted in propositions and theories to account for their status cross-culturally or in specific types of societies. Here, some of the "general circumstances" referred to above are examined with regard to the past and the future.

First, where women control the production of valued goods, their social status is higher than in societies where they have no such control. If women are to gain power, they need to produce valued goods and/or provide valued services, and to control the disposition of them.

Cross-cultural comparisons have shown that women's economic activity is an important prerequisite for gaining equality in the broad social sense (Bossen 1975; Martin and Voorhies 1975).

Peggy Sanday suggests that "female productive activities may be a necessary but not sufficient precondition for the development of female power," which is likely to develop where women control what they produce, "if females are actively engaged in producing valued goods" (1973:1697). In many societies women are active producers, but control of the distribution of goods and services outside of the domestic unit resides in men (Stack et al. 1975; Friedl 1975).

Among Malays of the east coast, women have engaged in the production of rice for generations. In Rusila both wet and hill rice were grown during the 1970s. Men and women cooperated in both types of cultivation: men cleared or prepared land, and repaired bunds around lowland plots; women planted or transplanted, and harvested, both types of rice. On the hillsides women did all of the weeding; men assumed most of the responsibility for putting fertilizer in the lowland plots, a periodic chore. Women also grew a variety of vegetables and fruits and controlled the marketing of all produce, although rice was and is grown for household consumption rather than for sale. Female work in the home and the fields is valued; women control marketing or distribution of produce.

Second, with regard to power, a distinction is drawn between activities and influence in the private or domestic domain (the family/household) and the public domain, "activities which take place or have impact beyond the localized family unit and relate to the control of persons or things" (Sanday 1974:190). Women are more likely to have domestic than public power. Sexual asymmetry is most pronounced in the public domain (Rosaldo 1974; Martin and Voorhies 1975).

The working wife whose income or produce (such as rice) is used for family/household consumption may gain parity in the domestic domain, but such usage "does nothing for her prestige and power outside it" (Friedl 1975:136).

Traditionally, Rusila women are the financial jugglers for their households. The average man gives the bulk of his income to his wife to run their household; she has the problem of stretching it, and of supplementing it when there is not enough to meet a family's needs. Ideally, whatever she earns in her own right is hers, to do with as she will, but a woman whose husband engages in village work must use some of her earnings for family support. And through their work in the fields, women provide food for their families. Rusila women do have parity in the home, and in some households they have more influence than their husbands with regard to financial matters. It is not unusual for a man to state that his wife is more clever than he about handling money. Women get the compliments and the responsibilities; their control over household funds also gives them some leverage in the home. There are at least two instances where local women secured loans when their husbands could not because it was the women who had reputations for astute financial decisions and reliability. Outside the economic arena Rusila women are not directly active in the public domain except as voters. Leadership positions are filled by men and membership on village committees is exclusively male, a situation common to villages elsewhere in Malaysia (Nash 1974; S. Husin Ali 1964, 1975).

Indirectly, women can influence men—their sons, husbands, brothers, and fathers—who then act in the public domain, but variation is great. Women are most likely to take strong stands and push their views about matters affecting their children, such as education.

Third, women can produce valued goods and control their distribution, exert power directly in the domestic domain and indirectly in the public domain, and still remain structural inferiors because of the way their rights are defined by other social institutions, such as religion or the law, or are embedded in social class organization.

Among Muslims women are equal to men in their rights to own, buy, and sell property, but they do not have equal rights with regard to inheritance, marriage, and divorce, as legal guardians of their children, and in other ways.

In class-structured societies female status is also a function of class position. In developing nations "class barriers are equally if not more important obstacles to genuine equality than sexual oppression" (Safa 1977:24).

Fourth, as development proceeds, women in traditional occupations are disadvantaged or displaced. Boserup's pioneering work (1970) alerted social scientists (and planners?) to the fact that women are often the victims of development because their productive role in traditional occupations is diminished and the levels of knowledge and training between women and men is widened, with men gaining the advantage.

Although both men and women may become victims of development, it is more difficult for women to adapt to new conditions because family obligations make them less mobile than men, their occupational choice is more narrowly limited by custom, they usually have less education and training, and even without these handicaps they often face sex discrimination in recruitment. Moreover, in

Third World countries a much larger percentage of the female than of the male labor force is engaged in traditional occupations, which are precisely those gradually replaced by modern enterprises in economic development (Boserup 1977:xii).

As agriculture becomes mechanized, for example, men are favored because they are the ones who are taught to operate, and therefore to control, machines. In some societies an examination of the local economy shows that women are producing subsistence crops with traditional techniques, such as hoes and digging sticks, while men are producing cash crops with the assistance of mechanized plows and cultivators. Or, as is the case in Rusila, where both men and women are engaged in rice production, land preparation—men's work—has been mechanized while women continue to plant and harvest with traditional hand tools. "In short, men represent modern farming in the village, women represent the old drudgery" (Boserup 1970:65). Women may be grateful if mechanization is extended to their traditional tasks, thus relieving them of "the old drudgery," but the result can be that they also lose control over the crops that they formerly produced. Recent findings support Boserup's observations (Bossen 1975; Tinker 1976; Manderson 1977, 1978; Kallgren n.d.).

Fifth, constraints are placed on development through the control of markets and technology at the international level by the industrialized nations, a persistence of neocolonialism.

Within developing nations, urban and landed elites forge economic programs to their own advantage—encouraging investment in export-crop agriculture, heavy industry, and urban growth. Power relations between men and women cannot be understood unless they are seen "in the context of the mode of production. . . . but how the mode of production affects Third World women is part of an international system based on dependency," the contrived dependency of developing nations on those that are highly industrialized. Women's options are severely limited "by the economic position of the whole community, which is ultimately determined by the international system" (Elliott 1977:5-8).

With regard to these ideas, in summary, the women of Rusila traditionally produced (and many of them still produce) valued goods (such as rice), and they control the distribution of those goods outside the domestic unit. They have power in the domestic domain, but their public influence is most likely to be on other women or else to be exercised privately, on husbands and sons who then act in the public domain. Income and goods produced are often used for family consumption, supporting parity in the domestic domain but not extending power beyond it. Local women are all Muslims, subject to the Islamic code of laws with regard to family matters. The great majority of them are also at the bottom of the social class system, although education has enabled some younger women to be upwardly mobile. Those who have stayed in the village, following traditional occupations, may become disadvantaged vis-à-vis men and mechanization, but the economic position of the entire community is tied to what is happening in Trengganu, Malaysia, and the rest of the world.

RUSILA WOMEN'S OCCUPATIONS

The fundamental occupation of Rusila women for the greater part of their adult years is ahli rumah, usually translated into English as "housewife"—but ahli in other contexts means "expert" and rumah can mean either "house" or "home," so "home expert" is a possible usage. Apprenticeship for this occupation, with its focus on child care and housework, begins early, and involvement with it may continue into old age, particularly among women who continue childbearing into their forties or who adopt grandchildren. Being an ahli rumah is seen by local women as a natural concomitant of being a wife and mother, which are natural stages of adult life.

All local women but one assume the responsibility for work in their homes, with or without the aid of children or grandchildren. The exception is a secondary school teacher who employs a neighbor as a full-time housekeeper. Housework is demanding even in a fairly small home. And, as suggested in Chapter 2, while toilets (outdoor or indoor) and sitting room furniture may be very desirable, they also create extra work for the women of the house. Routines vary considerably among women because they have different types of homes and furnishings, different numbers of children of different ages to care for (or get assistance from), and different social and work commitments outside the home. Nevertheless, women perform similar chores, most of which would be familiar to the average Western woman—cooking, cleaning, laundering, scrubbing—although the way of doing them might be unfamiliar.

Most women draw their water from a well rather than turning on a faucet; they scrub their laundry by hand rather than tossing it into a washing machine; they obtain fresh foods on a daily or meal-by-meal basis rather than relying on canned, packaged, and frozen foodstuffs; and some of them do all of their cooking over dapu fires, although kerosene stoves have become rather common.

Chores that are less likely to be familiar to Western women include the sunning of all bedding—mattresses, pillows, and linens—and furniture cushions several times per week to prevent mildew, a

common problem caused by high temperatures and humidity. Some
things can be propped in windows or draped over sills, but others
must be dragged outdoors onto verandahs. Neither mattresses nor
cushioned furniture is found in every local home; generally, the
more affluent the family, the more bedding and sitting room furniture there is to be sunned and cleaned.

Women do not work continuously, day in and day out, but it is
not unusual for a woman with a large, young family and no conveniences (such as piped water and refrigerator) to be engaged with
housework and child care from around 5:30 A.M. to approximately
9 P.M., with "time out" only for bathing, praying, eating—one
friend prepares breakfast for her family, sees everyone off to
work or school, cleans up the kitchen, and then sits down to enjoy
a quiet, solitary meal—and perhaps chatting with a passing neighbor
or just sitting on the verandah for a few minutes at midday to enjoy
the cooling breeze from the sea.

A large majority of women look after homes and families and
also engage in one or more remunerative occupations outside the
home and/or produce food on their own or a husband's land for
household use. It is often possible for women within the village
milieu to combine income-producing work with their child care
functions. Primary income-producing occupations, listed below,
are those done on a daily or regular and frequent basis, and reflect
responses to a question about the most important source of a woman's
cash income (thus eliminating food/goods produced only for household use). But primary occupations are only a part of the work picture. Many women also have seasonal, periodic, spare-time, and/or
occasional sources of income, do not have to make expenditures because of getting needed or at least useful goods free, do produce
goods/food for household consumption, and participate in kinship-
based cooperative networks that exchange goods and services.

Seasonally, and importantly, women transplant and harvest
rice—some annually, others occasionally, as when a friend or kinswoman needs help. In the spring of 1979, for example, an unusually
long period of hot weather brought much of the padi crop to the harvest point simultaneously. Even some women who normally do no
remunerative work were called upon for assistance by friends and
worked for a day or two, accepting a few dollars for their help or
acting within the reciprocity system. No one in Rusila sells rice;
only six couples produce enough to meet the needs of their families
for one year, and the rest must purchase some or all of the grain
they require.

The production of copra (dried coconut) is carried out several
times per year by those who own enough palms to accumulate 300-
400 nuts or by someone who has bought a batch of them cheaply.

Production can be a family enterprise involving a married couple and their children, often with casual help from neighbors, or an individual of either sex may hire a man to husk the nuts and then do the remaining work—essentially, splitting the nuts and drying the coconut meat on a platform under which a fire is kept burning continuously for a minimum of six hours.

A woman can have a primary occupation as a gardener, selling much of her produce locally, but when there is a surplus, she becomes a marketer in Marang or Kuala Trengganu. A shopkeeper spends many hours tending her shop and gets the bulk of her income from that work, but when there are no customers, she will likely use her time weaving pandanus mats for sale.

Figure 5. Two Roles: Mother and Paid Worker (Rusila, 1979). 'Timah strings tobacco, a seasonal occupation, while her two-year-old son plays nearby. Remunerative work performed in the village milieu often can be combined with child care.

A few women take advantage of opportunities to make extra income or to avoid making a cash outlay that others fail to recognize or ignore. During 1965 a group of village women went to the island a few miles offshore for a picnic. One of them spent part of her time filling several gunnysacks with a type of fruit that does not grow in Rusila or nearby, and later made a few dollars from selling it. No one else had been prepared to exploit the opportunity. During 1979 a young woman whom I accompanied on a visit to her parents' village took along sacks that she filled with rice husks at a friend's mill. Her mother-in-law used the millings to feed her ducks for several weeks. A woman whose husband drives a pickup truck got a garlic windfall after her husband delivered a consignment of the product. One of the baskets broke, and the dealer did not want to bother about the spillage. The driver's wife told me that she salvaged more than $10 worth of usable garlic. Two women who have refrigerators sell ice frozen into quart-size bags for $.20 each, making "enough to pay the electricity bill." Small amounts of income or savings through getting free what is usually purchased are probably far more important in many households than what I have recorded. It is difficult to keep track of income or savings that occur so irregularly because they are usually forgotten after a short time.

Gift exchanges fall into the category of generalized reciprocity, more or less equitable through time. Perishables such as fish, fruits and vegetables, and turtle eggs are among the foods shared with (or sold to) kin and neighbors when a woman has more than her own family needs. The surplus may be the result of a "good buy" or of gifts: I took mangoes to a friend who had received a sackful of them from her brother on the same day. The abundance was shared with my friend's mother and her brother-in-law's family. Or a surplus can result from luck: a family member goes walking on the beach during the season when giant leatherback turtles lay their eggs, sees one of the great creatures lumber ashore, waits, and (illegally) takes the 100 or so eggs.

Women also provide cooked food for nonresident kin, usually in cases where the recipient is ill. Assistance with child care is more common, particularly a grandmother caring for her grandchildren while their mother works or makes a trip to the town. In any emergency there are always women (and men) ready to help. The loosely organized cooperative networks of women are largely based on consanguineal and/or affinal ties, but also include neighbors who are not kin. They are activated for ceremonial and special events and when the unexpected—early ripening of the padi crop or a death in the family—happens. Women give and take moral/emotional support, time, efforts, and food; they borrow and loan kitchen equipment, small amounts of money, ceremonial paraphernalia, and clothing and jewelry for special occasions.

The general occupational categories for the 1965-66 and 1979 research periods are shown below.

	1965-66		1979	
	No.	Percent	No.	Percent
Able-bodied women; married or formerly married	137	100.0	184	100.0
Women performing remunerative work on a regular basis	127	92.7	144	78.2
Primary occupation, weaver of pandanus mats and basketry	97	70.8	78	42.3
Other primary occupation	30	21.9	66	35.8
Women who have the ahli rumah saja status (no remunerative work)	10	7.2	40	21.7

There were two notable shifts between 1965-66 and 1979. First, a smaller percentage of women performed remunerative work on a regular basis in 1979 than in the 1960s (from 92.7 percent to 78.2 percent); more women proudly claimed the ahli rumah saja status ("homemaker only"). Second, fewer women were reliant on pandanus weaving as a primary occupation (although many more than shown do weave for household use, make gifts for friends, and also sell something occasionally); more women had other primary occupations.

The primary occupations other than pandanus weaving during 1965-66 were ten: shopkeeper (N = 8), food hawker and other food sales outside home or shop (N = 5), vegetable and fruit gardener (N = 4), rubber tapper working cooperatively with a husband on land owned by either of them (N = 4), rubber tapper working individually for income on someone else's land (N = 3), wage earner: one pandanus-weaving instructor and one clerk at the Weaving Center (N = 2), mat and cloth dealer (N = 1), rubber grove laborer (N = 1), coconut-sugar maker working cooperatively with husband (N = 1), village midwife (N = 1). The last is somewhat misleading because, however important midwifery is to local women, the occupation is an occasional one. The respondent considered her work as a midwife to be far more important than anything else she did (seasonal work in the padi fields, weaving, raising ducks, and so on). For her it was a primary self-identity occupation if not the most important source of income.

By 1979, although more women were engaged in primary occupations other than weaving, new options were few: tobacco

grower (N = 31), shopkeeper (N = 11), tobacco laborer—one who
sorts, grades, strings, and bales (N = 4), food hawker and food
sales outside the home (N = 3), vegetable and fruit gardener (N = 3),
brocade cloth weaver (N = 2), village midwife (N = 2), seamstress
(N = 1), cloth dealer (N = 1), and coconut dealer (N = 1). Besides
the clerk and the teacher at the Weaving Center, there is a woman
who teaches pandanus weaving at another center in Kuala Trengganu.
And there are primary school teachers (N = 2), a secondary school
teacher, and the government midwife who runs the clinic in the village.

New occupations for women are mostly associated with tobacco
growing and processing, promoted since the early 1970s by the district officer, who also encouraged the establishment of a tobacco
growers' cooperative in the village. Four women and 18 men are
members. And there are now local professional women: teachers
and a government midwife. Brocade weaving on looms has long been
a traditional occupation for women in several villages north of Rusila;
the women producing brocade locally married into the village from
that area. Only two men were tapping rubber during 1979. Some
people owned trees that had passed the productive stage but others,
who had younger trees, were not tapping because the price of rubber
was too low to make the work worthwhile. When the price goes up,
several women and men plan to resume tapping.

Unmarried, dependent women were not included in the above
enumeration. During the 1960s they assisted their mothers with the
full range of housekeeping chores and care of younger siblings, and
a few helped in the fields or did other work ancillary to that performed by their mothers. Their only means of earning cash income
was through sale of pandanus mats and basketry or, if they were
selected, they could earn $.50 (later, $1) per day as students at the
Weaving Center. The 20 girls from Rusila and nearby villages who
were in the program were delighted to be paid for an activity they
would have performed at home anyway, and to work in the company
of friends. The training program at the Weaving Center was sus-
pended during part of 1975, but by August 1978 there were 11 young
women working under the guidance of a local instructress, and earning $40 per month each.

Neither the teacher nor the students were from Rusila; all
came from neighboring villages. One unmarried Rusila woman is
a full-time seamstress, working from her parents' home. Four
others also live with their parents but are employed outside the
village, two as pandanus weaving instructors and two as office
clerks. Another young woman works as an assistant clerk at the
Weaving Center in the village. Most of the young women who are
no longer in school are engaged in the traditional women's tasks,
helping their mothers and weaving mats and baskets for sale.

Pandanus weaving is an important source of income for many women, although the amounts earned are generally small—less than $25 for a mat that has taken a woman's every spare minute, for two or three or more weeks, to weave. Local women do not calculate time:income ratios; rather, one often weaves instead of just relaxing, doing nothing. The choice between weaving and not weaving is most dependent upon a family's needs or a woman's personal wants and plans.

Among women who do not own land, and even some who do, pandanus weaving is an important source of income although the amounts earned are generally small. The craft has been practiced by women in Rusila and nearby villages for generations. It is a spare-time specialty that can be carried on throughout the year, requires no investment except a few cents for dyes, can be done indoors or out, at any time of day or night, for a few minutes or several hours. It is highly congruent with household chores and child care.

Traditionally the craft was learned by girls through observation and imitation of their mothers and other adult women. Knowledge was imparted informally, usually within the context of the family, until 1957 when the Medan Anyaman (Weaving Center) was opened in the village under the auspices of RIDA (later MARA). It was a multifunctional place where young women learned to weave and were paid for doing so, and where women of all ages could gather to work in the company of friends. There were storage facilities (important for those with playful toddlers and living in small houses), and the Medan was a sales outlet. During the early 1970s a new center was built in the village, a modern structure designed more as a tourist attraction than as a place where women could or would gather. It continues to be a place of learning and a sales outlet, but its other functions have ended. The old center was converted into a midwife's clinic, and thus is still serving women. And now, in response to increased tourism, shopkeepers feature woven goods in their shops in competition with the Medan, so local women have a choice of outlets for their products.

Regardless of increased demand for woven products, the individual involved in handcrafting any item is able to produce only a limited quantity. Once the peak of individual productivity is reached, increased demand is meaningless to the individual unless it serves to increase the worth of the items produced.

The prices of mats and baskets have risen but have not kept pace with inflation. A finely woven prayer mat sold for $13 in June 1966. The same weaver was asking $21, an increase of almost 62 percent, for a similar mat in August 1978 if she sold it from her own home. It would cost the purchaser more at a shop, but the amount realized by the weaver would be approximately the same.

Figure 6. Trimming Pandanus (Rusila, 1966). Hajjah Fatimah trims pandanus, used for weaving mats and baskets. Her grandson, Ramli, and a neighbor, Hajjah Aminah, chat with her while she works.

During the same time period, top-quality rice (preferred by local women when they can afford it) rose from $1.70 per gantang to $3.80, an increase of 124 percent. A medium-quality sarong that was $5 in 1966 was $12—a rise of 140 percent—at the same shop in 1978. Thus income from weaving has not increased at the same rate as the cost of household and personal necessities that many weavers must buy.

During the Conference on Women in Development held at Mexico City in 1975, there was a debate in the Education Workshop concerning handicrafts. Participants were split between those who favored handicraft production as a means for poor women to earn income and those who saw handicraft production as an activity with "no future and low income." The overview was that probably both attitudes were accurate but that local situations of women needed consideration before including handicraft training in development schemes (Tinker 1975).

Figure 7. Artistry (Rusila, 1965). Selamah weaving a fine pandanus mat with a very complex pattern.

A majority of Rusila women do not have the luxury of being ahli rumah saja or of holding jobs that pay wages. Fewer women are reliant on mat and basketry weaving as a primary occupation than was the case in the 1960s, but more women engage in that work as a source of cash income than in any other occupation. The facts that the craft is a spare-time specialty that can be combined with household chores and child care, and that it requires no investment, mean that even the poorest woman whose responsibilities keep her at home can still earn income. No one will get rich from this form of work—prices have not kept up with inflation—but even small amounts of cash are important in the village context, especially to women who have skills only for village work.

More impressive than the shifts from rubber to tobacco, both agricultural cash crops, and the presence in the village of four professional, salary-earning women, is the increase in the number and percentage of women who identify themselves as ahli rumah saja. When a Malay village woman says, "Saya ahli rumah saja," she says it with pride. She is conveying the information that her husband is a very good provider and, as a result, she does not have to work outside her home. Both she and her husband are fulfilling their ideal adult roles, he as the supporter of his family and she as full-time wife and mother. In recent years it has become equally prestigious for a woman to hold a salaried position—for instance, teacher, midwife, government dentist, or white-collar office worker, all of which now require completion of five years of secondary school or more education. Few village women have thus far fulfilled the qualifications. Men are in the same position, and their failures may be the more frustrating because of the ideal image of the male as the family supporter, but men have a wider variety of local occupational opportunities than women have.

A comparison of the list of women's occupations with one for men reveals these greater opportunities for men and the diversification and specialization that are occurring, and also indicates how more women can have the luxury of being full-time home makers because husbands are regularly employed. In 1966 village men were engaged in 17 primary occupations and, like women, many had other seasonal or occasional work. Rubber tappers accounted for 32.8 percent (N = 44) of working men; another 23.1 percent (N = 31) were fishermen. Wage earners and salaried men (the penghulu, secular and religious teachers, clerks and public works employees; N = 12), carpenters (N = 12), fish peddlers (N = 9), gardeners and other agricultural producers (N = 9), and laborers at Rompin who load ore on ships (N = 6) made up the majority of the remainder. Three men received the bulk of their income from owning land or capital equipment used by others; they are now deceased and their holdings divided among children. There were also several men involved in sales of various goods (lumber, cement blocks produced by a wife, coconut sugar, dry goods, livestock, coconuts), and one rubber grove laborer. Most primary occupations were not wage-based; income was never assured.

By 1979 only 2 men were tapping rubber and 24 (14.4 percent) were fishermen, 3 as members of a co-op based in a nearby village. The largest number of men were engaged in growing and processing tobacco (N = 37, or 22 percent) and many of them also had other agricultural work. Twenty-six men held wage-paying jobs in a saw-mill or with the government as mechanics and heavy equipment operators. There were teachers and a headmaster, policemen and soldiers. Nine men worked as drivers, several in business with their own pickups, others of trucks and buses, and one man as the owner-operator of a trishaw. There were carpenters and building contractors, hawkers, shopkeepers, and land brokers. And each of the following occupations engaged a local man: coconut dealer, cook, cloth dealer, motor repair shop boss, watchman, driving instructor, forestry worker, furniture maker, bus conductor, and batik maker. Altogether respondents named 34 occupations, including kerja sendiri (my own work), a jack-of-all-trades kind of category that includes some agriculture, individual fishing (rather than as part of a big crew), this and that. The number of occupations that men claimed had doubled during 14 years, and many more men were enjoying a steady and higher income, thus allowing their wives to devote themselves to home and family on a full-time basis.

However desirable it is to be a "home maker only," and despite the increase in the number and percentage of women claiming that status because their husbands are able to fully support their families, the average woman does one or several types of remunerative work as well as being an ahli rumah. Many help to support their families; a few earn in order to provide themselves and their children with luxuries. Some manage to save enough to buy land or gold jewelry.

SAVINGS AND INSURANCE

One of the obvious signs of increased affluence among Rusila people in the 1970s as compared with the 1960s was the amount of gold jewelry worn by many women: elaborate and heavy gold chains, earrings, bangles and other bracelets, and rings were all in evidence. Gold jewelry is the basic insurance of peasants and, for Muslim women, it can be particularly important in case of divorce or the death of a spouse (see Fernea 1965:134). Since I left the village in the summer of 1979, the price of gold on the international market has almost trebled, making it an even more desirable commodity as both status symbol and as insurance and savings—but one that will now be more difficult to afford.

Pawning gold jewelry (with Chinese brokers in Marang or Kuala Trengganu) has become less frequent than in the 1960s, which suggests a general increase in prosperity, although the increase is uneven in the village. Women who are least likely to own much gold jewelry are also the ones who may have the greatest need to pawn it during any given year. They are the ones who have few economic assets, are married to men who do village work, and themselves do village work that is seasonally unreliable. The period of the monsoon sees the greatest drain on savings and the least income to households dependent on village work. If the monsoon is harsh, fishermen cannot go to sea, rubber tappers cannot tap, crops can suffer damage or destruction, and so on. A family can be forced to depend on savings, both cash and gold. The monsoon varies from year to year. During 1966, a particularly disastrous monsoon period, most of the gold jewelry in Rusila was pawned and some was never redeemed; during 1979 the monsoon was barely discernible, meaning that village work was not disrupted and no strain on the finances of most families occurred for that reason. Cash reserves and gold "insurance" may also become particularly important for funerals and weddings, for although the kindred and women's cooperative networks are then activated, some cash outlays are usual.

Although more women were saving money in Post Office accounts in 1979 than in 1965 (24 versus 3), it was still more common to find men using that facility and women adhering to the old practice of caching money in the home. The existence of these emergency funds is kept secret from a husband but, since the practice of having secret savings is common, a man usually assumes that his wife has some money in reserve. During 1979 two Rusila homes were robbed of cash and gold jewelry, and stories about similar crimes in nearby villages were circulating. Such events will probably encourage more people to use Post Office accounts as a way of safeguarding savings.

LAND OWNERSHIP AND INHERITANCE

Land for productive use is the most desirable commodity to the average villager of either sex. And it is now both scarce and expensive. There simply is no unowned land of any type in Rusila or nearby villages. Some house plots and the stands of coconut palms around them can, and probably will be, subdivided to accommodate an owner's children as they establish their families. But in parts of the village, houses are already built within a few feet of one another. Productive land divided below a certain size results in plots that cannot possibly provide more than a small supplement to family income. For this reason, despite Islamic partible inheritance rules, the government will not register individual ownership of plots below a specified size, which varies according to the type of land. Thus accommodations among heirs are usual, although the forms vary.

If a plot of land cannot be subdivided and the owners live in the village, joint exploitation may work best for everyone. But perhaps one or more of the owners live elsewhere or hold wage-paying jobs. Then it is more likely that one person, either an owner or someone hired for the purpose, works on the land and the others get a small share of the produce or the income from sales. When emotional ties between inheritors are close and needs differ, those who are in need may be given a larger share or, in the case of a house, a person who owns no home or a less desirable home is given preference.

Accommodations are often, but not always, amicable. In 1979 a Rusila woman died, leaving almost three-quarters of an acre of padi land to be divided between a son and a daughter, half siblings. The son is not a Rusila man and has never lived in the village. The daughter is a Rusila woman and has lived there all her life. She had worked the land with her mother for many years and wanted to buy her brother's share, approximately one-half acre. She offered him the current value for the land but needed to pay for it in installments. The brother, who was said to be financially well-off, would agree to installments only if a much higher price were paid, a demand that was interpreted as bordering on usury. There was much wrangling and ill will; the matter was unsettled when I left Rusila.

Even full siblings may insist on a meticulous property division and may need their rights badly. Generally, the more that people are dependent on productive land as their source of income, the stronger their demand for exact inheritance rights and the less they are willing to make accommodations. When agreement cannot be reached, the alternative is to sell the land and divide the proceeds. Villagers normally sell land as a last resort or, in a few cases, to finance a pilgrimage to Mecca.

While Muslims can will as much as one-third of their property, it is still unusual for village Malays to make wills. There is an idea that to make a will is to tempt fate and, more important, almost everyone accepts the Islamic rules of inheritance.

Ownership of house plots, rice land, and rubber is reckoned by extent, while coconuts and tobacco are reckoned by the number of trees or plants owned. It was noted previously that, unlike the Western assumption that a house and the land where it is situated form a unit, among Malays house and house land are two distinct entities, although both can be owned by the same person. Further, coconut palms near a house may appear to be one grove growing on the house land when in fact they may be owned by several other people. Joint but unequal ownership of individual trees is not unusual.

House and House Land Ownership

Ownership of both a house and its land is more often vested in men than in women (64 properties in contrast with 32 properties), and the owner is usually a resident of the house. There is one example where house and land are owned jointly by a married couple, and another where a woman and her son share the ownership of both

TABLE 7.1

Rusila House/House Land Ownership, by Sex and Residence: 1979

Owner	House Only		House Land Only		Both	
	Number	Percent of Total	Number	Percent of Total	Number	Percent of Total
Household resident						
Female	15	16.0	27	29.0	28	28.0
Male	76	82.0	2	2.2	62	63.0
Joint ownership	1	1.0	1	1.0	2	2.0
Subtotal	92	99.0	30	32.2	92	93.0
Nonresident						
Female			20	21.5	4	4.0
Male	1	1.0	41	44.0	2	2.0
Wakaf			2	2.2		
Government	1	1.0			1	1.0
Subtotal			63	67.7	7	7.0
Total	93	100.0	93	99.9	99	100.0

house and land. The government owns one house and its land, the residence of the official midwife and her family.

Where there is separate ownership of house and house land, more men than women own houses (77 to 15) and, again, the owner is usually a resident. But more women than men own house land although the difference is not great (47 to 43). Combining male and female ownership of house land only, more nonresidents than residents are owners (61 to 29). In almost all cases the land is owned by a parent or grandparent of the home owner, and may be part of the resident's inheritance expectation. One house is jointly owned by a married couple, and another couple shares the joint ownership of a house plot but does not own the house. Two families have their own houses on land that is wakaf, a gift to the community in the name of Islam.

Rice Land Ownership

There are 112 wet rice plots, ranging in size from less than one-half acre to ten acres, in the village, with 92 percent of them less than two acres in size. The vast majority of the plots are individually owned, reflecting both purchase patterns and the tendency of heirs to divide land for individual registry or to sell small plots to one of their number. There are five small plots where there is acknowledged joint ownership, whether it is registered as such or not. The ten instances of joint ownership shown in the table all involve men and women, either married couples (purchase), siblings, or mothers and sons (inheritance).

Women are represented equally with men in only two acreage categories: one-quarter to one-half acre and ten acres; in the latter an older couple, married for many years, shares ownership. Overall, women are 43 percent of the total owners of padi fields, owning a total of 48 plots.

Rubber Land

During 1965-66 rubber was an important part of the Rusila economy that was dormant in 1975. Many sections now have trees that are beyond the productive stage; replanting would be a major undertaking, but the land is still an asset. Almost everyone stopped tapping younger trees when the price of rubber was low, and found alternative sources of income; some stated they will resume tapping if the price rises. Thus, tappable or not, rubber assets were dormant until 1978, when the federal government purchased extensive

TABLE 7.2

Rusila Rice Land Ownership, by Amount and Sex: 1979

Amount of Land (acres)	Total Owners	Female Owners		Shared Ownership by Male and Female		Females as Percent of Total in Category
		Number	Percent of Total Owners	Number	Percent of Total Owned Jointly	
1/4 to 1/2	50	22	19.6	3	30	50.0
1/2 to 1	33	10	8.9	3	30	39.3
1+ to 2	20	4	3.5	2	20	30.0
2+ to 4	7	2	1.8	1	10	42.8
4+ to 9+	0	0	0.0	0	0	0.0
10	2	0	0.0	1	10	50.0
Subtotal	112	38 10*	33.8	10**	100	42.8
Total	112	48	43.0			

*10 shared ownership.
**10 cases, 20 people.

216

TABLE 7.3

Rusila Rubber Land Ownership, by Amount and Sex: 1979

Amount of Land (acres)	Total Owners	Female Owners		Shared Ownership Female and Male	Females as Percent of Owners in Category
		Number	Percent of Total Female Owners		
1/4 to 1	6	1	6.6		16.6
1+ to 2	5	2	13.3		40.0
2+ to 3	10	2	13.3		20.0
3+ to 4	7	2	13.3		28.6
4+ to 5	4	3	20.0		75.0
5+ to 6	10	3	20.0	1 (2 persons)	40.0
6+ to 7	2	0	0.0		0.0
7+ to 10	3	0	0.0		0.0
More than 10 acres	2	1*	6.6	1 (2 persons)	50.0
Subtotal	49	14	93.1		
		1**	6.6		
Total	49	15	99.7		30.6

*16 acres.
**shared.

217

tracts of old rubber on the hill west of Rusila and another village
where a telecommunications center is planned. Even so, there
were more owners of rubber groves in 1979 than in 1965 (49 compared with 34).

Women are 30.6 percent (N = 15) of the owners of land with
rubber trees. And, like their male counterparts, some of them
own trees that are no longer productive. Women own less than 50
percent of the tracts in all acreage categories except 4+ to 5 acres,
where they are three of the four people owning that amount, and in
more than 10 acres, where a man and wife jointly own 16 acres.

Tobacco

Tobacco ownership is reckoned by the number of plants a person has rather than the amount of land. Much of the tobacco is
planted in plots where padi, vegetables, and fruits are seasonally
grown. Altogether 64 people own tobacco, more than half of them
having fewer than 2,000 plants and 95 percent owning fewer than
3,000 plants. There are 22 women owners (34.4 percent), including 13 who share ownership with a husband. The largest holding,
4,800 plants, belongs to a woman who is one of four female members of the 22-person tobacco cooperative that operates its own
kilns, processes leaf, and sells.

Coconut Palms

Coconut palms are the only form of productive property in
which ownership of a small part—a percentage of one palm—is useful. Coconut cream (the liquid squeezed from coconut meat that has
been soaked in a small amount of water) is an ingredient in many
Malay dishes; the meat and water from green nuts are enjoyed as
snacks; and coconut oil, used for frying foods, can be made from
the meat of mature nuts. Many of the palms in the village are exploited only for these household uses. Equally important, the product is easily divisible among owners. For copra production to be
worthwhile, it is necessary to accumulate several hundred nuts.
People who make copra regularly own 30 or more palms, or they
have monkeys trained to pick the nuts and are paid in kind (10 nuts
for 100 picked) for the animal's work. Anyone who owns fewer than
30 palms is more likely to sell whatever surplus remains after the
needs of the household are met.

There are 125 persons who own one or more palms; 58 of them
are women. An additional 36 people own shares in one or more

TABLE 7.4

Rusila Tobacco Ownership, by Amount and Sex: 1979

| Number of Plants | Total Owners | Female Owners | | Shared Ownership Female and Male | Females as Percent of Owners in Category |
		Number	Percent of Total Female Owners		
1,000-1,999	35	5	22.7	5	28.5
2,000-2,999	26	3	13.6	7	38.4
3,000-3,999	2	0	0.0	1	50.0
4,000-4,999	1	1	4.5	0	100.0
Subtotal	64	9	40.8	13	34.4
		13*	59.1		
Total	64	22	99.9		34.4

*Shared ownership.

palms; 19 are women. One hundred and thirteen owners (90 percent) have fewer than 30 palms. Of the 12 people with more than 30 palms, four are women. One of them owns almost 300 palms.

Generalizations

Several generalizations are obvious from the above land ownership data.

First, more men than women own land of all types, and men own larger pieces of land than women own. The pattern results not only from the male bias of partible inheritance rules (although that is certainly important) but also from the past practice of some men registering deeds of purchased land in their own names even when a wife had contributed her efforts and earnings to buying it. That practice, in combination with divorce patterns in which a woman might give up land rights to obtain a divorce or might run away from a husband and refuse to resume cohabiting with him, meant that some women were left landless although they should have had a share.

Second, shared ownership by spouses is higher for tobacco than for any other category; it is lowest for rubber, although the largest local tract is jointly owned by a married couple. Tobacco is a short-term investment, a cooperative venture for a season. Rubber is a very long-term investment, for it is years before the trees can be tapped. A house and house land also suggest a long-term commitment, and there is little joint ownership in that category. Where joint ownership of rubber is found, the owners have been married for at least ten years before the venture is made. Marital stability is not the total explanation, but I suggest that it has a bearing on joint ownership. However, tobacco plants are also cheap compared with rubber and can be planted on land that is used for other crops, while rubber is a separate system.

Although the information is not reflected in the tables, there are two more generalizations to be made about land ownership.

Third, the vast majority of landowners are over 35 years of age. Very few people below the age of 35 own land of any type, although they do own houses. Most younger people have not yet inherited anything, and almost no land goes on the market for purchase.

Fourth, ownership is concentrated. Over 40 percent of the people who own productive land own more than one kind of productive land or crop—for example, a woman owns one-quarter acre of padi land, 1,000 tobacco plants, eight coconut palms, and house land. Her husband of 17 years owns only their house. He is a fisherman.

Two women owners have impressive holdings: the woman who has more than 4,000 tobacco plants, Lijah, and the one who owns almost 300 coconut palms, 'Mak 'Mas. While men own more land and larger amounts of land generally, these two women own the most in the tobacco and palm categories. And both of them own other productive property. Aside from that, they have little in common except their drive, intelligence, a keen eye for economic opportunity, and their Rusila birthplace. Compared with a majority of Rusila women, each has had an economic advantage: 'Mak 'Mas was a moneylender—not a respectable occupation in the view of her peers, although many used the service; Lijah's husband was among the few men who had a wage-paying job in 1965, enabling Lijah to save all of her own income from weaving mats, raising poultry and selling the birds and their eggs, and selling vegetables grown on a small plot. Both women invested their earnings in land.

THE DIVISION OF LABOR

The sexual division of labor in Rusila is not rigid. Women are responsible for home and child care, but in emergency situations a man will cook, clean, do the laundry, and perform child care functions. One young Rusila bachelor living in Kuala Lumpur regularly cooked for himself and cleaned his apartment without any feeling that it was peculiar. At home his mother did those chores, but he was not living at home. When he marries, if his wife also works outside the home, he says he will help around the house; if she stays at home, then she should do the work at home.

In contrast with the practices of villagers in Boserup's Malaya sample, where under single-cropping women work only 45 percent of the hours per week worked by men (1970:25), in Rusila the percentage was the opposite in 1965, when men still prepared land with hoes or buffalo-drawn plows. By 1979 male input was even less because most land was prepared by disk plows, leaving men only the chore of repairing the bunds around the fields. Women continued to transplant rice from the nurseries to the fields, back-breaking or at least back-aching work, and to harvest with the hand-held reaping knife, which allows cutting only one rice stalk at a time. Women transport the harvested grain, thresh it (with the feet), remove the husks (at the mill or by use of mortar and pestle), and winnow.

The division of labor in rice production is clear-cut, but women who have no men to plow land can prepare a small plot with hoes. Otherwise, they have to hire a man to plow with buffalo or machine. And there is no taboo that keeps men from transplanting or harvesting. Both men and women say that women are more adept at these tedious chores.

Figure 8. Workers in the Rice Fields (Rusila, 1965). A woman transplants seedlings into one part of the padi field (sawah) while her husband and his brother prepare another section of land. By 1979, although women continued to transplant manually, most land was prepared with mechanized plows.

Fishing is a men's activity. There is no concept among Malays that women are unlucky at sea, but women do not work aboard large boats as members of crews. Prior to the 1960s some Rusila women went fishing with their husbands in two-person boats, and they were often called upon to help fishing crews using a type of net in which the catch was hauled ashore rather than into the boat. Fish processing on a small scale, is a women's specialty, an extension of meal preparation.

Thus the division of labor for traditional occupations is fairly clear-cut but not rigid. Women are responsible for their homes and child care. Men prepare land; women transplant, harvest, and process rice. Men fish.

Figure 9. Harvesting Rice (Ru Dua, 1966). Suri harvesting padi with a small hand knife (tuai or ketaman). Women still used the tuai in 1979.

There is some carry-over from traditional agricultural practices to production of cash crops, but not much. Men usually engage in the preparation of the land for rubber trees, but both men and women have worked as laborers cutting undergrowth. Women as well as men performed all of the processes required for rubber production during the 1960s: tapping, collecting the latex, setting the latex, running the rubber blocks through manual presses to make sheets, drying the sheets, selling them. The same observation holds for tobacco. Men generally prepare the land; weeding the plants is done more by women than by men. Beyond that, all of the labor can be done by either sex, and I have observed both men and women engaging in the various tasks. However, men usually operate the kilns. Women string tobacco and grade it; men weigh it. Both are involved in sales.

Figure 10. Winnowing Rice (Rusila, 1979). Kulsum winnowing rice near her home in hamlet Gong.

Among the other traditional occupations, men dominate some and women, others. Most of the shopkeepers in Rusila are women. This is an extension of their role in the home, especially in the coffee shops, and many shops are extensions of the house, allowing a woman to be at home and still attend to the shop. But outside the village one man has a coffee shop and another works as a cook. Women also are seamstresses (part-time in most instances) for other women; men must seek tailors outside the village. Men and women work in sales, men dominating fish peddling and women in the sale of home-cooked foods. Both deal in cloth, coconuts, and other goods. In the newer occupations men are carpenters, other building specialists and contractors, mechanics, and heavy equipment operators. Throughout Malaysia one can see women and men working in petrol stations, pumping gas, but I have never seen a woman mechanic. Women drive cars but not trucks. A small sprinkling of women can be found in many, perhaps almost all, of the professions, but as noted at the beginning of this chapter, they are concentrated in those that are an extension of their role as nurturers: in teaching, nursing, and midwifery.

8
CONCLUSIONS

There is no one route to development. Malaysia and other

> . . . developing countries are seeking rapid economic
> growth in a wholly different total environment from
> that in which the main thrust of growth took place in the
> West. . . . [Such development] can in fact only mean
> following a path which is possible for each nation in its
> current circumstances, using to the best advantage the
> common stock of scientific knowledge which is avail-
> able. . . (Hunter 1969:ix, 296).

Nor can we suppose that scientific knowledge and technology
are sufficient. Commenting on the revolution in Iran, Chedli Klibi,
the Tunisian secretary of the Arab League, commented:

> The Shah understood technology and the need to end
> illiteracy, to train people in new skills. But beyond
> this, he lacked the sense of need to offer people a
> satisfying place in their new environment (Lewis
> 1980).

The spread of scientific knowledge and technology continue at
a rapid if uneven pace in Malaysia, giving rise to what some see as
excessive concern with materialism and a consequent loss of spiritual
values, a negation of the "satisfying place" of the past, with no replacement. The Islamic revitalization movement is, in part, a
response to such feelings, but one that in its more radical elements
seeks a return to the past, to the way of life of the Prophet. Many
lament the loss of traditional values that they see resulting from

development. Yet not all traditional values are in a state of decay and, as Alex Inkeles points out, the ". . . presumption that supporting most modern modes necessarily implies rejecting all traditional ones" (1976:125) is erroneous.

Women in Rusila, for example, have readily accepted the "modern mode" with regard to services and conveniences—when such are affordable—while continuing to act within traditional cooperative kin-based networks. They sometimes put the services and conveniences they enjoy to use for members of the cooperative network—for instance, making ice in one's refrigerator for use by a kinswoman at a <u>kenduri</u> (small feast). The traditional values that are questioned may not be universally rejected. Young people who have had post-secondary education and others who have been influenced by their model are changing the mate selection procedure and undermining the control of parents in the matter. But not all of the young have taken this position, and many parents still hold to the old values.

One reflection of development in the village is housing: a number of new, well-constructed homes, and extended and improved homes; the use of more costly materials; and a different architectural style. The changes are away from the practical, elevated, wooden structure typical of Malay houses and toward a more enclosed, less airy, structure of cement that is less practical in a tropical climate. Poorer families live in the smaller, more traditional houses.

Within some homes there are now services and appliances unknown a few decades ago, and a significant increase in the number of homes that have electricity. Furnishings have proliferated and have created new work for women, but are also prestigious. Some of the kitchen additions indicate a shift in the type of entertaining that is done as well as showing a level of prosperity that allows coffee and food to be routinely offered to guests.

Children are socialized for different sex-role behavior and many adult activities are segregated by sex, be they religious, social, or economic. All Malays are taught to be polite and to have an appreciation for the concept of shame, to show respect for superiors, and other values important in their culture. Training is more stringent for females because they can bring shame upon their families more easily than men, and because a greater degree of obedience to parents is expected from them.

Girls and boys go to the local primary school, almost 100 percent of them even in 1965. The importance of basic learning is well established in the village. There is less agreement among adults about the need for secondary education, particularly for females. But increasing development, land scarcity, the limited

reliability of agriculture, and the realization that many job opportunities are inexorably tied to post-primary education has led more
families to encourage daughters as well as sons to get as much
education as they can. An examination of percentages of secondary
students, by sex, indicates that a significant advance from 35 percent to 45 percent was made by women during the decade 1965-75,
and that by 1979, 62 percent of women between 13 and 18 years of
age were still in school.

As students, females are disadvantaged when compared with
males, because they have more household and child care responsibilities in the home and may have to sacrifice their studies to meet
parental demands. Children of a literate parent have a great advantage, in that the need for a youngster to study is recognized and
the student's work can be monitored by the parent.

There has been a shift from a majority of students attending
"Arab schools" in 1965 to a majority enrolled in Malay-language
schools today, suggesting greater appreciation for academic rather
than religion-oriented studies. But the proximity of the new Malay-
language school, and hence the reduced transportation costs entailed
in getting to it, is also a contributing factor to the shift. The reason most commonly given for denying children secondary education
continues to be an economic one, although an underlying fear of
female-male friendships influences some families who have
daughters.

Provision of secondary, post-secondary, and special technical education for the young, particularly Malays, continues to be a
part of well-publicized government policy. One result is an increased demand for education that facilities are still inadequate to
meet. Many young people have occupational hopes that are tied to
secondary or post-secondary education. They have rejected the
idea of becoming agriculturalists or fishermen or performing other
village work; they picture themselves in offices, working as clerks,
or in higher-better-paying positions as government officers. Failure to pass secondary school exams can smash the dreams and
result in frustration. Men show their frustrations far more than
women, a pattern that is not unrelated to the ideal that a man should
support his family. I do not suggest that women are unaffected;
more of them are thinking about wage-earning jobs. And not only
for the income potential. Women who earn wages or have the education for such jobs are the ones who will marry men in the same
category and enjoy a very high standard of living. Nevertheless,
a woman's primary goals of being wife and mother will be realized
whether she passes exams or not.

The ahli rumah saja still has high prestige in the village,
prestige that from an outside observer's view can be said to be a

reflection of her husband's economic position. The female worker with a regular income of her own enjoys similar prestige, gained by her own accomplishments.

Mothers holding salaried or wage-paying jobs, whether they live in towns or commute to their jobs from the village, are filling two demanding roles: wife/mother and paid worker. They are experiencing role conflict, and worry about not devoting enough time to their children. Traditionally village women with young children who worked outside of the home pursued their occupations on a part-time basis in the village, where they were readily available to their families if they were needed. Now young women are holding positions that require their presence at regular hours, thus creating a new pattern of nonavailability to their families. Young children are placed in the care of housekeepers or "mother's helpers" on a daily basis, another new pattern of behavior that raises questions about socialization as well as creating both a new occupational role for village women engaged in such work and a new social relationship—employer-employee—between women from the same village area or with similar village backgrounds.

The lifestyle changes for town-dwelling, educated persons are enormous, especially for those coming from average village families where both parents are illiterate. There is intergenerational mobility coupled with a tendency for the newly mobile individual to be pulled by two sometimes conflicting sets of values and norms. The conflict is heightened for the mother who holds a full-time job outside the home. And she may experience a degree of social isolation in her urban/suburban neighborhood that is unknown to village women. The young urbanites are cut off from the ready social security of the kindred and women's kin-based cooperative networks, although these can be activated in any emergency—with mother, grandmother, siblings, and/or affines arriving on the next bus. It is the day-to-day assistance when needed, or even the knowledge that it is there, that is missing. There are fewer interactions with female peers on any regular basis.

Despite their role conflicts and the problems of living in two worlds simultaneously, educationally/occupationally successful individuals serve as role models for younger people in their home villages. Male "success stories" in terms of education and regular income have been known in Rusila for several decades. Young women have ventured far from the village for education and jobs for only a decade.

Islam has been established in Trengganu since 1386 (1964:76). People in Rusila are proud that they built and maintain their own mosque and prayer houses, and that they have more Hajis and Hajjahs than any nearby village. I have not attempted to devise a measure of religiosity, but impressionaistically theirs is very strong. In 1965 some men used excuses for not working on secular public projects such as the road to the primary school—but all of them turned out to help construct a prayer house, and even the poorest family made a contribution to the purchase of materials. Recently the villagers refused government funds for a new mosque, in part because the old one symbolizes their community spirit and their willingness to make economic sacrifices for their beliefs, but also because some of the money would come from sources they define as contaminated, such as taxes on liquor. Their refusal of the funds has earned them the reputation among local government officers of being unprogressive. Nor does the imam accept a stipend from the government. Yet government-supported imams and mosques built at government expense are found widely in other parts of Trengganu and Malaysia. Generally, Rusila people take their religion seriously but continue to modify some Islamic rules, such as those pertaining to inheritance, with pre-Islamic adat and to practice some ancient rituals, such as the Hindu-derived bersanding. Women dress modestly, but no one wears the veil or other garments of Middle Eastern origin.

Islam allows polygyny; local people generally accept it, and women affected personally by the practice are usually stoical, although one middle-aged woman actively balked when her husband took a second wife; and many younger women and men make negative comments about the practice. The local polygyny rate is very low. The former imam is credited by local people with influencing some village men to remain monogamous. But the limited extent of the practice was reported for other areas (Djamour 1965; Rosemary Firth 1966), and economic and social reasons suggested. Nevertheless, the former imam and his son, the present imam, are referred to as learned men and the present imam has advanced formal education in Islamic studies. Thus the gap between the theological level of Islam and its practice in the village is probably much less than in many rural areas where religious leaders are neither especially learned nor formally educated.

Even when practices are fully illumined by theological knowledge, women are structural inferiors.

By the standards of the twentieth century, the religious sanctioning of polygamy and concubinage, divorce at will by the husband, guardianship of children to the father, unequal weight of female inheritance, unequal weight to the legal testimony of women, are hardly consonant with a woman's equitable position in the modern world. . . . Any voice that religious leaders

would have concerning the structure of control over
women would be to confirm and reinforce female sub-
jugation to the authority of male[s] . . . (Youssef
1974:100).

The gap between theology and practice can support the inferior
status of women, but it is clear that even when theology is applied
to practice, women are denied some important and fundamental
rights.

A woman must be given in marriage by a male guardian, usually with her agreement. It may be recalled, however, that a virgin
can be given in marriage without her consent by her father or paternal grandfather, according to the Shafi'aite interpretation of
Muslim law, which is "the universal doctrine of the Malays" (Rauf
1964:85) although the followers of the Hanafi school, including
Muslim Indians (Shaltout 1958:143), hold that a woman can marry
without parental consent once she reaches puberty (Foo 1976:27).
Malay women who want to exercise their own choice regarding
marriage must convince their male guardians to allow them to do
so. As village women have become more educated and/or economically independent, they have begun to take firmer stands about
mate selection. There are many differences between young women
as to how forceful they are prepared to be. There are also differences from one family to another with regard to how sternly a father
wants to exert prerogatives, how much support a woman can get
from her older siblings (particularly brothers), whether a mother
will support her daughter's choice in trying to convince a reluctant
father, and so on.

Thus, during the 1970s some Rusila women followed traditional patterns, marrying without demur men who were selected
for them by parents; others made their own choices and obtained a
male guardian's agreement. Regardless, the father (or legal male
guardian) has the right, whether or not he exercises it, to give his
daughter in marriage: "To the extent that women do not have control over the decision making involved in marriage and sexuality,
they are subordinate" (Lamphere 1977:621).

The main difference between the sexes with regard to mate
selection was illustrated in the text in some detail. By tradition
parents selected mates for sons as well as daughters. But an adult
son was not legally required to accept the choice, although many
"good" sons bowed to parental pressure backed by parental provision of bridewealth. Economic independence favors men and women
in influencing mate selection, but men have the advantage of the
law and greater economic opportunities.

Islam abhors divorce, but accepts the practice as a last resort when a couple cannot resolve their marital problems. Men have the right to divorce by simply pronouncing a talak; women's rights are far more narrowly defined. Some Malay religious leaders think that men have abused their privilege, but I have seen no concrete suggestion of ways to reduce the abuse while adhering to the law. The divorce rate has been highest among Malays in rural sections of the nation, and has greatly declined in those areas that are industrializing or modernizing generally, a reversal of the U.S. pattern. A related factor to a lowered divorce rate appears to be that child support payments can be deducted directly from wages when men are regularly employed. Men engaged in village work have never made child support payments, nor would it be easy to enforce a legal judgment awarding them to a mother when the father earns on an irregular or sporadic basis and can conceal some income. Concealment of resources is a long-established pattern among rural women too, most often taking the form of secret savings.

The highest divorce rate was found among the very young, the same group who married spouses selected by parents. A shift in mate selection patterns, along with increased education and delayed marriage, can be expected to further affect divorce rates. In Rusila, while the divorce rate was high, there was also a great deal of marriage stability between 1965 and 1979. Many people were already divorced and had married someone else before the 1965 village survey. But a survey of the same villagers in 1979 found most of them still married to the 1965 spouse or that the marital ties were severed by death rather than divorce.

Muslim women receive no financial support from husbands following a divorce, although they may be entitled to share property; Rusila women have never received child support. It is customary for all children to stay with their mother rather than for the father to exercise his legal rights with regard to custody. A father has legal guardianship of his children even though they reside with their mother, unless such guardianship is deemed by the courts to be disadvantageous to any child.

The situation of divorced women can be disastrous. Rural women have had more options than their poor urban sisters, which is not to suggest that a divorcée (or widow) in Rusila has an easy time supporting herself and her children. Kin, particularly parents and siblings, will help, and may take the woman and her children into one of their homes on a more or less permanent basis. And various familiar means for earning income are available.

Remarriage within a year or two of a divorce or the death of a spouse is usual for women who have not reached menopause (and a few who have), and is typical for men of all ages. Older women

may opt against remarriage if they have their own homes and income from land or assistance from children. Remarriage can
increase a woman's work burden without significantly improving
her life situation. Aged women who cannot look after themselves
are taken into the home of a child or grandchild; an aged man is
likely to have a younger spouse to look after him.

Within the intact family/household, the husband is defined as
the head, yet because of her economic contributions in food, goods,
and cash, the wife has traditionally enjoyed parity or near parity in
the domestic domain. Formal authority in a family is vested in the
husband; influence in decision making is shared by husband and wife;
and responsibility for managing the household and its budget is
vested in the wife. Where family life is characterized by stability,
affection and loyalty are expressed among members in many ways,
but the relationship between older children and their father is more
formal than their relationship with the mother. If divorce occurs,
children develop even closer ties with mother (assuming they live
with her rather than other kin) and may see their father rarely,
even when he lives in Rusila. In some instances it would not be
an exaggeration to claim that a man has divorced himself from a
wife and their children.

In times of crisis the kindreds and women's cooperative networks (which have some overlap but are not identical) can be relied
upon. Mothers and daughters often have very warm and close relationships, and help one another in myriad ways. While the larger
reciprocity networks function, the need for many women to cooperate is occasional, as for a feast. Women's information networks
also function, on both the intravillage and intervillage levels. But
in Rusila a change in activities has led to a reduction in regular
daily contacts: more women have their own wells near their homes
or piped water indoors, thus eliminating the shared time associated
with the daily laundry chores in 1965-66.

Considering the amount of water used for laundry—everything
except school uniforms is washed after one (or at the most, two)
wearings, food preparation and cooking, dish washing, bathing young
children and babies, and scrubbing floors or "laying the dust" when
it is windy, piped water is indeed a luxury. No wonder the first
woman to have piped water in her home had acquaintances from
other villages as well as Rusila women coming by to admire the
sink, bathing room, and available water supply. Even a well close
to the home is a great improvement over having to cross the highway or walk a quarter of a mile to the nearest well, lugging heavy
buckets each time and making several trips to get the water for a
day's household use. No woman would willingly revert to the old
pattern even though the new one has reduced regular, daily contacts

among women in parts of the village. Information transmission still takes place, but now requires more conscious effort. Nevertheless, women have a more comprehensive sense of what is going on in the village than men, although men (as a category) are better informed about events outside the village.

Casual visiting among neighbors, another but less regularized situation for transmitting information, was the favorite use of leisure time for men (with men) and women (with women) in 1965, and is still enjoyed, despite the advent of television. When a special program is scheduled, television can draw 20-30 people to a home that has a set. Men and women automatically segregate themselves by sex, with men taking the seats and women sitting on the floor. If refreshments are served—if one has a television set, surely one can afford to offer coffee? seems to be the consensus—they are served only to men. Large catherings of 20 or more were less common in 1979 than in 1975 because of the proliferation of television sets. As a category women who are ahli rumah saja have the most leisure time, especially if they have piped water and refrigerators, which save the time normally used for drawing water and transporting it and daily (meal by meal) getting fresh foods.

It was shown in Chapter 7 that more women are claiming the ahli rumah saja status because more husbands can provide full economic support for a family, usually as wage earners, without a wife's help. Both gain prestige through fulfilling ideal sex-role behavior for adults. Even so, not all women who could do so have opted for the ahli rumah saja status: three continue to do remunerative work on a regular basis. None of them has young children; all of them have teen-age daughters who are attending school but still help with household chores. One woman's reaction when I asked her about it was that she would look forward to "just sitting on the verandah" when she no longer enjoyed growing tobacco and participating in the co-op. The other women who could eschew remunerative work are mat weavers. Neither works if she does not feel like it, but both want their own income, however small the amount. The ahli rumah saja is more dependent on her husband than women who contribute to family support.

Although three women who could do so have not opted for ahli rumah saja status, many women workers would readily accept it and whatever dependency goes with it in exchange for dependable support. I am using the term dependency even though I have never heard a Malay woman express the idea that her husband's support puts her in such a position. She has her work as wife and mother; he has his work. The two are complementary. "Lip-service" dependency results from Islamic prescription of the husband as the head of the family and the requirement that a woman get her husband's permission to absent herself from the home. But women do not ask permission to go about their business; they do give public recognition to husbands as family heads.

As long as the ahli rumah saja is also the family treasurer, she continues to have domestic influence buttressed by the stereotype that women are more clever in financial matters than men are. But more men are working outside the village, enjoying a broader range of experience than the wives who stay at home in the village. Today's economic options are becoming more and more tied to the towns. Thus the question of how long it will be before men stop expecting wives to be more astute about finances, and stop looking to them for advice. If men stop expecting wives to perform managerial and advisory functions vis-à-vis financial arrangements, will they begin to control the purse strings?

There is already one instance where a man gives his wife the weekly pay packet, following the usual village practice, but takes money from her daily to make food purchases at the big Kuala Trengganu market during his lunch hour or after work. Sensible. Food of all types, except vegetables grown in the village gardens (fewer since the introduction of tobacco as a cash crop), is cheaper in the central market. This man also buys cloth or clothing for wife and children because he can monitor the shop sales on a daily basis. His wife does not need to make trips into town by bus unless she wants to, and she rarely does. Her sister-in-law envies her: how nice it would be to have a modern (moden) husband who takes care of the chores and gets things at bargain rates. The wife has the wages in her keeping; she and her husband discuss what is needed in the home; he makes the selections. The example is suggestive, but not more than that.

If male management of family funds becomes an established pattern, as it has among Malays elsewhere (Swift 1964), women may begin to lose their parity in the domestic domain. The change seems most likely to occur when men are engaged in work for regular income outside the village while their wives are ahli rumah saja, devoting themselves to home and children and spending the bulk of their time in the village milieu. Women who earn money will continue to control it, a practice supported by Islam.

Only one woman in the village, a teacher, employs another woman as a full-time housekeeper and surrogate mother. Two trends seem likely to increase the demand for housekeepers, both full-time and part-time: the creeping suburbanization of villages near Kuala Trengganu because of the current scarcity of urban, middle-class housing in the city, and the proposed building of a government telecommunications training center just west of the village. The facility will employ various white-collar and blue-collar workers, mostly men, who will need family housing in the area. Working for middle-class families or in food preparation or cleaning at the training center would be welcomed by many local women as a means of assuring regular income. Other benefits will be for men: jobs available, beginning with the construction itself, and possibly as trainees. The impact on the village should be multifaceted.

Male control of machines related to work is common. A woman can be part owner of a truck, as one local woman is, with her husband, but she is unlikely to drive it. Heavy machinery is thus far the undisputed province of men. If one sees a road construction crew working anywhere in Malaysia, the graders and other big pieces of equipment are operated by men. Women on the crew are hauling rocks in baskets atop their heads or doing other nonmechanized labor. Fishing boats operating along the Trengganu coast are all motorized, and many are equipped with power-driven winches to haul in the nets. Disk plows that are brought into the village are operated by men. In this case a Rusila man who once earned part of his livelihood with his buffalo and wooden plow has been displaced. Women still engage in traditional techniques of transplanting and harvesting, using hand tools. Thus the real contrast in Rusila is between men's labor, which has become largely mechanized, and women's agricultural work, which has not. If transplanting and harvesting are mechanized, women will be displaced from those tasks.

Women who rely on earning rice for their work as harvesters or who grow it for their own families would be disadvantaged, but other women would welcome mechanization if the cost was not too great. Transplanting and harvesting rice by hand are exhausting chores, and there is the unpleasantness of leeches and the danger of snakes in the sawah. While woman's role as food producer is idealized and can be important, many women would give it up if they and their families did not suffer as a result.

Handicraft production continues to provide a majority of women with some income, although fewer women practiced pandanus weaving in the 1970s than in the 1960s. Craftswomen received higher prices for their products in recent years, but income did not keep pace with inflation. Demand is lowest during the monsoon months and highest during the dry season, when tourists—Malaysians and foreigners—come to the region. The Medan Anyaman draws buyers, and shopkeepers now stock woven goods and advertise them with brightly painted signs along the roadside. Increased demand is meaningless to a woman once she has reached her production peak and can sell everything she weaves. The only means of increasing income then is to raise prices. The best weavers have always asked more for their work than women who produce mediocre goods, but a purchaser may not be aware of the differences, and take the cheaper one. Whatever the quality, the cheapest mats will always find a buyer or can be used in the weaver's home.

Pandanus weaving will not be mechanized. Traditional handicrafts are defined by the government as part of the nation's cultural heritage, so even if mechanization were possible, such a step would be extremely unlikely.

Income from the craft is low, but it can be important for women who own no land, have no salable skills for work outside the village, must contribute something to family support, or want extra income. Most important to women with young children is the high congruence of work with this craft and the demands of child care. For these reasons alone, government encouragement of the craft among women who already have a long tradition with it, through the Medan Anyaman and other training and marketing facilities, has been positive. Introduction of the craft into areas where it has no tradition has met with marked lack of enthusiasm (Mohd. Taib Osman 1978:45).

It would be unfortunate in the extreme for the government to equate the establishment of craft training facilities and outlets for products with sufficient attention to the role of these women in the nation's development plans, because only low income is possible for even a very productive woman. Craft activities should be seen as supplementary and spare-time rather than as ones from which women can derive a decent standard of living. But "spare-time" and "supplementary" seem to characterize the government's view of rural women's economic behavior. For example, Felda schemes do not make provision of income-generating skills for women integral to their programs; women's FOA-supported ventures have been highly traditional—such cottage industries as duck rearing and the like.

These and many other programs appear to have an integral assumption: women have support within the family structure from their husbands, so that their own economic activities need not be more than spare-time or supplementary, or women have child care responsibilities that preclude their working outside the home. While these assumptions have some validity, they ignore the realities of the widow, the woman whose husband is disabled or has low income, the divorcée, the woman whose children are older—in other words, a large number of the women in any village. The ideals that men are able to fully support their families and that women are wives and mothers who might like to earn "small money" underlie the planning even though they conflict with acknowledgment of widespread poverty in rural areas.

Growth with equity for women and men appears to be more common in the initial stages of development, particularly where women have been active in a nationalist movement, as in Malaysia. Everyone with skills is needed: elite men and women are the first to benefit because they are the ones who have the education and training. As the economy and education expand, rural women and other nonelite women, as well as men, have employment opportunities their parents never dreamed could be possible. As more people become better educated, qualifications for many forms of work are raised. Jobs that could be secured in the 1960s with two or three years of secondary education now require a high pass in the fifth-year exams or more. Competition for higher education increases. Admissions personnel in Malaysia's universities are said not to discriminate against women, and that may well be so. But women are underrepresented in many fields and in higher educational institutions generally.

Women who do get the secondary or higher education to qualify for a desired job are competing with men for what is available except in sex-specific occupations, such as midwifery. The tendency is for women to be hired for "ancillary occupations" (Manderson 1978) or to have to show qualifications superior to those for men for the same job. Men are preferred to women as employees by many firms because they do not require maternity leaves, crèche arrangements, or time off to look after ailing children. As long as women are defined as the ones wholly responsible for child care, the bias in hiring and in the type of programs designed for rural women will remain unchanged.

The problems of women may be more apparent than their rights, although Malaysian women are legally assured many rights.

> In Peninsular Malaysia all women, whether married or single, have no disabilities in public life [that is, of a legal nature; the ways in which women are restrained are sociocultural]. They are able to vote, to stand for election, to serve as jurors (although they are rarely called). They also have the right to education and may enter into government service. Furthermore, they have the same rights, duties and liabilities regarding property as men (Foo 1976:25).

Malaysian women in Rusila as well as Kuala Lumpur are turning their rights into realities. The transformation of rights into realities for more Malaysians can be a function of the development process if that process is made to serve a broad spectrum of the population, men—and women.

APPENDIX

All figures are for the 23 villages, collectively, in the administrative district of Marang but do not include the town of Marang. (Information is from Federation of Malaysia 1972).

Tables 1 and 2: Living Quarters, Classified by Number of Persons per Living Unit (pp. 251-59)

Number of occupied living units (including hotel, office, mosque)	4,206
Number of private occupied living units	3,641
Number of persons	16,914
Average number of persons per living unit	4.64

Note: During 1966 there was an average of 4.58 persons per occupied dwelling in Rusila. In 1975 the average was 4.67 per household, and in 1979 the average was 4.96.

Unless otherwise noted, the following tables refer to private living units only.

Table 6: Material of Outer Walls (p. 273)

Plank only	2,979
Atap, woven bamboo, or similar material	378
Brick, concrete, metal, or brick and plank	38
Other	246

Table 7: Material of Roof (p. 27 5)

Tiles	1,541
Atap, woven bamboo, or similar material	1,872
Zinc or corrupgated iron	114
Asbestos sheets	82
Other	32

Table 9: Period of Construction (p. 278)

0-4 years (ago)	983
5-9	1,096
Subtotal, 1961-70	2,079
10-29	1,245
30+	208
Not known	109

Note: New houses may indicate prosperity of families already established in the area, recently married couples moving from parents' home to own home, and/or outsiders taking up residence in a village. However these reasons for new construction balance, it is impressive that more than 50 percent of all houses in villages of this district were built in the decade prior to the census. In 1970 the town of Marang had 663 private living units and 299 had been built during the prior decade.

Table 10: Ownership of Occupied Private Quarters (p. 279)

Nongovernment	3,614
Government	27

Note: There were no government-owned living units in Rusila in 1966. In 1975 the midwife and her family lived in government quarters.

Table 11: Water Supply (pp. 286-87)

Piped	23
Exclusive well or pump	762
Shared well or pump	2,832
River, canal, other	24

Note: In Rusila during 1966 wells—both exclusive and shared—were the only source of water for household use. By 1979, 26 homes had the convenience (luxury!) of piped water.

Table 12: Lighting (p. 289)

Public electricity	244
Private generator	10
Pressure/gas lamp	264
Oil lamp (pelita)	3,123

Note: By 1966, 32 (24 percent) Rusila homes had electricity, and by 1979, 120 (62.8 percent) had this convenience. Even using the 1966 Rusila figures for comparison with all district villages in 1970, we find a disparity. In the district there were 3,641 private dwellings and 244 (6.7 percent) had public electricity. What accounts for the disparity? I suggest that the following, taken together, provide an answer: Rusila was among the first villages in the district to have public electric power available; some of the inland villages in the district (like two of the Rusila hamlets) are so far from the power lines that the cost of having any home wired may be prohibitive; compared with some of the other villages, Rusila may have a larger number of relatively affluent residents.

Table 14: Toilet Facilities (p. 297)

Exclusive to living quarters	
Flush	70
Bucket	4
Pit	189
Over river or sea	11
Subtotal	274
Shared facilities	
Flush	14
Bucket	2
Pit	44
Over river or sea	307
Subtotal	367
Grand total	641

Note: There were 3,000 village homes in the district that had no toilet facilties in 1970. People continued to use beach and bush, as their forebears had done. In Rusila in 1966 there were public pit toilets in outhouses only in association with the school and the weaving center. By 1979 such facilities were found near 86 homes (45 percent) and there were 14 flush toilets (7.3 percent); a total of 100 homes (52 percent) had toilet facilities, some of which were also used by neighbors. No houses are situated so that indoor toilets over the sea can be used.

GLOSSARY OF MALAY WORDS

abang – elder brother

adat – Malay custom

adat perpateh – system of customary practices with a matri-bias found in the west coast states of Negri Sembilan and Malacca, Peninsular Malaysia

adat temenggong – system of customary practices with a patri-bias, found throughout Peninsular Malaysia except in parts of Negri Sembilan and Malacca on the west coast

adik – younger sibling of either sex

ahli rumah saja – homemaker only

akhad nikah – official Muslim marriage ceremony

akikah – thanksgiving feast to celebrate the birth of a child

anak – child

anak angkat – "carried child"—a child who is adopted, often informally

anak dara – virgin female

ayah – father

bahasa Malaysia – the national language of Malaysia (Malay)

bahasa Melayu – the Malay language

baju – blouse, shirt

baju kurung – a long-sleeved, loose-fitting woman's garment that reaches below the knees; formally it is worn with a matching ankle-length skirt

banyak berani (colloq.) – very brave, "gutsy"

bapak, 'pak – father

bapak saudara, 'pak saudara – uncle

batik – textile and art medium using a wax-resist technique on cloth

bersanding – traditional wedding ceremony, the "sitting in state," of Hindu origin; in Rusila, except for the bridegroom and young boys, it is attended only by women

bersilat – artistic Malay form of self-defense

bidan kampung – village midwife

bidan kerajaan – government midwife

bin – son of; for example, Daud bin Ahmad

bini – wife

binti – daughter of; for example, Hasnah binti Ahmad

bodoh – foolish, silly

bomoh – Malay medical-magical practitioner

buah spring – a form of "cradle" for young children

budak - young person of either sex

budak kacau - "bad boy"; the term could also be applied to a female; used seriously or in a semi-jocular sense

bumiputra, bumiputera - "son of the soil"; broadly the term encompasses Malays and indigenous peoples, but is sometimes used to refer only to Malays

bunga telor - "flower egg," a traditional ornament for nasi semangat ("the rice of the spirit of life") used for ceremonies and celebrations, and given to guests afterward

Cina buta - literally, "blind Chinese"; colloquial term for muhallil, a man who serves as an interim husband to a woman divorced with three talak who expects to remarry her former spouse

cucu - grandchild of either sex

cukor kepala - "to shave the head," a customary rite for infants

dakwah - Islamic missionary movement

dapu, dapur kayu - cooking "table" for wood fires

Dewan Negara - Senate; together with the Dewan Rakyat, Parliament

Dewan Rakyat - House of Representatives; together with the Dewan Negara, Parliament

dua pupu - second cousin of either sex

duduk di dapur saja - "just sit in the kitchen," an expression used in reference to a woman's role as housewife

emak, 'mak - mother

emak saudara, 'mak saudara - aunt

fasah - divorce granted to a woman because of a husband's physical or mental incapacity

gantang - a measure of quantity equal to approximately eight pounds of milled rice

gila - insane

gotong royong - mutual aid, cooperation for the good of all; a Malay ideal

haj - pilgrimage to Mecca; one of the five pillars of Islam, and thus a Muslim obligation

Haji - a man who has performed haj

Hajjah - a woman who has performed haj

halus - fine, superior quality

harta - wealth of any type; one's children

idda (old spelling form, eddah) - the period following a divorce during which a woman is not permitted to marry: three months and ten days; 100 days

imam - prayer leader in a mosque; in Rusila, the religious leader in the community

jahat - wicked, evil

jamuan - a feast

Jawi - Arabic script

jijak tanah - "footsteps on the earth," customary rite for infants

kain sembahyang - woman's hooded prayer robe of white cloth that covers the entire body and head except the face

kakak - elder sister

kampung - village

kasar - crude, coarse, of inferior quality

kathi (kadzi) - Muslim registrar of marriages and divorces

kebangsaan - national

kerajaan - government

ketua kampung - village headman

khalwat - "proximity," an offense under the Islamic legal code

kuala - a confluence

ladang - a form of swidden horticulture

laki-laki - man

lapuran tahunan - annual report

Madrasah Arabiah - Arab School

mahr - bridewealth

malu - ashamed, shy; embarrassment, shame

masjid - mosque

'mas kawin, emas kawin - "marriage gold," bridewealth

masuk Melayu - to become a Malay

Medan Anyaman - literally, "woven pandanus goods market," which I have taken the liberty to translate as "Weaving Center"

melenggang perut - "to sway the stomach," a customary ceremony held for a woman during the seventh month of her first pregnancy

moden (colloq.) - modern

modin - a man who performs circumcisions

muhallil - see Cina buta

mukim - an administrative unit comprising several villages

musim gelora - monsoon

nafkah - maintenance to which a Muslim wife is entitled from her husband

nasi - cooked rice; the word is often used as a synonym for food

nasi semangat - "the rice of the spirit of life," used in customary ceremonies and celebrations

orang - person

orang asli - a member of one of the aboriginal populations of Malaysia: Semai, Mah-Meri, and others

orang Cina - a Chinese

orang Melayu - a Malay

orang putih - a white person

padi - rice while it is growing

pantang - taboo, proscribed behavior

penghulu - official in charge of a mukim

perempuan - woman

pertanian - agriculture
Raja Permaisuri Agong - the queen
rodat - type of dancing and singing performance indigenous to
    Trengganu
Rumi - Romanized script
sains - science
saya - I, me, my
sekolah agama - school of religion; type of secondary school with
    a curricular focus on Islamic studies
senang - feeling of contentment, pleasure, peacefulness
sirih - leaves used in making a betel quid (a light stimulant); a
    traditional symbol of hospitality
sombong - arrogant, snobbish
suami - husband
susah - difficult, worrisome, unhappy
syariah - Islamic legal code; Islamic courts
taklik (formally, cerai taklik) - conditional divorce provision
    granted to a woman at the time of marriage
talak - divorce or repudiation of a woman by her husband
tebus talak (formally, cerai tebus talak) - divorce gained by a woman
    through payment to her husband; tebus = redeem
teknologi - technology
telekong - hood worn by female students attending religious schools
    and by some other women
tengok menantu - "look at the daughter-in-law," customary practice
    associated with welcoming a newly married woman to the home
    of her husband's parents (menantu = son- or daughter-in-law)
teruna - virgin male
tidak ada guna - useless
tidak apa - never mind; it doesn't matter
tiga pupu - third cousin
tok - grandmother (in some parts of the Federation, tok means
    grandfather and nek designates grandmother [Nagata 1979:156])
tokki - grandfather
towkay, taukeh - entrepreneur, usually in reference to Chinese
tukang - specialist—tukang bersanding = bersanding specialist;
    tukang kayu = wood specialist or carpenter
tunku, tengku - hereditary title for members of royalty of either
    sex, usually rendered in English as "prince" or "princess"
wakaf - land or building given to the community as an Islamic
    endowment
Yang di Pertuan Agong - the king
zinah - adultery

BIBLIOGRAPHY

BOOKS AND ARTICLES

Abdul Kadir bin Yusof (Tan Sri Datuk Haji Abdul Kadir). 1975. "Women and the Law." Kuala Lumpur: NCWO Seminar. Mimeographed.

Abdul Rahman bin Yusop. 1964. Collins Malay-English/English-Malay Dictionary. London: William Collins Sons.

Ahmad Ibrahim. 1965. The Status of Muslim Women in Family Law in Malaysia, Singapore and Brunei. Singapore: Malayan Law Journal.

_____. Undated. "Islam—Customary Law: Malaysia." Intisari 2, no. 2:47-74.

Ahmad Kamal. 1961. The Sacred Journey, the Pilgrimage to Mecca. New York: Duell, Sloan and Pearce.

Ajami, Fouad. 1980. "Islamic Ideas." New York Times Book Review, March 2, 1980, pp. 6, 25.

Allen, J. de Vere. 1968. "The Ancien Regime in Trengganu, 1909-1919." JMBRAS 41:23-42.

Amru'llah, H. A. M. K. 1968. "A Deserted Child." In Six Indonesian Short Stories, translated by Rufus S. Hendon. Southeast Asian Studies, Translation Series, no. 7. New Haven: Yale University Press.

Anonymous. 1977. "Malaysia to 1980: Economic and Political Outlooks for Business Planners." Hong Kong: (attributed to) Business International. Mimeographed.

Baldwin, Stephen C. 1977. Policies and Realities of Delayed Marriage. Population Reference Bureau Report, vol. 3, no. 4. Washington, D.C.: Population Reference Bureau.

Barber, Elinor. 1979. "Some International Perspectives on Sex Differences in Education." Signs 4:584-92.

Berelson, Bernard, and Gary A. Steiner. 1964. Human Behavior, an Inventory of Scientific Findings. New York: Harcourt, Brace, and World.

Boserup, Ester. 1965. The Conditions of Agricultural Growth: The Economics of Agrarian Change Under Population Pressure. London: George Allen and Unwin.

_____. 1970. Woman's Role in Economic Development. New York: St. Martin's Press.

_____. 1977. "Preface: Women and National Development." Signs 3:xi-xiv.

Bossen, Laurel. 1975. "Women in Modernizing Societies." American Ethnologist 2:587-601.

Burkholz, Herbert. 1980. "The Latinization of Miami." New York Times Magazine, September 21, 1980, pp. 46-47, 84-100.

Chan Su-Ming. 1965. "Kelantan and Trengganu, 1909-1939." JMBRAS 38:157-98.

Chung, Betty Jamie, and Ng Shui Meng. 1977. The Status of Women in Law: A Comparison of Four Asian Countries. Singapore: Institute of Southeast Asian Studies.

Cohen, Ronald. 1967. The Kanuri of Bornu. New York: Holt, Rinehart, and Winston.

Cooke, Elena M. 1961. Rice Cultivation in Malaya. Singapore: Malaya Publishing House.

Dadzie, K. K. S. 1980. "Economic Development." Scientific American, September 1980, pp. 59-65.

Daly, Mary. 1978. Gyn/ecology: The Metaethics of Radical Feminism. Boston: Beacon Press.

Das, K. 1978. "All the Premier's Bright Young Men." Far Eastern Economic Review, November 3, 1978, pp. 29-32.

_____. 1979a. "The Inner Thoughts of Hussein Onn." Far Eastern Economic Review, January 26, 1979, pp. 18-23.

_____. 1979b. "A Judge's Verdict on Islamic Law." Far Eastern Economic Review, November 23, 1979, pp. 22-23.

_____. 1980. "The Threat of the Holy Warriors." Far Eastern Economic Review, April 11, 1980, pp. 24-25.

Das, K., Anthony Rowley, and Pat Pfeiffer. 1979. "Malaysia 1979—Overview." Far Eastern Economic Review, August 31, 1979, pp. 35-68.

Davies, Derek. 1980. "Traveller's Tales." Far Eastern Economic Review, July 18, 1980, p. 17.

Djamour, Judith. 1965. Malay Kinship and Marriage in Singapore. London: Athlone Press.

Elliott, Carolyn M. 1977. "Theories of Development: An Assessment." Signs 3:1-8.

El-Zayyat, Mohammed. 1954. Questions to a Moslem—An Exposition of Islam. Washington, D.C.: National Publishing Co.

Enloe, Cynthia H. 1973. Ethnic Conflict and Political Development. Boston: Little, Brown.

Fernea, Elizabeth Warnock. 1965. Guests of the Sheik. New York: Doubleday.

Firth, Raymond. 1964. "Capital Saving and Credit in Peasant Societies: A Viewpoint from Economic Anthropology." In Capital, Saving and Credit in Peasant Societies, edited by Raymond Firth and B. S. Yamey, pp. 15-34. Chicago: Aldine.

_____. 1966. Malay Fishermen. 2nd, rev. ed. London: Routledge and Kegan Paul.

Firth, Rosemary. 1966. Housekeeping Among Malay Peasants. 2nd, rev. ed. New York: Humanities Press.

Foo, Gillian Hwei-Chuan, et al. 1976. Women Today in Peninsular Malaysia. Kuala Lumpur: Federation of Family Planning Associations.

Fox, Robin. 1967. Kinship and Marriage. Baltimore: Penguin.

Fraser, Thomas M., Jr. 1960. Rusembilan: A Malay Fishing Village in Southern Thailand. Ithaca, N.Y.: Cornell University Press.

_____. 1966. Fishermen of South Thailand: The Malay Villagers. New York: Holt, Rinehart, and Winston.

Freed, Stanley A., and Ruth S. Freed. 1969. "Urbanization and Family Types in a North Indian Village." Southwestern Journal of Anthropology 25:342-59.

Friedl, Ernestine. 1975. Women and Men: An Anthropologist's View. New York: Holt, Rinehart, and Winston.

Gamst, Frederick C. 1974. Peasants in Complex Society. New York: Holt, Rinehart, and Winston.

Geertz, Clifford. 1960. The Religion of Java. Glencoe, Ill.: The Free Press.

_____. 1968. Islam Observed: Religious Development in Morocco and Indonesia. New Haven: Yale University Press.

Goldschmidt, Walter, and Evalyn Jacobson Kunkel. 1971. "The Structure of the Peasant Family." American Anthropologist 73:1058-76.

Gordon, Shirle. Undated. "Marriage/Divorce in the Eleven States of Malaya." Intisari 2, no. 2:23-32.

Hammond, Dorothy, and Alta Jablow. 1976. Women in Cultures of the World. Menlo Park, Calif.: Cummings.

Hareven, Tamara K. 1976. "Modernization and Family History: Perspectives on Social Change." Signs 2:190-206.

Harris, Marvin. 1975. Culture, People, Nature: An Introduction to General Anthropology. 2nd ed. New York: Thomas Y. Crowell.

Haub, Carl, and Douglas W. Heisler. 1980. 1980 World Population Data Sheet of the Population Reference Bureau. Washington, D.C.: Population Reference Bureau.

Ho, Robert. 1964. "The Environment." In Malaysia, edited by Wang Gungwu, pp. 25-43. Singapore: Donald Moore Books.

Hunter, Guy. 1969. Modernizing Peasant Societies: A Comparative Study in Asia and Africa. London: Oxford University Press.

Inkeles, Alex. 1976. "Understanding and Misunderstanding Individual Modernity." In The Uses of Controversy in Sociology, edited by Lewis A. Coser and Otto N. Larsen, pp. 103-30. New York: The Free Press.

Jackson, James C. 1972. "Rice Cultivation in West Malaysia." JMBRAS 45:76-96.

Jamillah Ariffin. 1978. "Industrial Development in Peninsular Malaysia and Rural-Urban Migration of Women Workers: Impact and Implications." Xth International Congress of Anthropological Sciences. Mimeographed.

Kallgren, Joyce K. Undated. "Enhancing the Role of Women in Developing Countries." AID/CM/ta-147-350. Berkeley: University of California. Mimeographed.

Kane, Thomas T. 1979. 1979 World Population Data Sheet of the Population Reference Bureau. Washington, D.C.: Population Reference Bureau.

Kessler, Clive S. 1980. "Malaysia: Islamic Revivalism and Political Disaffection in a Divided Society." SEAC 75:2-11.

Khadijah, Muhamed. 1978. "Women in Malaysian Politics." Kuala Lumpur: University of Malaya. Mimeographed.

Kiefer, Thomas M. 1972. The Tausug: Violence and Law in a Philippine Moslem Society. New York: Holt, Rinehart, and Winston.

Kottak, Conrad Phillip. 1978. Anthropology: The Exploration of Human Diversity. 2nd ed. New York: Random House.

Kraar, Louise, and Stephen Blank. 1980. "Malaysia: The High Cost of Affirmative Action." Asia, March/April 1980, pp. 6-9.

Lamphere, Louise. 1977. "Review Essay—Anthropology." Signs 2:612-27.

Lawton, John. 1979. "Arab Aid in Malaysia." Aramco World Magazine 30:33-36.

Leeds, Anthony. 1977. "Mythos and Pathos: Some Unpleasantries on Peasantries." In Peasant Livelihood, edited by Rhoda Halperin and James Dow, pp. 227-56. New York: St. Martin's Press.

Lewis, Flora. 1980. "Learning from Shah's Tragedy." New York Times, "Week in Review," reprinted in The Ledger (Lakeland, Fla.), August 3, 1980, p. 4C.

Manderson, Lenore. 1977. "Malay Women and Development in Peninsular Malaysia." Kabar Seberang 2:61-84.

_____. 1978. "Women and Work: Continuities of the Past and Present." Asia Teachers' Association Bulletin 6:6-24.

Martin, M. Kay, and Barbara Voorhies. 1975. Female of the Species. New York: Columbia University Press.

Matthiasson, Carolyn, ed. 1974. Many Sisters—Women in Cross-Cultural Perspective. New York: The Free Press.

Mauss, Marcel. 1967. The Gift. New York: W. W. Norton.

Mazidah Zakaria and Nik Safiah Karim. 1978. "Women in Development: The Case of an All-Girls Youth Land Development Scheme in Malaysia." Xth International Congress of Anthropological and Ethnological Sciences. Mimeographed.

McIntyre, David. 1964. "Political History 1896-1946." In Malaysia, edited by Wang Gungwu, pp. 138-48. New York: Frederick A. Praeger.

Mernissi, Fatimah. 1975. Beyond the Veil: Male-Female Dynamics in a Modern Muslim Society. New York: Schenkman.

_____. 1976. "The Moslem World: Women Excluded from Development." In Women and World Development, edited by Irene Tinker and Michele Bo Bramsen, pp. 35-44. Washington, D.C.: Overseas Development Council.

Mohammed Din bin Ali (Haji). Undated, a. "Islam and Adat Surrounding Puasa." Intisari 1:22-25.

_____. Undated, b. "Malay Customary Law/Family." Intisari 2, no. 2:33-45.

Mohd. Salleh Daud and Dr./Prof. Asmah Haji Omar. 1973. Kamus Pelajar Federal. Kuala Lumpur: Federal Publications.

_____. 1977. Kamus Harian Federal. Kuala Lumpur: Federal Publications.

Mohd. Taib Osman. 1978. "A Place for Traditional Technology in Industrialization Planning, Peninsular Malaysia." Malaysian Geographers 1:37-58.

Moore, Mick. 1973. "Cross-Cultural Surveys of Peasant Family Structures: Some Comments." American Anthropologist 75:911-15.

Murdock, George Peter. 1949. Social Structure. New York: Macmillan.

_____. 1960. "Cognatic Forms of Social Organization." In Social Structure in Southeast Asia, edited by G. Murdock, pp. 1-14. Chicago: Quadrangle.

Nagata, Judith A. 1974. "What Is a Malay? Situational Selection of Ethnic Identity in a Plural Society." American Ethnologist 1:331-50.

_____. 1979. Malaysian Mosaic: Perspectives from a Poly-Ethnic Society. Vancouver: University of British Columbia Press.

Nash, Manning. 1964. "The Organization of Economic Life." In Horizons of Anthropology, edited by Sol Tax, pp. 171-80. Chicago: Aldine.

_____. 1966. Primitive and Peasant Economic Systems. San Francisco: Chandler.

_____. 1974. Peasant Citizens: Politics, Religion and Modernization in Kelantan, Malaysia. Athens, Ohio: Center for International Studies, Ohio University.

Nash, Nancy. 1978. "Pilgrims' Progress, Asian Style." Far Eastern Economic Review, November 17, 1978, pp. 32-36.

Nortman, Dorothy. 1977. "Changing Contraceptive Patterns: A Global Perspective." Population Bulletin 32:3.

Ortner, Sherry B. 1974. "Is Female to Male as Nature is to Culture?" In Woman, Culture and Society, edited by M. Z. Rosaldo and Louise Lamphere, pp. 67-88. Stanford: Stanford University Press.

Orvis, Pat. 1978. "Illiteracy Is a Growing Global Problem." New York Times, April 30, 1978, p. 23.

Parmer, Norman J. 1964. "Malaysia." In Government and Politics of Southeast Asia, edited by George M. Kahin, pp. 281-371. Ithaca, N.Y.: Cornell University Press.

Peyman, Hugh, and K. Das. 1980. "Focus: Malaysia '80." Far Eastern Economic Review, August 22-28, 1980, pp. 33-56.

Pickthall, Mohammed Marmaduke. 1959. The Meaning of the Glorious Koran. New York: Mentor Books.

Puthucheary, Mavis. 1975. "Women in Employment." Kuala Lumpur: NCWO Seminar. Mimeographed.

Rasjidi, Mohammad. 1958. "Unity and Diversity in Islam." In Islam, the Straight Path, edited by Kenneth W. Morgan, pp. 403-30. New York: Ronald Press.

Rauf, M. A. 1964. A Brief History of Islam with Special Reference to Malaya. Kuala Lumpur: Oxford University Press.

Raybeck, Douglas. 1975. "Kelantanese Divorce: The High-Price of Village Harmony." American Anthropological Association 74th Annual Meeting. Mimeographed.

Razman, M. A. 1975. "Malaysian Women Win Reforms." Asia Magazine. July 13, 1975, pp. 14-16.

Reiter, Rayna R., ed. 1975. Toward an Anthropology of Women. New York: Monthly Review Press.

Robinson, Harry. 1967. Monsoon Asia, a Geographical Survey. New York: Frederick A. Praeger.

Roose, Hashimah. 1965. "Changes in the Position of Malay Women." In Women in the New Asia, edited by Barbara Ward, pp. 287-95. Paris: UNESCO.

Rosaldo, Michelle Zimbalist. 1974. "Woman, Culture and Society: A Theoretical Overview." In Woman, Culture and Society, edited by M. Z. Rosaldo and Louise Lamphere, pp. 17-42. Stanford: Stanford University Press.

Rule, Sheila. 1980. "Women Still Knocking on the Door." New York Times, "National Recruitment Survey," October 12, 1980, p. 43.

Safa, Helen. 1977. "Introduction: Women and National Development." Signs 3:22-24.

Sanday, Peggy R. 1973. "Toward a Theory of the Status of Women." American Anthropologist 75:1682-1700.

_____. 1974. "Female Status in the Public Domain." In Woman, Culture and Society, edited by M. Z. Rosaldo and Louise Lamphere, pp. 189-206. Stanford: Stanford University Press.

SEAC. 1979. "Changing Role of S.E. Asian Women." Southeast Asia Chronicle 66 (January/February):1-27.

_____. 1980. "Race and Class in Malaysia." Southeast Asia Chronicle 72 (April): 16-23.

S. Hasnah binti Mohammed Ali. Undated. "Islam and Adat—Effect on a Basic Attitude—Health." Intisari 1:27-36.

S. Husin Ali. 1964. Social Stratification in Kampong Bagan. Monographs of the Malaysian Branch of the Royal Asiatic Society, 1.

_____. 1975. Malay Peasant Society and Leadership. Kuala Lumpur: Oxford University Press.

Shaltout, Mahmud. 1958. "Islamic Beliefs and Code of Laws." In Islam—The Straight Path, edited by Kenneth W. Morgan, pp. 87-143. New York: Ronald Press.

Siraj, Zaibun Nissa. 1975. "Women and Adult Education: A Case Study of the Women's Institute Movement in Peninsular Malaysia 1952-1974." Masters of Education thesis, University of Malaya.

Skeat, Walter William. 1967. Malay Magic. New York: Dover.

Smelser, Neil J. 1967. "Toward a Theory of Modernization." In Tribal and Peasant Economies, edited by George Dalton, pp. 29-50. New York: Natural History Press.

Smith, T. E. 1961. "Marriage, Widowhood and Divorce in the Federation of Malaya." [Proceedings] International Population Conference 2:302-9.

Stack, Carol B., et al. 1975. "Review Essay—Anthropology." Signs 1:147-59.

Stenson, Michael. 1976. "Class and Race in West Malaysia." Bulletin of Concerned Asian Scholars, April-June 1976, pp. 45-54.

Strange, Heather. 1971. "The Weavers of Rusila: Working Women in a Malay Village." Ph.D. dissertation, New York University.

_____. 1976. "Continuity and Change: Patterns of Mate Selection and Marriage Ritual in a Malay Village." Journal of Marriage and the Family, August 1976, pp. 561-71.

_____. 1977. "Education and Employment Patterns of Rural Malay Women 1965-1975." Journal of Asian and African Studies (Toronto) 12:42-58.

_____. 1980. "Some Changing Socio-Economic Roles of Rural Malay Women." In Asian Women in Transition, edited by Sylvia Chipp and Justin Green, pp. 123-51. University Park, Pa.: Pennsylvania State University Press.

Strauch, Judith. 1979. "Multiple Ethnicities in Malaysia: The Shifting Relevance of Alternative Chinese Categories." Cambridge, Mass.: Harvard University. Mimeographed.

_____. 1980. "Malaysia's Response to the Boat People: The Ethnic Factor." Southeast Asia Chronicle 72:24-26.

Sundaram, Jomo. 1977. "Class Formation in Malaysia." Ph.D. Dissertation, Harvard University.

Swift, M. G. 1963. "Men and Women in Malay Society." In Women in the New Asia, edited by Barbara E. Ward, pp. 268-86. Paris: UNESCO.

_____. 1964. "Capital, Saving and Credit in a Malay Peasant Economy." In Capital, Saving and Credit in Peasant Societies, edited by Raymond Firth and B. S. Yamey, pp. 133-56. Chicago: Aldine.

_____. 1965. Malay Peasant Society in Jelebu. London: Athlone Press.

Tasker, Rodney. 1979. "The Explosive Mix of Muhammad and Modernity." Far Eastern Economic Review, February 9, 1979, pp. 22-29.

_____. 1980. "Keeping Islam in Balance." Far Eastern Economic Review, November 28, 1980, pp. 34-36.

Tham Seong Chee. 1977. Malays and Modernization. Singapore: Singapore University Press.

Tinker, Irene. 1975. "A Report on AAS Seminar on Women in Development, Mexico City, June 15-18, 1975." Washington, D.C.: American Association for the Advancement of Science. Mimeographed.

_____. 1976. "The Adverse Impact of Development on Women." In Women and World Development, edited by Irene Tinker and Michele Bo Bramsen, pp. 22-34. Washington, D.C.: Overseas Development Council.

Turnbull, Mary. 1964. "The Nineteenth Century." In Malaysia, edited by Wang Gungwu, pp. 128-37. New York: Frederick A. Praeger.

Wallerstein, Immanuel. 1976. "Modernization: Requiescat in Pace." In The Uses of Controversy in Sociology, edited by Lewis A. Coser and Otto N. Larsen, pp. 131-35. New York: The Free Press.

Wharton, Clifton R., Jr. 1967. "Recent Historical Developments in Malaysia." Asia 7:30-40.

Williams, Louise. 1979. "WFS Reports Confirms Changes in Asian Breastfeeding Patterns." Intercom, April 1979, pp. 7-9.

Wilson, Christine S. 1973. "Food Taboos of Childbirth: The Malay Example." Ecology of Food and Nutrition 2:267-74.

Wilson, Peter J. 1967. A Malay Village and Malaysia. New Haven: Human Relations Area Files Press.

Winstedt, Richard. 1961. The Malays, a Cultural History. London: Routledge and Kegan Paul.

Winzeler, Robert L. 1974. "Sex Role Equality, Wet Rice Cultivation, and the State in Southeast Asia." American Anthropologist 76:563-67.

Wira, Pekirma (Tunku). Undated. "Islam and Adat in Trengganu." Intisari 1:37-48.

Wise, Donald. 1979. "Malaysia." In Asia Yearbook 1979, pp. 237-46. Hong Kong: Far Eastern Economic Review.

Youssef, Nadia Haggag. 1974. Women and Work in Developing Societies. Westport, Conn.: Greenwood Press.

PUBLIC DOCUMENTS

Federation of Malaysia

1953. National Association of Women's Institutes of Malaya Handbook. Kuala Lumpur: Cavton Press.

1970. Federal Constitution, Incorporating All Amendments up to 1st June, 1970. Kuala Lumpur: Government Printer.

1971a. Laws of Malaysia: Act 30: Universities and University Colleges Act 1971. Kuala Lumpur: Government Printer.

1971b. The Second Malaysia Plan. Kuala Lumpur: Government Printer.

1972. 1970 Population and Housing Census of Malaysia, vol. II, pt. 7: Trengganu. Kuala Lumpur: Jabatan Perangkaan Malaysia.

1973. Laws of Malaysia: Act 106: Women and Girls Protection Act, 1973. Kuala Lumpur: Government Printer.

1976a. The Third Malaysia Plan. Kuala Lumpur: Government Printer.

1977a. University of Malaya, Annual Report, 1975-76. Kuala Lumpur: University of Malaya.

1977b. 1970 Population and Housing Census of Malaysia, vol. I, pt. 7: Trengganu. Kuala Lumpur: Jabatan Perangkaan Malaysia.

1979. University of Malaya, Annual Report, 1977-78. Kuala Lumpur: University of Malaya.

Malaysian National Museum. 1978. Upacara Perkawinan Tradisional di Malaysia (Traditional Malaysian Weddings).

NACIWID. 1978. "Income Generating Skills for Women: Interim Report." Kuala Lumpur: Faculty of Education, University of Malaya. Mimeographed.

_____. n.d. "Women in Development: Plan of Action." Kuala Lumpur: NACIWID. (Circulated in January 1978.) Mimeographed.

National Family Planning Board. n.d. Report on West Malaysia Family Survey 1966-1967. Kuala Lumpur: the Board.

United Nations

1980a. Women 1980: Conference Booklet. "World Conference of the United Nations Decade for Women: Equality, Development and Peace." New York: Division for Economic and Social Information.

1980b. Women 1980: Newsletter #1. "Islam: Liberation or Oppression." New York: Division for Economic and Social Information. (No author or editor designated.)

1980c. Women 1980: Newsletter #2. "Improvements for Rural Women Wanted by Asian and Pacific Region." New York: Division for Economic and Social Information. (No author or editor designated.)

INDEX

Abdul Kadir bin Yusof, 105,
156, 162, 182
aborigines (orang asli), 5, 7
(see also bumiputra)
adat (Malay custom), 3, 6, 8,
21, 57-58, 60, 65, 70-71,
78, 87, 103, 130, 182
agriculture, horticulture, 2,
171-73, 206, 210, 215,
221-23, 236
ahli rumah (homemaker) and
ahli rumah saja (homemaker
only), 111, 201, 205, 209-
10, 228-29, 234-35
Ahmad Ibrahim, 156, 157, 161
Ajami, Fouad, 21
Allen, J. de Vere, 4

bomoh (Malay medical-magical
practitioner), 59, 72, 73,
77
Borneo (see East Malaysia)
Boserup, Ester, 185, 191, 199-
200, 221
Bossen, Laurel, 198, 200
bridewealth, 108, 111-12, 118
bumiputra, 7, 80, 81, 85, 174
(see also aborigines,
Malays)

Chan Su-Ming, 4
Chinese, 4, 5, 7-9, 11, 12,
15, 19, 43-44, 57, 74,
80-82, 85, 87, 139, 153,
174, 176, 177, 182, 187
(see also ethnic categories)

Chung, Betty Jamie, 141,
154, 158, 160, 162, 165,
182-83
colonialism (see Malaya)
cooperatives, 175-77, 193-94

dakwah (see Islam)
development, xvii, 1, 15-17,
68, 137-38, 170, 179-80,
208, 225, 226-28, 236-38
(see also economy, educa-
tion, Malaysia, Trengganu,
Rusila)
divorce, 149-69, 232; Chinese
and Malays (Trengganu)
compared, 153-55; costs of,
154; custody and support
of children, 165-66, 232;
grounds among Muslims,
156-57, 159-60; grounds
among non-Muslims, 153-
54, 168; and household
economy (Rusila), 165-67;
idda, 161-62, 184; initiated
by Muslim women, 156-60;
legal codes, 153-58, 168-
69; and Malay cultural patterns, 151-53; male pre-
rogatives (Muslim), 157-
58, 159-61, 231-32; and
marital stability (Rusila),
158-59, 232; and moderni-
zation, 149-51, 231-32;
muhallil (interim husband),
162-64; and property, 151,
154, 161-62, 164-65; in
Rusila, 158-68; statistics

ABOUT THE AUTHOR

HEATHER STRANGE is an Associate Professor of Anthropology at University College, Rutgers-The State University of New Jersey. During 1978-79 she was a Senior Fulbright Lecturer in the Department of Malay Studies and the Southeast Asia Program, Faculty of Arts and Social Sciences, University of Malaya. Dr. Strange's articles have appeared in Journal of Marriage and the Family, Society, Asian Journal of Medicine, Journal of Asian and African Studies, and others. She received her B.A. degree from the American University of Beirut in Lebanon in 1955 and her Ph.D. from New York University in 1971.